Christ's
Fulfillment of
Torah and Temple

Christ's Fulfillment of Torah and Temple

Salvation according to Thomas Aquinas

MATTHEW LEVERING

UNIVERSITY OF NOTRE DAME PRESS
Notre Dame, Indiana

Manufactured in the United States of America

Library of Congress Cataloging-in-Publication Data
Levering, Matthew Webb, 1971–
Christ's fulfillment of Torah and temple : salvation according to
Thomas Aquinas / Matthew Levering.
p.   cm.
Includes bibliographical references and index.
ISBN 0-268-02272-0 (cloth : alk. paper)
ISBN 0-268-02273-9 (pbk. : alk. paper)
1. Salvation.   2. Catholic Church—Doctrines.   3. Thomas, Aquinas,
Saint, 1225?–1274—Contributions in doctrine of salvation.   I. Title.
BT755 .L48   2002
234—dc21
2002000263

∞ *This book is printed on acid-free paper.*

Contents

Acknowledgments

This book began as a dissertation at Boston College, so I am especially grateful to the members of my board. I was unusually blessed to work with such teachers. Stephen F. Brown's enthusiasm for the project, and willingness to direct it, meant much to a young graduate student and improved the outcome enormously. Fr. Matthew L. Lamb guided me through the doctoral program and offered numerous suggestions and corrections for the dissertation. Fr. Romanus Cessario, O.P., mentored me in Thomistic theology and gave me my first insights into Aquinas's theology of Christ and salvation. His teaching inspired me to undertake this project. While in the doctoral program I was supported financially by a doctoral fellowship from Boston College and by summer grants from the Bradley foundation for the years 1997–2000. My colleagues and students at Ave Maria College, especially William Riordan and Dominic Aquila, enriched this work by their conversation and friendship.

Other teachers and friends who contributed, in various important ways, to this work include Barbara Appleby, Christine Bowie, Fr. Bevil Bramwell, O.M.I., Fr. John Connelly, Michael Dauphinais, Tomás Fernandez-Whipple, Shirley Gee, Timothy Gray, Fr. Robert Imbelli, Susan Keefe, Paul LaChance, Fr. Antonio Lopez, Fr. Edward P. Mahoney, Donald Mathews, Michael Miller, Jason Pannone, Fr. Louis Roy, O.P., Lillian Smith, Michael Terranova, David Vanderhooft, and Jeremy Wilkins. Fr. David

Burrell, C. S. C., Stanley Hauerwas, and Thomas Hibbs generously read the dissertation and gave valuable input as I was revising it for publication.

In the last stages before publication, Fr. Gilles Emery, O. P., and an anonymous reader at the University of Notre Dame Press greatly improved the book through their comments and criticisms; to them I owe heartfelt thanks. Jeffrey Gainey, associate director of the University of Notre Dame Press, did a magnificent job of guiding the book to publication. I am grateful to Gregory LaNave for reading the penultimate draft with his keen editorial eye.

Without the support given by my family, I would never have been able to undertake the work. To my parents, Ralph and Patricia Levering, along with my brother Brooks, I owe the greatest debt and deepest gratitude. My grandparents and aunts and uncles were also a cherished influence. My parents-in-law, Lynn and Ann Moretz, and sister-in-law, Jan Moretz, have shown extraordinary love. The generosity of my grandmother, Mrs. Irene B. Webb, made possible this book. To my children, David and Andrew, and my beloved wife Joy, I owe far more than can be expressed.

In short, the book, while its flaws are my own, is a result of many blessings. In gratitude to the author of all blessings, of which the foremost is salvation, I dedicate the book to our Creator.

Introduction

This book had its origins in a challenge posed to me by a friend. He remarked that no one had ever given him a coherent explanation of the belief that the acts of Jesus of Nazareth could be "salvific" for him today, two thousand years later. It seems to me that his question requires an answer consisting of at least six aspects.

First, my friend would need to be introduced briefly to the dynamic of salvation history. Since Christianity proclaims that God has acted in history, through the covenants with Israel and the New Covenant in Christ Jesus, to save humankind, an account would need to be given of God's overarching plan. Second, he would need an account of Jesus' person, and of Jesus' ministry in Israel, that would show how Jesus in particular was able to enact God's purposes for the salvation of the world. Third, he would need to understand Jesus' cross in a way that would place Jesus' suffering and death in the historical context of God's covenants with Israel and the prophets' proclamation that the whole world would be redeemed through Israel's Messiah. Fourth, he would need to grasp what is meant by the claim that those united to Christ become "temples" of the Holy Spirit by sharing in Christ's suffering and resurrection. Fifth, he would need to see how salvation in Christ, far from being an individualistic transaction, is a participation in the salvation of the world through inclusion in Christ's "Mystical Body." Finally, he would need to have a sense of the ultimate destination or goal, because "salvation" ends not in earthly existence but in eternal life in communion with the Trinity.

These six aspects correspond to the chapters of the book. In brief, the first chapter is about human history understood in light of the divine law and covenants, the second about Jesus the incarnate Son of God and Messiah of Israel, the third about Jesus' cross, the fourth about being transformed in the image of the risen Lord, the fifth about the Mystical Body of Christ into which all human beings are called, and the sixth about eternal life.

As such, this book is an introduction to Christian theology of salvation. Taking the doctrines of faith as my starting point, I hope to answer the questions of those (Christians and non-Christians) who desire to learn about how and for what end Jesus "saves" humankind. The book is also, however, an invitation to learn about these questions by studying in detail the theology of a Christian saint and teacher, Thomas Aquinas. The reader might wonder why I consider Thomas Aquinas to be such an important guide into the mystery of salvation. It might seem that expecting a thirteenth-century theologian to inform modern, historically minded persons about the significance of Jesus of Nazareth is a misguided endeavor, given the progress that theological and exegetical studies have made since Aquinas's day.

Other theologians have answered this question before me. Jean-Pierre Torrell perhaps has put the matter best: "It would be absurd to pretend that Thomas has the answer to all our questions, but we can be confident that his reading illumines the work of our salvation, and that, following him, one can speak of the work of salvation in a more sane and more balanced way."[1] Without suggesting that any theologian knows all the answers, one can affirm that Aquinas's answers—and the sapiential structure of his questions—draw the student into the heart of the theological task of pondering the mysteries of the work of salvation.

Furthermore, contemporary progress has made possible a renewed appreciation of Thomas Aquinas's theology of salvation. Spurred by contemporary biblical exegetes—some of whom I will discuss in these pages—most Christian theologians now recognize that no Christian account of "salvation" is possible that abstracts from the covenants and law of the people into which Jesus was born, the people of Israel.[2] At the same time, theologians today investigate medieval theology with a deepened appreciation of the fact that it derived primarily from *lectio divina*, the reading of Scripture. The recovery of this perspective in this century received its impetus from the contribution of neoscholastic theologians.[3] As M.-D. Chenu noted, Aquinas's "systematic Summa is implanted in and fed with a continuous study of Scripture . . . its most perfect rational structures are never an end, but a means to arrive at a better knowledge of the Word of God."[4] Theological interpretation of the *Summa Theologiae* cannot proceed without continual attention to the *Summa*'s scriptural fount.[5] As we will see, at the heart of Thomas Aquinas's scientific theology of salvation lies the narrative of Scripture—the fulfillment of Israel's Torah and Temple through the New Covenant in Christ Jesus. One can thus expect to find in Aquinas's theological questioning—his interweaving of dialectical enquiry and scriptural narrative[6]—a guide that reveals the meaning of the apostolic witness that the Scriptures have been fulfilled in Jesus of Nazareth.

By way of exploring the Christian meaning of "Jesus saves" and "salvation," I will therefore draw upon both Thomas Aquinas's theology, especially as found in mature form in his *Summa Theologiae*, and the work of contemporary biblical exegetes and theologians. It is worth noting that there already exist valuable commentaries on Aquinas's presentation of Jesus Christ in the *Summa Theologiae*, most notably Jean-Pierre Torrell's recent commentary.[7] These works generally follow the order of questions adopted by Aquinas and offer theological and historical insights into each question. My study, intended as a contribution to contemporary systematic theology in the Thomist tradition, complements these works by offering a reading of Aquinas's theology of salvation that focuses on his use of central motifs from the Old Testament: Torah and Temple. The chapters that follow are an invitation to a dialogue, with St. Thomas as the major but far from the only interlocutor, on the meaning of "Jesus saves" and "salvation."

Nonetheless, before we begin in earnest, a certain amount of strictly historical introduction is appropriate. The twelfth and thirteenth centuries were a period of enormously fruitful debate over the meaning of Christ's passion, death, and resurrection. The debate's starting point was Anselm's *Cur Deus Homo*, written at the prompting of his fellow monks, which attempts to provide a rational explanation for Christ's bloody death.[8] Why, Anselm asks, did God choose this bloody means, involving the death of an innocent man, to redeem human beings? Would it not have been more reasonable for God simply to redeem human beings by the command of his will? Furthermore, why did God choose that his Son should redeem us? Why couldn't we have been redeemed by the actions of a mere sinless man created for that purpose, or by an angel?[9]

In answer to such questions, Anselm develops his theory of "satisfaction." As Guy Mansini has shown, Anselm drew this term from the Rule of St. Benedict, where it refers to the guilty person's making amends for a violation of the communal rule of conduct.[10] For Benedict and Anselm, satisfaction differs from punishment because the person performs satisfaction by his or her own free will. Anselm notes that right order between the creature and the Creator exists when the creature's will is conformed to the Creator's holy will. When the rational creature turns away from God, this right order is destroyed. Punishment ensures that the creature who sins (and does not make restoration) is not equal to the creature who does not sin. For Anselm, it is impossible that God would simply ignore the disorder and raise all human beings to the ultimate "end" for which God created rational creatures, namely eternal life.[11] Anselm illustrates eternal life by comparing it to a treasury, and each rational creature to a treasure. The blessed angels are sparkling treasures; sinful human beings are muddied treasures. God would not place muddied treasures in the same treasury where he preserves his sparkling treasures.[12] Thus the disorder in sinful creatures must be healed interiorly, not extrinsically by divine command.

To restore right order, a human being would have to do three things. First, the human being would have to subject his or her will to God's will, thus returning what the first human being took away.[13] Second, the human being would need to return to God all the people who, because of original sin, were not subject to God's will.[14] Third, in addition to healing the disorder, the human being would need to compensate for the insult bound up with (yet distinguishable from) the disorder.[15] Anselm shows that a mere human being could not accomplish any of these three tasks. On the other hand, the incarnate Word, as God-man, achieves all three: his human will is perfectly in accord with his divine will; his undeserved death merits an eternal reward, which he transfers to those who are joined to him by faith and charity; and his free sacrifice of his bodily life, as the bodily life of the Word, compensates superabundantly for the insult bound up with the disorder.[16]

Almost immediately, Peter Abelard challenged Anselm's theory (without addressing its particular details) by rejecting its framework of justice.[17] For Abelard, Christ's cross cannot be properly interpreted by analogies based on human conceptions of justice. Rather, the cross manifests God's superabundant charity, leveling all conceptions of justice. Christ's suffering reveals God's charity, not God's will to have Christ make satisfaction for sins.[18] Abelard's challenge was answered in kind by his contemporary Bernard, who defended Anselm's perspective. Bernard argues that God's mercy operates by means of justice.[19] Christ's suffering is not simply a revelation of God's charity. On the contrary, it enacts God's charity by accomplishing our salvation through the restoration of justice.[20] Retrieving the Pauline theme of the Mystical Body, Bernard suggests that Christ, by his undeserved suffering and death (paying sin's penalty, which he did not owe), makes satisfaction as Head for the members of his Body.[21] In this way, Bernard attempts to show that while our salvation is due to Christ's suffering on the cross, nonetheless salvation is not an extrinsic event: by interior union with the Head, human beings receive the interior renewal that his suffering brings about.

Later twelfth- and thirteenth-century theologians attempted to overcome the apparent divide between the two approaches by uniting Anselm's emphasis on justice with Abelard's emphasis on charity. The great theologians of the thirteenth century, such as Albert, Bonaventure, and Aquinas, all incorporate into their accounts of salvation Anselm's theory of satisfaction (without Anselm's effort to arrive at "necessary reasons"), the centrality of Christ's charity, the role of merit, and the Mystical Body, as well as complex discussions of causality drawn from their reading of Aristotle. This wide conceptual agreement has led modern scholars to conclude that Aquinas's contribution lay in synthesizing and at times sharpening the insights of his well-known predecessors. Brian McDermott expresses this view in concluding his brief summary of Aquinas's doctrine of redemption:

"Aquinas's treatment of redemption, though not original, is a very balanced and tempered synthesis of many key contributions from biblical and patristic soteriology."[22]

Such depictions, although accurate as regards his sources, nonetheless underestimate his contribution. Most importantly, they do not appreciate the reemergence, during this period, of widespread Christian theological study of the Old Testament. As Chenu has pointed out, theologians in the twelfth century "did not treat the Old Testament as a bygone and defunct stage in the divine plan but on the contrary resorted to the Old Covenant somehow to illuminate or elaborate elements in the New by recourse to what had gone before."[23] Chenu identifies a growing enthusiasm (even over-enthusiasm) for the Old Testament among twelfth-century theologians.[24] Behind this surge of interest lay a number of factors, from combat with the Catharist heresy, which rejected the Old Testament, to the development of increasingly complex legal and political institutions.[25]

The growing interest in the Old Testament can be documented by tracing medieval theology from the eleventh century onwards, but I will not undertake that project here. The importance of the Old Testament for Aquinas's theology of salvation can be traced in large part to the influence of the *Summa Fratris Alexandri*, whose completion preceded Aquinas's *Summa Theologiae* by little more than a decade. The *Summa Fratris Alexandri* was finished around 1260 through a collaborative effort on the part of Franciscan theologians, among them Alexander of Hales (d. 1245) and his students John of la Rochelle and William of Middleton. As Beryl Smalley and more recently John F. Boyle have noted, this Franciscan compendium is an important source for the shift that took place in Aquinas's theology of salvation between his *Commentary on the Sentences* (finished in 1256) and his *Summa Theologiae* (the early 1270s).[26] Whereas the *Commentary on the Sentences* contains almost no discussion of the Mosaic Law and lacks a carefully organized exposition of the mysteries of Christ's life, Aquinas adds both to his mature theology of salvation in the *Summa Theologiae*.

In its massive treatment of the Mosaic Law, the *Summa Fratris Alexandri* proposes three classes of precepts: moral, judicial, and ceremonial (Maimonides had already anticipated this threefold division).[27] The author explains this threefold division by arguing that the purpose of the Mosaic Law was to confer goodness in accord with the "branches of charity," namely love of God and love of neighbor (moral precepts); punishment of evildoers (judicial precepts); and preparation for the worship of God (ceremonial precepts).[28] The *Summa Fratris Alexandri* then makes explicit the connection between the three kinds of precepts and Christ's fulfillment of the law. Citing Mt 5:17, the author addresses "The Fulfillment of the Law of Moses by Christ."[29] The author holds that Christ fulfills each class of laws in a different way.[30] Christ fulfills the moral laws by perfect knowledge of the good, perfect execution of the good, and perfect revelation of the good after the fall. Thus, Christ fulfills the moral laws by his teaching and example and by giving grace so that others can follow this teaching and example.[31] He fulfills the ceremonial laws *"per terminationem, per exhibitionem, per manifestationem"*: as the end or term of the ceremonial laws, he shows what they prefigure, and he manifests their inner meaning.[32] Finally, Christ fulfills the judicial laws by leading people away from evil; for instance, by abolishing divorce and by teaching people not to resist evil rather than exacting the retribution of "an eye for an eye."[33] The author concludes that Christ fulfills the Old Law especially by two modes: by revealing grace in his teaching and conferring grace through the effects of his sacrifice on the cross and by teaching the truth about the way to God (particularly in the Sermon on the Mount).[34]

Aquinas, in his *Summa Theologiae*, adopts from the *Summa Fratris Alexandri* both the threefold division of the Mosaic Law and the claim that Christ fulfills each aspect of the Mosaic Law. Unlike the authors of the *Summa Fratris Alexandri*, however, Aquinas argues that Christ fulfills[35] the Old Law precisely in his passion or suffering on the cross. Aquinas suggests that Christ's perfect obedience to the threefold law in his passion fulfills both the literal and the spiritual meaning of the Mosaic Law: Christ's passion manifests his perfect charity (moral precepts), through which he freely wills to suffer the penalty of sin for all sinners (judicial precepts) and to give himself as a perfect offering to God (ceremonial precepts).[36] While I will explain this fulfillment in detail in the body of the study, it should already be clear that viewing Aquinas's theology of salvation in light of the covenants opens up a new range of possibilities for contemporary appropriation of his theology of salvation. It should also be clear why the chapters that follow focus on Aquinas's *Summa Theologiae*. The sustained theology of salvation found in the *Summa Theologiae*—specifically its treatises on law and on Christ—moves beyond his earlier systematic work.[37]

Aquinas's biblical commentaries, the most important of which were given (as course lectures) at the same time that he was composing the *Summa Theologiae*, also influenced the direction of his systematic exposition. While it seems unlikely that he "rediscovered" the theological importance of Scripture late in his career, nonetheless his commentaries and his *Catena Aurea* certainly assisted his mature theological expression.[38] In his commentaries, as well as in his selection of patristic authorities in the *Catena Aurea*, he identifies Christ as the fulfillment of all that is recorded in the Old Testament.[39] Thus, commenting on Rom 3:31 (explicitly in light of Mt 5:17), Aquinas interprets St. Paul to mean that the Mosaic Law is established (*statuimus*) by being perfected and fulfilled (*perficimus et adimplemus*) by Christ.[40] This fulfillment is not a revocation. Commenting on Rom 11:29, he states, "someone could say that although the Jews were formerly most beloved of God on account of their fathers, nevertheless the enmity which they exercise against the Gospel would prohibit them from being saved in the future. But this the Apostle affirms to be false, in saying: 'For the gifts and the call of God are irrevocable.'"[41] Aquinas goes on to show that while God is frequently said to repent or change his mind in the Old Testament, St. Paul is here speaking of the permanent election of the Jews, which belongs to God's predestination.[42]

Approached in this way, Thomas Aquinas's theology of salvation can be linked with certain of the concerns and insights of current biblical exegesis. As we will see, Aquinas reads the Old Testament in terms of Torah and Temple, a reading that flows from the Psalms, chanted daily by Dominican friars, which continually refer to the beauty of God's law and of the Temple.[43] This reading is by no means a Christian imposition upon the text of the Old Testament. In his *Sinai and Zion: An Entry into the Jewish Bible*, Jon D. Levenson has argued that the Old Testament (Jewish Bible) should be interpreted through these two primary covenantal narratives about the relationship of Israel and God.[44] Along with Jewish exegetes such as Leven-

son, contemporary Christian exegetes have emphasized the significance of Torah and Temple for understanding the Messiah presented in the gospels and epistles of the New Testament. Luke Timothy
Johnson has remarked, "In Matthew's Gospel, Jesus is the teacher
of Torah, the fulfillment of Torah, and the very personification of
Torah."[45] As Richard B. Hays points out, it is now widely accepted
that "authentically Christian biblical interpretation would necessarily be an exercise in intertextual reading, attending with great care
to the way in which the canonical NT writers heard, echoed, and
transformed the voices of their precursors in the OT."[46]

In its current manifestation, the attention given to the importance of the Old Testament is a response to the attempt, originating
in Protestant liberalism but flowering in Roman Catholic transcendental theologies as well, to ground theology in universal anthropo-
logical categories abstracted from the history of God's revelation.
Classical Protestant liberalism was particularly eager to distance itself
from the Old Testament.[47] In his *Glaubenslehre*, Friedrich Schleiermacher remarks that "Christianity cannot in any wise be regarded
as a remodelling or a renewal and continuation of Judaism," and he
goes on to conclude that "the Old Testament appears simply a superfluous authority for dogmatics."[48] He adds that "whatever has a certain flavour of the Jewish or the Heathen is more in keeping with
the Roman Church, just as every opposition to these elements, even
in earlier times, contained something akin to Protestantism."[49]

I will propose that Thomas Aquinas's theology of salvation does,
as Schleiermacher might have predicted, revolve around the way that
Christ brings to fulfillment and thereby transforms God's covenantal relationship with Israel, concretized by law and liturgy.[50] Because
of the nature of *sacra doctrina* as integrative wisdom, Aquinas manifests Christ's fulfillment of Torah and Temple by bringing together
investigation of the nature of triune God, Christ's life, and human salvation: as Valkenberg has pointed out, the *Summa Theologiae*'s form
means that "theological, christological and soteriological considera-
tions [while distinct] are never separated."[51] By means of his systematic attention to the interplay of the Bible's central narratives, Aquinas
also avoids the kind of supersessionism (the view that the fulfillment
of Israel's covenants means that they are now *revoked*) that mars the
work of earlier medieval theologians such as Robert Grosseteste.[52]

I should note at the outset that Christ's fulfillment of Torah and Temple is not divided sequentially. Perfect fulfillment of the Torah (perfect holiness) is perfect fulfillment of the Temple (perfect worship). As we will see, this approach gives equal importance to the missions of the Son and the Holy Spirit. Similarly, this approach overcomes the dichotomy between "objective" and "subjective" redemption.[53] Through the grace of the Holy Spirit, human beings are enabled to share, by their own free will, in Christ's self-giving on the cross and in his resurrection into eternal life. Thus the entire Mystical Body, Head and members, fulfills Torah and Temple. The "objective" redemption accomplished by Christ is not isolated from the "subjective" appropriation of redemption by other human beings. As Aquinas remarks in discussing how Christ's merit causes our salvation, Christ's passion merited glory, and through his passion Christ "was glorified, not merely in Himself, but likewise in His faithful ones, as He says Himself (Jn 17:10)."[54]

The book is for theological readers who, with the perseverance requisite for entering into Thomas Aquinas's thought, seek to gain a better understanding of what Christians mean, or should mean, when they speak of salvation. As in Aquinas's own theology, voices from various traditions will be present throughout the work. The book is not a comparative study of how the various religious traditions understand "salvation."[55] Yet I should emphasize that the Christian approach presented here is inclusive in the sense of not ruling out the salvation of adherents of other religions. As a Christian theologian, I affirm the Christian confession that all salvation—understood as transformative and eternal communion with the Trinity—ultimately is received through the mediation of the incarnate Son of God. Precisely because salvation is primarily a divine rather than a human work, however, I do not pass judgment on the ways in which human beings, if unable to receive Christ explicitly, might nonetheless be joined to the blessings of his mediation.

Thomas Aquinas's theology of salvation flows from his intertextual or canonical readings of the Old and New Testaments, in which the New constantly sheds light on the Old, and vice versa. Fully appreciating Aquinas's theology is possible only when one recognizes, in the words of the Thomist theologian Servais Pinckaers, that

"Scripture is the primary source of all theology, and we need to return to it if we wish to make any kind of worthwhile contribution to the work of renewal."[56] For Aquinas, theology is the scientific expression of the sacred teaching authored by God in Scripture and summarized in the Church's articles of faith. The task of theology is to employ scientific reasoning in order to understand more profoundly God's teaching.[57] With this in mind, we are prepared to turn to the task of learning, guided by Aquinas, how the words and deeds of Jesus of Nazareth can be said to accomplish the salvation of the entire world.

PART 1

The Fulfillment
of Israel's Torah

1 Divine Law and Divine Pedagogy

What significance does the Mosaic Law have for Christians? Is the Old Law (Torah) merely a preparation for the New Law in Christ Jesus, whose passion, death, and resurrection *revoke* the Old Law? Christian theologians today often try to answer such questions. The medieval period, however, is generally not the place where contemporary theologians look for answers. A challenging exception is the work of the Jewish theologian Michael Wyschogrod. Because of his interest in Aquinas's work and his nuanced rendering of a paramount question for any contemporary Christian theology of salvation—namely the question of supersessionism—I will begin this study of how Christ fulfills Israel's Torah by seeking to enter into dialogue with the concerns posed by Wyschogrod.

The April 1995 issue of *Modern Theology* presents a symposium centered on a "letter" written by Wyschogrod and addressed to an unnamed Jewish convert to Roman Catholicism. The symposium includes the responses of seven theologians, Jewish and Christian.[1] In the letter, Wyschogrod proposes that from *both* a Jewish and a Christian perspective, Jewish Christians should continue to observe the Mosaic Law.[2] Wyschogrod first makes the claim from the side of Judaism: "Because you are a Jew, you are obligated, like all Jews, to obey the *mitzvoth* (e.g., tefilin [phylacteries] in the morning, kashrut, sabbath, etc.)."[3] He then seeks to explore the status of a Jewish convert from the side of *Christian* theology. He begins by pointing out that the Catholic Church, in the Second Vatican Council, has affirmed that God's covenant with Israel "has never been revoked."[4] Jewish converts, however, are not allowed to continue practicing the *mitzvoth*, so they are generally assimilated within a generation. How then can the Church claim to recognize God's continuing covenant with Israel, which would quickly disappear as a visible reality if all Jews heeded the Church's evangelical call? The covenant remains a reality today, in Wyschogrod's view, only because there are still Jews who obey the Mosaic Law.

Having identified this apparent tension in the Church's teaching, Wyschogrod briefly describes the theological grounds on which converted Jews have been prevented from obeying the Mosaic Law. He selects Aquinas as a notable representative of the traditional view. Following Gal 5:2 ("If you receive circumcision Christ will do you no good at all"), Aquinas concludes that obeying the "ceremonial" precepts of the Mosaic Law after Christ would be a mortal sin for Jewish Christians, although the "moral" precepts have permanent validity. Wyschogrod challenges this position on two grounds. First, he argues that Aquinas's distinction between "ceremonial" and "moral" precepts ignores the unity of the Mosaic Law, which God gave to Israel as a single entity to be obeyed. Second, he points out that the original Jewish Christians, as depicted in the book of Acts, either continued to follow the entire Mosaic Law or at least did not consider doing so to be a mortal sin. Along the same lines, he notes that many of the original Jewish Christians held that the Gentiles, too, were obligated to follow the entire law. He concludes by suggesting that observant Jewish Christians should once more find a place in the Church. Were this to happen, "a profound clarification of the Church's attitude to the Hebrew bible and its Jewish roots will have taken place."[5] The Church, in short, would be recognizing in practice what it affirmed theoretically at Vatican II: the existence of a perpetual covenant between God and the Jews that is not superseded by the new covenant in Christ.

Although many of the responses to Wyschogrod's letter were insightful, none of the theologians selected by *Modern Theology* took the occasion to explore in depth the view that Wyschogrod attributes to Aquinas. This oversight is unfortunate because Wyschogrod's "letter" has its roots in an essay he wrote a few years earlier entitled "A Jewish Reading of St. Thomas Aquinas on the Old Law."[6] The essay reveals Wyschogrod as a perceptive reader of Aquinas, and it also presents in detail the concerns, noted briefly in the later "letter," that Wyschogrod has about the "traditional Christian view."[7] Wyschogrod specifically seeks to bring Aquinas into the contemporary Jewish-Christian dialogue.[8]

The bulk of Wyschogrod's essay surveys Aquinas's treatment of the Old Law. On the basis of this survey, Wyschogrod offers some criticisms from his perspective as a Jewish theologian. First, he notes that St. Paul is notoriously difficult to understand on the issue of the Mosaic Law. Jesus claimed to observe the law but was accused (perhaps justly, Wyschogrod thinks) by a number of Pharisees of breaking it. Paul's situation is even more ambiguous. In Wyschogrod's view, Aquinas gets around the difficulties in Paul's thought by dividing the one Mosaic Law into three aspects—moral, ceremonial, and judicial. This division enables Aquinas to separate the law into permanent and nonpermanent parts.

The permanent part is the "moral" law, which contains precepts (such as "honor your father and mother") that are the foundation of right living and would have been known immediately by the rational creature had reason not been obscured by sin. The ceremonial and judicial precepts are related to this moral law. They constitute the way in which God, at a particular time, chose to arrange—in accordance with the general and universal precepts of the moral law— the specific details of divine worship (the ceremonial law) and of communal life (the judicial law). The ceremonial and judicial precepts come to an end in Christ.

Wyschogrod identifies two flaws in this position. First, even accepting (for the sake of argument) the threefold division, Wyschogrod cannot agree that the ceremonial precepts are not permanent, since to some of them the Old Testament attaches the phrase "it shall be a statute forever unto their generations." Second, Wyschogrod argues that the ceremonial law should be accepted as valuable on its own terms. For Aquinas, the ceremonial law has significance in two ways: in relation to the moral or "natural" law, which it expresses (by divine decree) in a particular time and place; and as prefiguring Christ. Aquinas holds, therefore, that after Christ it would be a "mortal" sin for a person, professing that Christ has come, nonetheless to continue to observe the ceremonial law that God gave in preparation for Christ. Wyschogrod, in contrast, argues that the ceremonial law should be understood as the permanent way that God intended for *Jews* to worship God. Jewish Christians (among whom Wyschogrod does not, it should be noted, count himself) should then continue to obey the ceremonial law even after Christ, simply as a sign that the covenant of God with the Jewish nation remains in force and will remain in force (along with the new covenant in Christ) until the time of the "final fulfillment that both Jews and Christians await."[9]

As in "Letter to a Friend," Wyschogrod next discusses the passages from the book of Acts (particularly Acts 15) that show that Jewish Christians did indeed continue to observe the Mosaic Law in the early Church. On this basis, he argues that Aquinas should have considered "the possibility that Jewish Christians ought to maintain a Jewish identity in the Church by continuing to live under the Mosaic Law, while sharing with Gentile Christians their faith in Christ."[10] This situation would not, Wyschogrod thinks, compromise the fundamental equality of Jews and Gentiles; rather, it would simply constitute a special task reserved in the Church for Jews, in the same way that the priesthood is reserved for men even though in Christ "there is neither male nor female" (Gal 3:28). Nor would it mean that Jewish Christians would be "justified" by the Mosaic Law. Wyschogrod argues that, from the Jewish perspective, only *God* justifies. The law simply sets forth God's will for Jews. Observant Jewish Christians could still believe that they were justified by Christ (as God incarnate), not by the law.

It should be clear from this earlier essay that Wyschogrod's later "Letter to a Friend" can be read as addressed not only to his Jewish friend but also to Catholic theologians, and in particular to those who study the theology of Aquinas. The central task of the present chapter will be to examine Aquinas's views on the Mosaic Law. In interpreting Aquinas, I will seek to show more fully why he divided the law in the way that he did, why and in what sense he considered some of the law's precepts to have been superseded, and why he (unlike some of his Christian predecessors and successors) placed the law within the heart of his theology of salvation. The chapter will proceed in two steps. Following the order of Aquinas's treatise, I will begin by examining 1–2, qq.90–92, where Aquinas discusses law's essence and effects and briefly sketches the various kinds of "law." Here we will see how the Mosaic Law fits into the *Summa Theologiae*'s broader *exitus-reditus* pattern. Second, I will turn to a detailed examination of Aquinas's extensive treatment of the Mosaic Law in 1–2, qq.98–105.

Aquinas on Law

In the code of law given to Israel, Aquinas recognizes the form and structure typical of law in all societies. Certainly the Mosaic Law is more than a mere human production, since it is composed and promulgated by God; but it is nonetheless recognizably "law." Therefore, Aquinas begins his treatise on law, which culminates in his discussion of the Old (Mosaic) Law and the New Law, by asking what constitutes the essence of law.[11] He notes first that law pertains to the reason, not to the will. Law, properly speaking, is composed of precepts that guide and direct human acts toward the end recognized by right reason.[12] Aquinas argues that the ability of right reason to recognize this end is due to the participation of human reason in the divine reason. All creaturely being is a finite, created participation in infinite Divine Being, but as rational creatures human beings image God in a special way. By means of the rational soul, human beings are able to grasp the intelligible order that characterizes the universe. This ability constitutes the human being's participation in the "eternal law," the Creator's idea of the government of things in the universe.[13] The end fitting to human beings, as Aquinas has already shown, is happiness, which consists in the "common good" (which must be a rational good, a perfection fitted to the rational creature) of the whole community, to which each member is ordered as a part.[14] Law, whose precepts direct human actions to this common good, thus seeks to make each person, and finally the whole community, good or virtuous.[15] Since law is directed to the whole community, it must be promulgated or made known publicly, and it must be promulgated by someone, or some entity, who possesses the power to enforce it, so that it will truly be able to shape the community.[16]

For Aquinas, law is rational and positive, not arbitrary or constricting. Law is meant primarily to aid people in their quest to know and do the good, although certainly law also has the secondary role of restraining the wicked.[17] From this understanding of law, it is easy to understand why God, in order to manifest his covenantal love for Israel, gave Israel a *law*. Aquinas identifies the Torah given to Moses as the center around which revolve the Old Testament's historical, wisdom, and prophetic books, which either prepare for the law or describe Israel's arduous effort to live out the law fully and to grasp its inner dynamic.

God wishes Israel to become, through the gift of the law, a uniquely virtuous community. But why would not natural law (the law known by human reason) or human positive law suffice for this purpose? Aquinas's answer derives from his understanding of history. As the narrative of Genesis relates, God made human beings to be in communion with him, but the first human beings turned away from him, cutting off this integral communion.[18] Lacking this communion, human beings fell deeper and deeper into the disorder of sin. Overwhelmed by disordered desires, human beings no longer chose the good identified by reason, and indeed the light of reason itself became obscured.[19] With reason obscured, human beings could no longer efficiently discern the natural law. Human positive law, which applies the general principles of the natural law to particular cases, was correspondingly affected.

Yet why did not God simply give Israel a perfect human law? By entering into a free covenant with Israel, God shows that he means to restore human beings to closer communion with him than would have been naturally possible. Natural and human law are therefore not enough, since they are not directed to the supernatural end that God reveals by entering into the covenant.[20] The uniqueness of the Mosaic Law is that its precepts, promulgated by God, direct human beings to this supernatural end. On the other hand, Aquinas thinks that the Mosaic Law does not fully direct human beings to this end (thus the promise of a "new" law). First, the end is not explicitly put forward by the Mosaic Law, which refers instead to temporal punishments and rewards that do not express the fullness of communion with God. Second, the Mosaic Law, like human law, regards exterior acts; the Mosaic Law instructs people on how to act justly, but it is not an inner law that guides and perfects the movements of the soul. As the prophet Jeremiah suggests, the Mosaic Law is dynamically ordered toward a new law (and new covenant) that will make explicit the communion that God has in store for us and that will interiorly guide and perfect our actuating powers so that they will cleave, entirely out of self-giving love, to the true and the good.

In summary, Aquinas in qq.90–92 argues that all laws, and especially the one that God establishes for Israel, direct human beings to acts that are perfective of human nature; in this sense, all true laws are connected with the rational "natural" law that enables us to identify what is good in matters of action. Second, Aquinas notes that all laws serve an end that the lawgiver has in mind. The divine lawgiver gives law to human beings with an end in mind that he has specifically chosen as perfective of the kind of creature that human beings are. Law itself is possible because it is grounded in God's eternal law for the government of the universe (not merely the ordered arrangement of things but also their progression and development in time). Finally, by means of his covenant with Israel, God has revealed a hidden aspect of his eternal plan: the end of the rational creature will be a supernatural perfection—participation, through knowing and loving, in the divine life. God promulgates the twofold divine law to enable human beings to attain this supernatural aspect of his eternal law.[21]

Aquinas on the Old (Mosaic) Law

Aquinas begins his analysis of the Old Law by asking whether, in a technical sense, the Old Law was "good." Something is good if it leads the person to the end of human *being*, namely, the perfection fitting to human nature.[22] This perfection, as we have seen, is a supernatural one; still, it should be noted that in the state of supernatural perfection, human nature will not lack its "natural" perfection, since, as Aquinas says elsewhere, grace does not destroy nature but perfects and elevates it. On this basis, the Old Law is indeed good, since it leads Israel toward the supernatural perfection that God has ordained for human beings.

The Old Law conduced to this end by forbidding sinful acts and by restraining disordered desires, which are opposed to the perfection of the rational creature. On the other hand, Aquinas notes, the Old Law was not "sufficient in itself" to achieve the supernatural end, which perfects the rational creature by enabling him or her to share in the very life of God by means of knowing and loving. For this end to be achieved, not only must exterior acts be ordered, but also human beings must receive an interior principle that will be able to direct human acts, at their root, toward the supernatural end of knowing and loving the triune God. This interior principle, since it must have the power to give us a participation in God's trinitarian life, must itself be divine. Aquinas explains that the divine law, to which the Old Law (as promulgated by God) belongs, "should make man altogether fit to partake of everlasting happiness. Now this cannot be done save by the grace of the Holy Spirit."[23] Thus, in its end, the divine law is one. Yet it requires two parts, since the structure established by the Old Law (which forbids sin, those acts that draw human beings away from their perfection) must be completed and perfected by the interior principle of the grace of the Holy Spirit.

The giving of this interior principle cannot fittingly be done in an external way. The God of the *covenant* has already shown that he does not wish to simply "zap" human beings from on high. In promulgating the Mosaic Law, God has in view the promulgation of the New Law, the grace of the Holy Spirit, which (since the Holy Spirit is God) only God can give. God will promulgate this interior principle from within the people that receive the Old Law. For this reason, Aquinas argues that the Old Law is intrinsically ordered to Jesus Christ, the Messiah of Israel.[24] This order appears in two ways. First, the Old Law "bears witness" to Christ by prefiguring him; second, it prepares for Christ by turning people away from idolatrous worship and toward the one God. In both ways the Old Law, far from being a husk that is to be thrown out, possesses a permanent goodness.

For Aquinas it is not the case that if the Old Law is figurative, then one no longer needs to pay attention to it.[25] The figurative aspect of the Old Law is crucial for Aquinas not because he wishes to disregard the Old Law but because he wishes to establish the *unity* of the divine law. In this regard, Aquinas makes use of a distinction between the "New Law" and the "state of the New Law."[26]

The state of the New Law begins after the Incarnation, while the New Law itself, as the grace of the Holy Spirit, is found in all places and times.[27] Given this distinction, it follows that the "state of the Old Law" does not preclude the New Law's already being active. The sacraments of the Mosaic Law, while they do not *cause* grace, nonetheless belong to the movement whereby men and women under the state of the Old Law participated in the New Law. As Aquinas remarks, "The ancient Fathers, *by observing the sacraments of the law*, were brought towards Christ through the same faith and love by which we are still brought towards him."[28] The Mosaic Law and the New Law are thus intrinsically related.

Aquinas's conception of God's action in history has two levels. On the one hand, following St. Paul, he views the Mosaic Law as a "pedagogue" that, at a time when the entire human race had fallen into idolatry, sought to withdraw a particular nation from that idolatry in order to make ready a nation from which Christ might be born.[29] Human history had to be made ready for Christ so that he could truly enter it and transform it from within. The covenant with Israel, therefore, involved real historical development as the people (and individuals among the people) progressed in holiness of life and spiritual insight.[30] On this level, Aquinas views the Old Law as gradually making people better by teaching them their state of sin and by aiding them to recognize the virtuous course of action, although this progressive movement truly flowers (in terms of numbers of people changed) only through the public preaching of the Gospel.[31]

On another level, however, Aquinas views God's action in history as radically unified. He argues that in all places and times there are "two kinds of men," good and evil, and that in all places and times the good accept God's call and the wicked reject it.[32] Furthermore, he does not conceive of a time before Christ that lacked grace. On the contrary, as we have seen, the New Law (which is the grace of the Holy Spirit) infuses the period of the Old Law, even though grace does not belong to the Old Law per se.[33] The integral unity of divine law is brought about by the fact that faith in Christ, who by his passion (to which we are united by faith) enables us to receive the grace of the Holy Spirit, can be implicit or explicit.[34] Aquinas suggests that in attempting to follow the precepts of the Old Law, members of the people of Israel made a twofold discovery. First, they realized that to be able to obey the precepts, they needed an interior principle (the grace of the Holy Spirit).[35] Second, in the ceremonial precepts, they found a figurative outline of the manner by which the disorder that obstructed human beings from receiving God's grace would be healed. By participating in this figurative drama (through the sacraments of the Old Law), they could be proleptically, and implicitly, united to the future Messiah who, by perfectly fulfilling all aspects of the Law, would make this grace available to all.[36] Such "implicit" faith (itself a supernatural gift) joined the person, in advance, to Christ, thereby indicating that the person had already received the interior principle of the grace of the Holy Spirit.[37]

Nonetheless, it should equally be noted that Aquinas does not "flatten" history, as if all times were really the same and the historical enactment of the passion hardly mattered.[38] Aquinas holds that the ultimate reward of the New Law (beatific communion with God in heavenly glory) is received by the souls of the holy men and women of the Old Testament only *after* Christ has undergone his passion.[39] Similarly, as we have seen, he argues that Christ's passion inaugurates the period of history in which grace is given most abundantly because the state of the New Law instantiates grace in the sacraments of the Catholic Church.[40] The historical event of Christ's passion is the decisive act of God's love that transforms everything. Yet Aquinas does not allow this undeniable discontinuity to overshadow, in his theology of history, the fundamental continuity of God's active love throughout history, and especially in the covenantal history of Israel.

In Wyschogrod's view, however, Aquinas does not sufficiently allow for true continuity. For Wyschogrod, the primary requirement is that Jews, whether or not they have converted to Christianity, should continue to observe the Mosaic Law as a sign of God's perpetual covenant with Israel.[41] For this reason, Wyschogrod focuses his critique upon the aspects of Aquinas's treatment that enable Aquinas to hold that observance of the Mosaic Law is not binding upon Jews (Wyschogrod agrees that it is never binding on Gentiles) after Christ. Foremost among these aspects is Aquinas's division of the Mosaic Law into three kinds of precepts, moral, ceremonial, and judicial, of which the latter two come to an end with Christ.

Aquinas justifies this threefold division by referring back to his earlier discussion of the nature of law, where (as we have seen) he argued that the divine law is no exception to the rule that laws are made with particular purposes or ends in view. The Mosaic Law is ordered to one end: communion or "friendship" with God.[42] Since the Mosaic Law directs various aspects of life toward this one end, however, it is composed of various precepts, which are distinguished according to the aspect of life that each one directs. On this basis, Aquinas identifies three broad categories of precepts. First are the precepts that command the universal acts of virtue, which can be known naturally by reason (but are included in the law because sin has obscured reason), but do not specify the exact way in which these acts are to be carried out—for example, "honor your father and mother." These precepts are the unchangeable core of the Mosaic Law.

Human beings are "good"—that is, their being is perfected—when they perfectly obey the moral precepts. The purpose or end of the law, then, is uniquely bound up in the moral precepts. Aquinas's explanation is worth quoting in full: "just as the principal intention of human law is to create friendship between man and man, so the chief intention of the Divine law is to establish man in friendship with God. Now since likeness is the reason of love . . . there cannot possibly be any friendship of man to God, Who is supremely good, unless man become good: wherefore it is written (Lev. 19:2, cf. 11:45): *You shall be holy, for I am holy.*"[43] Included in the moral precepts, as their foundation, are love of God and love of neighbor (out of love of God).[44] The two other kinds of precepts in the Mosaic Law flow from this twofold commandment of love.

Aquinas first discusses the "ceremonial" precepts, which are those that direct the particular way in which Israel is to express love of God.[45] This particular way is, in a certain sense, changeable. For example, God might have commanded that Israel slaughter two sheep instead of a red cow in a particular ceremonial offering without distorting the basic act of worship. Yet in another sense the way is not changeable—or, better, is changeable only by God—since God, as a wise lawgiver, has reasons for determining that Israel should worship in this particular manner.[46]

Second, Aquinas turns to the precepts commanding the particular ways in which Israel is to express love of neighbor. Love of neighbor is not an abstract concept for the Mosaic Law (or for Aquinas):

true love of neighbor requires the just arrangement of such aspects of community life as government, courts of law, war, relations to foreigners, legal punishments, wages, trade, loans, possessions, and so forth. Detailed precepts regarding all these aspects can be found in the Torah. As lawgiver, God gives Israel judicial precepts that are in conformity with the universal moral precepts, although in some cases, Aquinas thinks, God chose to tolerate (not to sanction) an injustice from which the people would be gradually weaned.[47] As with the "ceremonial" precepts, the precepts governing Israel's community are changeable in a certain sense. God could have affixed a different punishment than stoning to the crime of gathering sticks on the Sabbath.[48] But they are changeable only by God, to whom alone it belongs to establish the mode of life of his covenantal people.

From the above, it should be clear that Aquinas's threefold distinction is not an example of oversystematizing. The three categories delineate, as simply as possible, the various objects of the law that God gave Israel.[49] By using these categories, Aquinas is able to explain why the Ten Commandments were specially engraved upon stones, while the remainder of the precepts were given orally.[50] It should also be clear why Aquinas argues that the ceremonial and judicial precepts are not unchangeable in the sense that the moral precepts are. However, I have yet to reach the heart of Wyschogrod's criticisms. Wyschogrod is concerned especially to challenge Aquinas's view that Jewish Christians should no longer observe the Mosaic Law. It remains, therefore, to explore the theological grounds upon which Aquinas bases this view.

One of these grounds, as Wyschogrod recognizes, is Aquinas's claim that the ceremonial and judicial precepts are figurative. This claim is based upon the Old Testament itself, especially the prophetic books, which promise (among other things) a Messiah who will justify the people, a new interior law, and the extension of God's covenant with Israel to the Gentiles as well. Since the prophets were shaped by their participation in the practices of the Mosaic Law, Aquinas reads the Mosaic Law in light of the promises. He believes, of course, that these promises refer to Jesus of Nazareth. For each precept, therefore, he gives figures that relate in some way to Jesus Christ or to the Church.

Determining the precise figures, however, is not Aquinas's real concern. Apart from the obvious figures, such as the connection of the Passover sacrifice to the self-offering of the Messiah, only God knows the precise figures.[51] Aquinas seeks only to give possible examples. Instead, the main purpose of his emphasis on the figurative causes of the ceremonial and judicial precepts is to draw attention to the fact that these precepts can and should be read in light of the prophetic expectation. In this light, the precepts concerning the government of Israel, for example, can be seen to be binding for their time but not necessarily binding for the future time in which the covenant with Israel has been extended to the Gentiles as well. To take another example, the precepts concerning sin offerings, which command that each day certain animals be slaughtered ritually to atone for sins, could be recognized as inadequate to express the full perfection of human communion with God.

I should emphasize again that Aquinas does not think that the "figurative" causes of the ceremonial and judicial precepts mean that one can ignore the history of Israel and simply focus on the figures. On the contrary, the figurative sense upholds the integral unity of the divine law. In recognizing that Israel prefigures Christ, one does not therefore dismiss Israel as a reality in itself. Rather, as Aquinas explains, each aspect of Israel's history takes on importance in a way that no other ancient people's history does: "The Jewish people were chosen by God that Christ might be born of them. Consequently the entire state of that people had to be prophetic and figurative. . . . Thus, too, the wars and deeds of this people are expounded in the mystical sense: but not the wars and deeds of the Assyrians or Romans, although the latter are more famous in the eyes of men."[52] The importance of Israel's figurative role, indeed, explains why Aquinas grants so much space to discussing the "literal" causes of the precepts—that is, the suitability of the precepts for making Israel into a holy people.[53]

Granted that the precepts are in some sense figurative, however, why cannot Jewish Christians—if only as a way of reminding Gentile Christians of Israel's role—continue to observe the law established by God for Jews? Here one should recall two of Wyschogrod's most telling points. First, to some of the ceremonial precepts that Aquinas claims are no longer to be observed, God attached the command that the precept be observed forever. Second, the early Jewish Christians, as described by Acts, continued to observe the Mosaic Law.

Aquinas's fundamental answer to these two challenges is that the Mosaic Law, in a real sense (though not one that would be recognized by Wyschogrod), *is still observed by Christians*. This reality lies at the heart of Aquinas's treatment of the relationship of the Old Law and the New Law, but as an apparent paradox it requires explanation. Aquinas's account of salvation is built around the idea that Christians, as members of the Mystical Body of Christ, share in the redemptive acts of their Head (Christ). Christians share, and all human beings potentially share, in Christ's fulfillment of all aspects of the Mosaic Law.

Aquinas holds that this fulfillment occurs supremely in the work by which Christ redeems humankind, his passion.[54] In Aquinas's view, as chapter 3 will discuss in more detail, Christ's passion not only fulfills but also perfects and elevates the Mosaic Law: Christ fulfills and transforms the moral precepts through his most perfect (supernatural) love of God and, in God, of all human beings; his perfectly free and loving self-sacrifice on the cross fulfills and transforms the animal sacrifices and purity laws; and his suffering and death (as the suffering and death of the God-man) fulfill and transform the judicial precepts by paying an interior "penalty" that is sufficient to rectify, from the inside, all the disorder caused by sin in human history.[55]

However, Aquinas does not limit Christ's fulfillment of the Mosaic Law to his passion, as if Christ had decided to obey the Mosaic Law when faced with death, having ignored it before. Rather, Christ's suffering and death on the cross are the culmination of a life lived in obedience to the Mosaic Law. Discussing Christ's manner of life, Aquinas argues that "Christ conformed His conduct in all things to the precepts of the Law."[56] Aquinas is aware of Jesus's disputes with the Pharisees, who criticized him for allegedly breaking the law. In this regard, Aquinas notes that one effect of Jesus' obedience to the law was that it enabled him to defend himself against those of his fellow-Jews who criticized him. Examining the various instances in which the gospels record that the Pharisees accused Jesus (or his disciples) of breaking the law, Aquinas seeks to show that the Pharisees were mistaken, largely because they did not understand the nature of Jesus' work.[57]

But Aquinas is more concerned to show *why* Jesus obeyed the Mosaic Law. As we have seen, Aquinas thinks that Jesus fulfilled the Mosaic Law to "perfect it and bring it to an end in His own self, so as to show that it was ordained to Him."[58] In Christ, the Mosaic Law (and the covenant with Israel) is not revoked. Instead, the Mosaic Law is brought to its proper "end"—Christ—*in whom* all people (Jews and Gentiles) now may perfectly fulfill the law. This distinction between revoking and fulfilling (or consummating) is crucial if one is to understand Aquinas's position that Jewish Christians should no longer observe the Mosaic Law. For Aquinas, the Mosaic Law has been fulfilled by Christ, so people observe it by conformity with Christ in the community of the Church. Christians (including Jewish Christians) no longer observe, as Israel did and (where possible) still does, the ceremonial and judicial precepts. From the perspective of a community that holds that Israel's Messiah has come, these precepts were ordained to Christ and fitted, as the judicial precepts make especially clear, for preparing *one* nation to receive him. Yet Christians, by sharing in Christ's passion, will forever observe the ceremonial and judicial precepts—although now in the way proper to a universal "body" that enjoys trinitarian communion through Christ the "Head."[59] In Aquinas's view, Jewish Christians, sharing in Christ's Jewish fulfillment of Mosaic Law, do not lose their identity. Rather, they enter into the (supernatural) fullness of their identity.[60]

We are now in a position to understand how Aquinas responds to Wyschogrod's point that some of the ceremonial precepts are followed by the injunction that "it shall be a statute forever unto their generations" (Ex 27:21 and elsewhere).[61] Aquinas holds that the ceremonial precepts are indeed to be observed forever, but only in their *fulfilled* reality, the end that God has had in view from the beginning. Answering an objection that cited a text similar to the one Wyschogrod gives from Exodus, he explains, "The Old Law is said to be *for ever* simply and absolutely, as regards its moral precepts; but as regards the ceremonial precepts it lasts for ever in respect of the reality which those ceremonies foreshadowed."[62] The ceremonial and judicial precepts are taken up and fulfilled, not revoked, by Christ. They come to an end in the positive (teleological) sense of attaining their ultimate end, in which they rest or last forever.

Yet if this is true, why did the early Jewish Christians continue to follow the Mosaic Law in the old way? Aquinas replies to this question by again turning to his distinction between revoking and fulfilling. When Christ fulfills the Mosaic Law, he does not simply discard it as a mere tool. Rather, the Mosaic Law retains its honored place, although it is observed by sharing (by faith) in Christ's passion. For this reason, Aquinas thinks, "the Holy Ghost did not wish the converted Jews to be debarred at once from observing the legal ceremonies," since then the Gentiles might assume that the Mosaic Law was on par with their own idolatrous rites.[63] The situation described in Acts, therefore, constituted a "middle period" that served to emphasize the fundamental unity of the divine law, during the time in which the Gentiles were being brought into the new covenant. After the Gentiles had been brought in, Aquinas argues, Jewish Christians who continued to observe the ceremonies of the Mosaic Law would be in a state of "mortal" sin—that is, no longer in communion with God— because such observance would constitute a "false profession" of faith in Christ.[64]

In dialogue with Wyschogrod, this chapter has served to introduce my study of Aquinas's account of Christ's fulfillment of the Mosaic Law.[65] The chapter first sought to grasp the significance that Aquinas gives to law. Second, it explored Aquinas's view of the relationship of the Mosaic Law to the New Law. Many of the aspects briefly touched upon in this chapter will need to be further elucidated in the following chapters. In the next chapter, however, I will turn from law to the *source* of law, the Wisdom of God, who became incarnate in Christ Jesus. Only in light of Christ's identity as the incarnate Word and Wisdom of God can his fulfillment of the Mosaic Law be accurately understood. Chapter 2, therefore, will present Aquinas's conception of the Incarnation. Rather than focusing upon the metaphysics of the Incarnation, I will address the achievement of Aquinas in balancing two themes: the Incarnation of divine Wisdom and the historical development in Israel of Christ's humanity.

2 *Incarnate Wisdom in Israel*

The claim that divine Wisdom, the Word of God, took on flesh and died on the cross for our sins lies at the heart of Aquinas's account of salvation. The first verse of the Gospel of John teaches, "In the beginning was the Word, and the Word was with God, and the Word was God" (Jn 1:1). Among New Testament scholars, it is now generally agreed that, as Ben Witherington III puts it, John's Gospel "must be read in light of this very first verse, for it means that the deeds and words of Jesus are the deeds and words of a divine being, and not a created supernatural being, either, for he existed prior to all of creation."[1] The attribution of divine status to Jesus does not begin with John. Indeed, as Craig A. Evans has argued, Jesus's frequent description of himself as the Danielic "Son of man"—a title found throughout the synoptic gospels but not in John—constitutes a multifaceted claim to divine authority.[2]

The Johannine approach guides Aquinas's theology of salvation, since Christ's fulfillment of the Mosaic Law, which (as divine law) expresses divine Wisdom, depends upon Christ's unique status as Wisdom incarnate. What does it mean to say that divine Wisdom has truly become incarnate in Christ Jesus?[3] In seeking to answer this question, the present chapter will explore how Christ's human wisdom harmonizes with his divine Wisdom and makes possible his salvific words and deeds.

As Jean-Pierre Torrell has noted, Aquinas never fully worked out, even to his own satisfaction, the issue of the relationship of Christ's divine knowledge to his human knowledge.[4] In the *Summa Theologiae*, Torrell shows, Aquinas secures Christ's beatific knowledge by arguing that Christ—unique in this way among human beings—had the ability to concentrate perfectly (without distraction) on each object proper to his rational powers and thus was able to contemplate God fully even while engaging fully with the world around him.[5] While admiring the genius of this solution, Torrell ultimately rejects it on the grounds that it makes a "flagrant exception" of Christ as regards his human psychology.[6] For Torrell, it is a mistake to distinguish Christ's human nature from ours except with regard to sin (cf. Heb 4:15). The question to which Torrell returns is that of whether this depiction of the "perfection" of Christ from his conception accords with the *witness of the New Testament* to the historical development of Jesus' humanity. Like Yves Congar, Torrell is convinced that the answer is no.[7]

The witness of the New Testament on this issue is by no means clear. Raymond Brown has noted that each of the four Gospels attributes to Jesus the ability to know what is in others' minds, to know what is happening elsewhere, and to know the future. In the synoptic Gospels, there are also passages indicating that Jesus had limited knowledge: for example, that Jesus did not know the time of the Second Coming or Parousia and that he grew in knowledge. There are also passages where Jesus' citation of Scripture involves him in an apparent error.[8] Finally, one finds passages throughout the Gospels that present Jesus as the embodiment of divine Wisdom who enjoys, as a human being, Wisdom's relationship with the Father: for example, Mt 11:27 (par. Lk 10:22), "All things have been delivered to me by my Father; and no one knows the Son except the Father, and no one knows the Father except the Son and any one to whom the Son chooses to reveal him." The Pauline corpus contains the same difficulty. On the one hand, there are texts such as Gal 2:20, where St. Paul makes the startling claim that Jesus "loved *me* and gave himself up for *me*" (emphasis added), and on the other, texts such as Heb 5:7–8, which describes Jesus' suffering in terms that seem opposed to the claim that he possesses beatific vision.

The difficulty in interpreting the scriptural evidence is paralleled by the controversy over the meaning of *beatific vision* and whether such vision can coexist with acquired knowledge. In contrast to the patristic and medieval position, most contemporary theologians hold that Christ did not possess this vision, but there are notable exceptions.[9] Bernard Lonergan and Karl Rahner have, in distinct ways, defended the claim that Christ, as man, possessed unique (beatific) knowledge of the Father by elaborating on the fact that for Aquinas, this "vision" is nonconceptual.[10] Romanus Cessario has suggested that "beatific knowledge can harmonize with human life in a way that infused knowledge, which requires capacities alien to the human mind, does not."[11] On this view, Christ's beatific knowledge would both allow for true acquired (discursive) knowledge and account for his extraordinary intimacy, as man, with his Father, without reducing this intimacy to infused (prophetic or angelic) knowledge. Without denying that Christ grew in human knowledge, this position makes sense of the claim that Christ possessed "intimate and immediate knowledge . . . of his Father" and "knew and loved us each and all during his life, his agony, and his Passion and gave himself up for each one of us."[12]

In light of the scriptural and theological grounds that exist for affirming that Christ's divine Wisdom intimately engaged his human wisdom ("beatific vision"), the "flagrant exception" that Torrell identifies as the basis of his disagreement with Aquinas deserves more sustained attention. I will undertake this task in two ways: by inquiring into how the grace of the Holy Spirit shapes Christ's human nature and by inquiring into how Christ's humanity, precisely as exceptional, shapes the historical structure of salvation. The *soteriological* claim that Christ's human knowledge "expressed the divine life"—that is, the divine Wisdom—is inseparable from the view that Christ fulfills Israel's Torah, which is the expression of divine Wisdom. Beginning with faith in the Incarnation of the Son of God, the chapter will examine Aquinas's understanding of the mission of the Spirit (in relation to the mission of the Son) in forming Christ's humanity. Second, it will discuss the mysteries of Christ's life between his Incarnation and his passion, to show how Aquinas conceives of the historical expression in Israel of incarnate Wisdom.

The Word, the Holy Spirit, and Christ's Humanity

Citing (pseudo-)Dionysius, Aquinas notes that "all things caused are the common work of the whole Godhead."[13] This is so because the divine Persons are distinguished solely by relations of origin. Were they to be distinguished by attributes of being, then they would no longer be one God. On the other hand, what Aquinas calls "the common work of the whole Godhead" cannot be abstracted from the Persons. There is only one work, but this work is characterized by the fact that God the Father works through the Son and through the Spirit, according to the Persons' order of procession.[14] The distinction of Persons is not extrinsic to the acts of God *ad extra*.[15] This balanced understanding of the triune God's action has implications for the Incarnation. Aquinas explains that while the assumption of the human nature terminated in the Person of the Word, the assumption itself was not an action of the Word alone. Rather, the triune God, by divine power, assumed the human nature to the Person of the Word.[16] Since the human nature subsists in the Person of the Word, however, Aquinas notes that the act of assuming a human nature is, in this sense, "more properly" said of the Person of the Word.[17] It cannot properly be said, for example, that the Father assumed a human nature (even though the Father did assume a human nature *to the Son*) because this would suggest that the Father became incarnate. For our purposes, the point is to keep in mind that the Incarnation involves the Son uniquely, as the term of the assumed human nature, but nonetheless is not an isolated act of the Son.

Given that the power to assume belongs to the divine nature, and that each of the divine Persons could have been the term of the assumed human nature, Aquinas seeks to explain why the Son alone is the term, rather than the Father or the Spirit or all three at once.[18] Perhaps the most intriguing possibility is the idea that all three could have assumed the same human nature. Since the Persons are equal in dignity, should they not share the same role in salvation history? In fact, Aquinas holds that two or three divine Persons could have assumed the same human nature, on the grounds that "such is the characteristic of the Divine Persons that one does not exclude another from communicating in the same nature, but only in the same Person."[19] The human nature thus assumed, Aquinas suggests, would not subsist in one Person but would share in the unity of each Person, in an analogous way to the sharing of the divine nature in the unity of each Person.[20]

Yet, in Aquinas's view, it was more *fitting*, for the purpose of human redemption, that the Son alone assumed a human nature. Aquinas adduces a number of reasons for this fittingness.[21] First, he points out that the Word has a special "agreement" with creatures, since God knows creatures by knowing his Word, which is thus the "exemplar likeness of all creatures."[22] Moreover, this "agreement" is even more in the case of rational creatures, since the attribute of Wisdom is specially appropriated to the Son. The human intellect, Aquinas notes, is a finite participation of divine Wisdom, so it is particularly fitting that human beings (having fallen by pursuing illicit knowledge) be restored and perfected by participating in the saving work of Wisdom incarnate. Second, the Son receives all that is the Father's, in a way analogous to the human event of receiving an inheritance. Christ's saving work is intended to enable human beings to receive a "heavenly inheritance" as adopted "sons" of God, so again it seems particularly fitting that the *Son* assume a human nature.[23] Finally, the Holy Spirit, who proceeds from the Father and the Son, is in a sense the "gift" of the Father and the Son.[24] Therefore, it is fitting that the incarnate Son's saving work should bestow upon human beings the "gift" of remission of sins by the inner working of the Holy Spirit, since the Holy Spirit is the Son's proper gift. As these reasons of fittingness make clear, Aquinas considers the value of the Incarnation of the *Word* to consist in its unique ability to reveal, in the "economic" realm (i.e., in the structure of our salvation), the characteristics appropriated to each divine Person on the basis of the relations of origin.

The question remains, however, whether the human nature's subsistence in the Person of the Word affects the human nature in a different way than if, for example, the human nature had subsisted in the Person of the Holy Spirit. In God, Aquinas holds, the relations of origin can be analogously described as "Persons" because as distinct relations, they subsist distinctly, even though they are distinct only by relation, not by essence.[25] Thus the human nature's subsistence in the Person of the *Word* means that the human nature shares in the Word's "subsistence"—that is, in the way that the Word is a distinct relation. The Word's subsistence becomes, through the union of the human nature and the divine nature in the Person of the Word, the human nature's subsistence.[26] Since the human nature is assumed at the very instant of its conception,[27] it always subsists in the Word (i.e., shares in the Word's subsistence), rather than subsisting on its own.[28] Christ's status as a *subject*, therefore, is defined by the unique relation of the *Son* to the Father and to the Spirit. Even in his human nature, he embodies this relation, although he does so in a fully human way.

Aquinas holds, therefore, that the grace of the Holy Spirit is not necessary for the assumption of the human nature to the Person of the Son. In his view, the subsistence of the human nature in the person of the Son is certainly a "grace," in the sense that it neither flows from nor is merited by the human nature.[29] The hypostatic union, however, *is* a grace; it is not the effect of grace. The grace of the Holy Spirit qualifies the human nature by giving it a new (supernatural) operation. In contrast, the grace of union simply *is* the subsistence, or the "personal being," of Christ's human nature.[30] Just as we do not need the infusion of the grace of the Holy Spirit to continue to have being (otherwise, falling out of the state of grace would entail the total destruction of human nature), Christ's human nature does not need an infusion of the Holy Spirit to subsist in the Word.[31] Thanks to the action of the triune God in assuming a human nature to the Person of the Word, the "personal being" of Christ's human nature is to subsist in the Word; Christ's human nature never has being in any other way. In short, Christ's human nature, insofar as it "subsists" or has being as a concrete subject, already (and permanently) is the human nature of the Son of God.

It would seem, then, that the Holy Spirit is excluded from a significant role in the Incarnation. While Aquinas holds that the action of assuming belongs to the (triune) divine essence, he makes clear that the Incarnation is sustained by the Word's subsistence.[32] Even so, Aquinas does in fact recognize a significant role for the Holy Spirit in the Incarnation. Aquinas draws this role from the promise to the Virgin Mary, "The Holy Ghost shall come upon thee" (Lk 1:35). On this basis, Aquinas suggests that the Spirit is the "active principle" who brings about the conception of Christ's human nature.[33] Aquinas is careful not to deny that the works of the Trinity *ad extra* are, as St. Augustine remarked, "indivisible."[34] But he holds, nonetheless, that the various aspects of the work of the Incarnation should be "appropriated" to specific divine Persons. Thus, he attributes authority in the work to the Father, the assumption of the human nature to the Son, and the formation of the human nature to the Holy Spirit.[35]

Aquinas's point is that the work of the Incarnation proceeded in a trinitarian way. In one sense, the Father is the ground of the Incarnation, since he is the source from which the work originates; in another sense, the Son is the ground of the Incarnation, since He assumes the human nature by subsisting in it; in yet another sense, the Holy Spirit is the ground of the Incarnation, since he conceives the human nature that is assumed. By means of an analogy, Aquinas explains why the role of conceiving the human nature is appropriated to the Holy Spirit: "just as other men are sanctified spiritually by the Holy Ghost, so as to be the adopted sons of God, so was Christ conceived in sanctity by the Holy Ghost, so as to be the natural Son of God."[36] The conception of Christ's human nature by the Holy Spirit is thus central to his human nature's having existence as "Son of God."[37] In this way, Aquinas shows that Christology is based not merely upon the action of the Word but rather upon the work of the whole Trinity in relation to Christ's human nature.

The interplay between Word and Spirit informs Aquinas's understanding of the sanctification of Christ's human nature. Aquinas, as we have seen, conceives of the Incarnation as "a condescension of the fulness of the Godhead into human nature rather than as the promotion of human nature, already existing, as it were, to the Godhead."[38] From the moment of his conception by the Holy Spirit, Christ's human nature was united to the divine nature in the Person of the Word. This union with God, far more intimate than that experienced by any merely human saint even in the state of glory, caused the effects of perfect union with God to appear in Christ's human nature at the moment of his conception, whereas in other human beings these effects develop gradually, as the person's (graced) union with God develops. Christ therefore possessed the "fullness of grace," or the spiritual effects of perfect (hypostatic) union with

God, from the moment of his conception.[39] Aquinas does not, however, simply state that Christ possessed the fullness of grace and leave it at that. Instead, before defining (in 3, q.7, a.9) Christ's "fullness of grace," Aquinas devotes the first eight articles of the question to outlining what he means by Christ's grace. His central point in these articles is that the purpose of the graces Christ received is to relate him to God and to all humankind.

Aquinas distinguishes three ways in which a person united to God experiences the activity of the Holy Spirit: habitual grace, the gifts of the Holy Spirit, and the "gratuitous" graces. Habitual grace is the new (supernatural) nature given to the graced human being by the Holy Spirit. Habitual grace enables the recipient to share, on a supernatural level, in God's knowing and loving. Christ, through the unique union of his human nature with the divine nature in the Person of the Word, receives this gift of the grace of the Holy Spirit in a perfect and preeminent way.[40] Thus Aquinas interprets Is 11:2, "The Spirit of the Lord shall rest upon Him," primarily as a reference to the experience of Christ as a human being.[41] In this sense, the work of the Word in assuming Christ's human nature is "prior"— though not temporally prior—to the work of the Holy Spirit in perfecting Christ's human nature.[42]

The meaning of this habitual grace is seen in the relation that Christ has, as a human being (and from the moment of his conception), to God and to his fellow human beings. In relation to God, Christ is united, through his soul, to the Word, so it follows that he should receive preeminently, in his human nature, the effects of participation in the Word.[43] These effects have to do with perfecting and elevating the soul so that the soul, by its proper (elevated) activities of knowing and loving, can participate in God's triune life. Thus Christ's uniquely perfect habitual grace makes him preeminent in knowing and loving. Aquinas emphasizes that Christ's habitual grace is relational first of all in relation to God because it is an effect in Christ's soul caused by God. Beatitude is union with God, and no union with God can be greater than Christ's, which he possesses from the moment of his conception: "Now the end of grace is the union of the rational creature with God. But there can neither be nor be thought a greater union of the rational creature with God than that which is in the Person. And hence the grace of Christ reached the highest measure of grace."[44]

In relation to human beings, Christ, as the God-man, is the one "Mediator of God and men" (1 Tm 2:5).[45] His perfect habitual grace is from his conception ordered to the salvation of other human beings, who receive, by means of Christ's mediation, this grace of higher knowing and loving. As the mediator between God and humankind, Christ, as a man, receives from God so as to give to his fellow human beings. It follows that Christ's habitual grace is of a character that enables Christ to be the unequaled fount of all grace.[46] Since grace is directed specifically to enabling the soul to know and love God (and everything else in relation to God) in a higher manner, Christ's habitual grace, as the fount, enables him to know and love in the highest human way possible. Only in this way, Aquinas explains, can it be true that Christ's *humanity* brings, as the mediator of grace, his fellow human beings to beatitude.[47]

Aquinas's view of Christ's unique knowing and loving presupposes a theology of history in which God's presence in historical agents—and uniquely in Christ—is seen not as constricting human freedom but rather as enabling human beings to experience time and suffering in the most profound way possible.[48] In this light, it becomes more clear why Aquinas thinks that possession of beatific vision does not imply a "docetic" Christ. Christ, at the moment of his conception by the Holy Spirit, is established in the end (beatitude), to which he is then able to lead, by his salvific actions and words, all other human beings.[49] The fact that Christ is established in the end of beatitude from his conception does not negate his historical development (for example, his bodily development and his experiential acquiring of knowledge) or the historical manner in which he brings about our salvation. Rather, his establishment in beatitude shapes and informs his historical deeds and words. By possessing the fullness of knowing and loving, he is able to *know* each person in light of God's plan for the salvation of all, and he is able to *love* each person who is included in God's plan for the salvation of all. Thus he does not need to wait to meet us in heaven before knowing and loving us; his personal love for each of us is given, in St. Paul's phrase, while we are still in our sins. In short, Christ's establishment in beatitude, far from making him an ahistorical figure, actually enables him, precisely in his historical life, to perform the historical work of salvation in the personal way that it must be performed.

In Aquinas's view, however, habitual grace does not suffice by itself for Christian perfection. Rather, the soul's (graced) powers must still be aided to perform acts of supernatural holiness. Therefore, the gifts of the Holy Spirit are present in the recipient of habitual grace in order to help make each particular action a perfect response to the Holy Spirit's prompting.[50] As an example, Aquinas cites Lk 4:1, where Christ, "full of the Holy Ghost," is "led by the Spirit into the desert."[51] The Spirit leads Christ, like other recipients of habitual grace, by means of the gifts, which reveal the way in which charity should be directed at a specific place and time.

The gratuitous graces also have to do with the ability of the Holy Spirit to engage particular historical situations. He explains that "the gratuitous graces are ordained for the manifestation of faith and spiritual doctrine."[52] They are spiritual gifts, such as prophecy, miracles, and speaking in tongues, that do not have the permanence of habits but are nonetheless ordained to the end of our salvation.[53] Since a central part of Christ's earthly ministry involved teaching spiritual doctrine and manifesting the truth of his teaching by miraculous signs (Aquinas describes Christ as "the first and chief teacher of the faith"[54]), Christ needed to possess the gratuitous graces in addition to his graced habits.

Finally, Aquinas explores the way in which Christ's perfect habitual grace is related to the Holy Spirit's activity before the Incarnation of the Son of God. He does so by examining Christ's mission in light of the Pauline image of the Church as a Mystical Body, with Christ as the Head.[55] As we have suggested above, Christ's preeminent "fullness of grace" does not simply involve his dignity as an individual. Rather, Christ's fullness of grace is directed toward the end of the salvation of all human beings, who are sanctified by receiving the grace that flows to them through Christ's saving work. Christ's habitual grace and his grace as Head of the Mystical Body, therefore, are the same.[56] From the moment of his conception, he enjoys this headship. Thus, the angel can rightly proclaim to the shepherds that "today in the city of David a savior has been born for you who is Messiah and Lord" (Lk 2:11), not who *will be* Messiah and Lord.

As a grace of headship, Christ's habitual grace unites him with the people who, in every historical place and time, receive the influx of his grace. Aquinas affirms that Christ's "grace is the highest and first, *though not in time*, since all have received grace on account of His grace."[57] Since grace is the effect of the working of the Holy Spirit, whose indwelling and sanctifying presence people receive insofar as they possess (implicit or explicit) faith in Christ as Savior, the "interior influx of grace is from no one save Christ,"[58] yet the influx cannot be restricted to the time after Christ. On the ground that Christ's saving work is the efficient (instrumental) cause, as well as the meritorious cause, of grace in all other human beings, Aquinas holds that grace flows, proleptically, through Christ even before he is born.[59]

The Messiah in Israel

As Richard Schenk has noted, most commentators on the *tertia pars*, in their examination of the mysteries of Christ's life, have jumped from Aquinas's treatment of Christ's baptism directly to his treatment of Christ's passion, a move that fails to appreciate Aquinas's view of revelation as encompassing all of Christ's deeds and words.[60] As Wisdom incarnate, everything that Christ does and says participates in the mystery of his fulfillment of God's law. By forming and informing Christ's human nature, the Word and the Holy Spirit reveal the triune God through all aspects of the human life of the incarnate Son. The Incarnation, then, is not abstracted from the *history of Israel*, as if the Incarnation were merely the pinnacle of the upward movement of humanity or the symbol of God's interior activity in man.[61] Rather, Aquinas's treatment of salvation accords with N. T. Wright's proposal that the New Testament witness to the Incarnation can be understood only in light of the fact that "Jesus is enacting the great healing, the great restoration, of Israel."[62]

To draw out this aspect of Aquinas's theology of salvation, I will examine Aquinas's account of Christ's life in light of Israel's three offices of prophet, priest, and king. While this approach is warranted by the *tertia pars*, it has not previously been pursued to the degree undertaken here. As Aquinas states, Christ came into the world for three purposes: to "publish the truth" (prophet), to "free men from sin" (messianic king), and "that by Him we might have access to God" (priest).[63] Ulrich Horst has shown that these three purposes constitute for Aquinas "a principle that determines all further details" of Christ's ministry in Israel.[64] By entering into and transforming these roles, Jesus reveals how these roles—so central in ancient Israel—belong to the intelligibility of his salvific fulfillment of the law.

Aquinas begins his treatise on the mysteries of Christ's life with Christ's manifestation to the shepherds, the Magi, and Simeon and Anna.[65] His manifestation reveals him as messianic *king*. In Luke's Gospel, the angel informs the shepherds that "today in the city of David a savior has been born for you who is Messiah and Lord" (Lk 2:11). The same Gospel also recounts the testimony of Simeon, who is described as "righteous and devout, awaiting the consolation of Israel, and the holy Spirit was upon him" (Lk 2:25). Simeon has been promised "by the holy Spirit that he should not see death before he had seen the Messiah of the Lord" (Lk 2:26). Prompted by the Spirit, Simeon enters the temple when the infant Jesus is being presented by his parents. Upon seeing Jesus, Simeon praises God for allowing him to see "your salvation, which you prepared in sight of all the peoples" (Lk 2:30–31). The prophetess Anna, who lived in the temple, confirms Simeon's words. Similarly, the Gospel of Matthew relates that the Magi ask to see "the newborn king of the Jews" (Mt 2:2). When the Magi find the infant Jesus, they bow down and worship him (Mt 2:8).

As Gerald O'Collins has pointed out, this "conception Christology" of the infancy accounts indicates that from the start, "Jesus fulfilled and expressed the presence of YHWH with his people" and therefore that Jesus' "total history discloses the God who is the Father, the Son, and the Holy Spirit."[66] In his discussion, Aquinas emphasizes the way in which even the manifestation of the infant Jesus mirrors the apostolic proclamation of the Messiah. He notes that just as all kinds of persons are contained in the Church, so also all kinds of persons—Jews and Gentiles, women and men, poor and rich, pious and superstitious—are represented in the manifestation of the infant Jesus.[67] Together, those who recognize the infant Jesus as Messiah demonstrate the fact that God wills "no condition of men to be excluded from Christ's redemption."[68] Aquinas also suggests that God condescended to manifest the Messiah by means appropriate to each "condition": the Jews, represented by the shepherds, heard (as frequently in the Old Testament) an angel of the Lord; the Gentiles, who often trusted in astrology, saw a star; and the most righteous Jews, who spent their time in prayer at the Temple, were taught by "the interior instinct of the Holy Ghost."[69] The manifestation of the infant Christ is thus a microcosm of the proclamation of Christ's kingship to the whole world.

In q.39, Aquinas discusses Christ's baptism in light of his *priestly* mission. Describing Christ's baptism, the Gospel of Matthew records that "John tried to prevent him [Jesus], saying, 'I need to be baptized by you, and yet you are coming to me?'" (Mt 3:14). Aquinas cites Christ's reply: "Allow it now, for thus it is fitting for us to fulfill all righteousness" (Mt 3:15).[70] This exchange reveals that Jesus received baptism as part of his priestly mission; by receiving baptism, Jesus sanctified the water and made ready the sacrament of baptism. Correspondingly, he began the public phase of his mission, culminating in the "baptism" of the cross.[71] The unity of these two ends is expressed, Aquinas suggests, by the opening of heaven and the descent of the Holy Spirit, which signified the effect of Christ's passion that is appropriated by baptism.[72]

In q.40, Aquinas's discussion of Christ's manner of life emphasizes Christ's *prophetic* mission. In answer to the first article (whether Christ should have lived a solitary life), he states, "Christ's manner of life had to be in keeping with the end of His Incarnation, by reason of which He came into the world. Now he came into the world, first, that He might publish the truth; thus He says Himself (Jn 18:37): *For this was I born, and for this came I into the world, that I should give testimony to the truth.*"[73] Christ is first and foremost the one who reveals the mystery of the Trinity and of human salvation to the world. In this respect, he was a prophet, although, unlike Moses—whom Aquinas considers to be the greatest Old Testament prophet—he did not give an exterior law but rather, by the power and truth of his preaching, converted people interiorly through the grace of the Holy Spirit (this interior conversion to the truth is itself a "New Law").[74] Since Christ's task was to reveal God and God's love for human beings, it was fitting that he traveled throughout the land of Israel and participated in everyday social functions, in addition to preaching to his disciples and the crowds. In this way, he ensured that people, both then and now, would have "confidence in approaching Him."[75] By approaching Christ and receiving his friendship, we come to know his Godhead through his human nature, as befits the fact that our intellects rely on sensibles.[76]

Like the prophets of the Old Testament, Christ did not spend all his time in public. He often retreated to pray.[77] Yet many of the saints led (externally speaking) far more austere lives than did Jesus, and among his contemporaries, Jesus faced negative comparisons of his life to that of John the Baptist (Mt 11:19). Since Christ's purpose was to associate with human beings, Aquinas suggests that it was fitting that he should conform his life "to their manner of living," at least in regard to bodily eating and drinking.[78] Austerity in eating and drinking is a spiritual discipline that can be useful but is not necessary, especially in the case of Christ, whose sinlessness meant that he did not need to practice asceticism as a means of avoiding the outbreak of disordered desires.[79] On the other hand, Christ did fast, although not in public. He fasted in preparation for his temptation in the wilderness, so as to give an example to sinners.[80]

While Christ did not lead an austere or ascetic life, he did lead a life of poverty. The Gospel of Matthew relates that he had nowhere to lay his head (Mt 8:20), and he seems to have had almost no possessions.[81] On the other hand, Christ did not experience the desolating poverty that many human beings experience. Aquinas notes that it was fitting that Christ not experience "extreme poverty" so that he would be able to associate freely with all classes of men.[82] Christ's poverty entailed a freedom from possessions rather than an inability to obtain the necessities of food and clothing. The wealthy members of Israel's society thus had a role in Christ's life. Aquinas notes, "A man may feed and clothe himself in conformity with others, not only by possessing riches, but also by receiving the necessaries of life from those who are rich. This is what happened in regard to Christ: for it is written (Lk 8:2–3) that certain women followed Christ and *ministered unto Him of their substance*."[83] The reasons that Aquinas gives for the fittingness of Christ's poverty, therefore, do not include the idea that Christ thereby mandated the same kind of poverty for all his disciples.[84]

When Aquinas examines Christ's poverty, he does so in terms of its relationship to Christ's prophetic mission. This mission, as we have seen, is to teach people the truth about God. For this reason, Aquinas holds that Christ's poverty is fitting first of all because poverty aids in the prophetic task of preaching.[85] Possession of wealth, he recognizes (his father was Count of Aquino), leads to numerous worldly responsibilities and temptations. Wealthy people have to devote time and energy to managing their money, land, and servants. Such a state of life, while not sinful in itself, hardly conduces to sustained and effective preaching. Citing Mt 10:9, where Jesus commands his apostles not to carry money with them on their preaching missions, he holds that effective preachers should "be able to give all their time to preaching" and therefore "must be wholly free from care of worldly matters."[86] He also points out that a wealthy preacher risks having his preaching ascribed to greed for more riches.[87]

In addition to these practical reasons, Aquinas gives another kind of reason for the fittingness of Christ's poverty: namely, that it better manifested the glory of God. First of all, Christ's poverty can be seen to be analogous to the "poverty" that the Word assumed by becoming incarnate. He quotes the Vulgate's translation of 2 Cor 8:9: "He became poor for your sakes, so that through His poverty we might be rich."[88] In comparison to Godhead, human nature is well characterized as "poverty." Second, he suggests that the lowliness and relative poverty into which Christ was born—and in which condition he lived his life—heighten the contrast with his Godhead.[89] When Jesus performed great deeds such as miracles, therefore, it was all the more clear that this was the work of the God-man rather than of a great man (as the world understands greatness). In this way, too, Jesus' poverty aided his prophetic mission to teach about God.

Finally, Aquinas notes that Christ's manner of life included, as would have been expected from a member of the people of Israel, obedience to all the commands of the Torah. He states that Christ "wished to conform His conduct to the Law, first, to show His approval of the Old Law."[90] Christ's prophetic mission did not entail rejecting the teachings of Moses and the other prophets of Israel; he himself lived under and submitted to the Mosaic Law. On the other hand, Christ, as the Messiah for whose coming Israel had been prepared by the law and the prophets, is the "end" to which the Mosaic Law is ordained by God.

In short, Christ was not merely another prophet, as if he had been sent simply to confirm the teachings of Moses. Rather, the Messiah's obedience to the Old Law enabled him to fulfill and to transform the Old Law. The Old Law points to the redemption that will be accomplished by the Messiah's perfect obedience to the law. Citing Gal 4:4–5, Aquinas concludes that Christ came "in order to deliver [*liberaret*] men from subjection [*servitute*] to the Law."[91] Christ does not revoke but rather fulfills—a distinction that is crucial to understanding what it means to be "in servitude" to the law, without being able perfectly to fulfill it. The experience of this kind of servitude, Aquinas suggests, was why Israel longed for a Messiah who would redeem both Israel and the world. This Messiah has come in the man Jesus of Nazareth.

The remaining questions leading up to Aquinas's treatment of Christ's passion can also be illumined by reference to Israel's threefold office. In q.41, he addresses Christ's temptation, after his baptism, by the devil in the wilderness as belonging to his *priestly* mission. Christ's temptation, he suggests, fits the context of his mission to suffer and thereby to triumph over evil.[92] Since all human beings suffer at the hands of the devil, who tempts them to evil, Christ's example of enduring such suffering (and of preparing for such suffering by the spiritual discipline of fasting[93]) inspires his followers to endure similar suffering. Christ thereby strengthens his followers against temptation and warns against pride by showing that all people will be subject to temptation. Since Christ has undergone the same suffering, human beings can trust him to be merciful. Aquinas cites the passage from Heb 4:15, "We have not a high-priest who cannot have compassion on our infirmities, but one tempted in all things like as we are, without sin."[94] Christ's suffering at the hands of the devil in the wilderness prepares for and prefigures his salvific suffering on the cross.

On the other hand, Christ's temptation is not absolutely the same as ours, because his is without sin. His temptation consists in suffering the pricks of an external enemy, not the pricks of internal disordered desires.[95] Christ, whose human will remains always in conformity with the perfect holiness of his divine will, does not suffer temptation by wavering internally. The experience of internal wavering is itself a result of sin: as Aquinas states, "temptation which comes from the flesh cannot be without sin, because such a temptation is caused by pleasure and concupiscence" insofar as such a temptation marks the rebellion of the flesh against the spirit.[96] To suppose that Christ's rational *will* could have wavered from the divine Goodness is to posit an internal struggle for control between Christ's human will and his divine will, which would impair the unity of action required for personal unity. Aquinas rejects this alternative.[97] It follows that Christ's temptation involves a real suffering, just as we likewise suffer by being tempted; but his suffering does not involve the internal wavering that we associate with temptation. In this way, Christ can be both victim and priest. As priest, he freely offers himself to suffer on our behalf.[98] Unlike sinners, he can offer himself with perfect freedom, since his will is not constrained by the wound of sin. Moreover, as a true priest, he wards off the temptation by "quoting the authority of the Law, not by enforcing His power."[99] As victim, he truly suffers for us.[100]

In q.42, Aquinas discusses Christ's *doctrina*—that is, his teaching or doctrine.[101] It would seem that this question would be the place for Aquinas to elaborate further on Christ's status as prophet, and indeed this is the theme of the third and fourth articles. However, he first explores Christ's teaching in light of his kingship. As the Messiah, Jesus brought the good news of God's kingdom first to the Jews, to whom it had been promised. Aquinas states, "It was fitting that Christ's preaching, whether through Himself or through His apostles, should be directed at first to the Jews alone. First, in order to show that by His coming the promises were fulfilled which had been made to the Jews of old, and not to the Gentiles."[102] Christ was first the king of the Jews, although *kingship* here refers not to temporal government but to the establishment of righteousness and justice in relation to God. Christ's mission to the Gentiles began only after his passion; Christ preached to the Jews during his earthly ministry because the Mosaic Law prepared the Jews, in contrast to the idolatrous paganism of the Gentiles, to worship one God. For this reason, the Jews were "nearer to God" than were the Gentiles, so it was fitting that Christ should teach the Jews, who would then (through the Jewish apostles) teach the Gentiles.[103]

Aquinas has to reckon with Christ's harsh words to a number of the Jewish leaders, most notably the scribes and Pharisees. If Christ came to establish justice between Israel (first) and God, why did Christ offend many of the Jewish leaders? He explains that Christ condemned the actions of certain of the leaders in order to advance the salvation of the multitude of Israel. He states, "The salvation of the multitude is to be preferred to the peace of any individuals whatsoever. Consequently, when certain ones, by their perverseness, hinder the salvation of the multitude, the preacher and the teacher should not fear to offend those men, in order that he may insure the salvation of the multitude."[104] As Messiah or true king of Israel, Jesus had authority to identify leaders who were leading the multitude astray, and his preaching against them was therefore justified. He compares Jesus' actions in this case with those of Daniel against the elders of the people (Dn 13).[105]

Aquinas inquires into two further problems with regard to Christ's teaching: why Christ often taught in parables and why he did not teach by composing a book. Both of these issues have to do with his prophetic mission. With regard to the first, Aquinas emphasizes that Christ's teaching was not esoteric. He affirms that "whatever things out of His wisdom He judged it right to make known to others, He expounded, not in secret, but openly; although He was not understood by all."[106] As a true teacher or prophet, he willed to communicate his message in a way that would be best understood by his listeners, and he took pains to teach the crowds. However, since he was communicating divine realities, many of his listeners inevitably would not be able to grasp the full meaning of his words. For this reason, Christ employed parables, so that his listeners might at least recognize that there was a deeper spiritual meaning to his words than they were able to understand. Christ taught the "unveiled truth of these parables to His disciples," whom he had specially prepared. His disciples were thereby enabled to communicate his message to others.[107]

The divine wisdom of Christ's teaching also guides Aquinas's response to the problem of why Christ did not write down his teaching in a book. Christ's teaching was not meant to be merely understood intellectually; rather, it was meant to be "imprinted on the hearts of His hearers" and to become an interior law.[108] Christ's teaching was so personally powerful that writing it down could only dilute its force. In the same vein, the realities taught by Christ were too profound to be fully expressed in writing. Aquinas cites Jn 21:25 to the effect that Christ's teaching is inexhaustibly rich and will never be plumbed by mere human books.[109] Had Christ written a book, "men would have had no deeper thought of His doctrine than that which appears on the surface of the writing."[110] The written word simply cannot contain all that Christ taught. Finally, Christ's choice not to write a book fits with his mission of forming a Church. He did not wish to teach people directly through his own written word. Rather, he willed to teach people through the testimony of his apostles and their successors. In this way, a fitting order is preserved: Christ is seen to be the highest teacher, rather than having his writings put on par with those of his followers.[111] On the other hand, Aquinas affirms Augustine's statement that Christ can be said to have written and spoken through his apostles, since they are his "members." The New Testament is, in this sense, written under the direct guidance of Christ and reveals to us what Christ wished us to know about his deeds and words during his earthly ministry.[112]

In qq.43–44, Aquinas treats Christ's miracles. He connects Christ's miracles largely with his *prophetic* office. The primary reason that God enables anyone to work a miracle is "in confirmation of the doctrine that a man teaches."[113] Only doctrines regarding divine mysteries, inaccessible to reason alone, require this kind of confirmation. Mysteries of faith cannot be proved by rational arguments, so they need to be "proved [*probentur*] by the argument of Divine power."[114] Such an "argument" is most fittingly a miracle, which is a change in the order of nature that can be worked only by God's power.[115] A human being who works true miracles, therefore, can be assumed to be teaching divine mysteries. Miracles are an explicit sign that the teaching is "from God."[116] Second, miracles of a certain kind demonstrate that God is dwelling by grace in the miracle worker.

These two reasons explain why Christ performed miracles as an integral part of his mission. Christ's miracles testified to the fact that his teaching about God was true, and they also testified to his divinity.[117] Unless Christ were in fact divine, his claim to divinity would not have been confirmed by miracles.[118] Likewise, Christ did not begin to work miracles until, at Cana, he inaugurated his teaching mission.[119] Unlike other merely human miracle workers,

Christ worked miracles as a human being through the power of his divine nature. His human nature can thus be described as an "instrument" of his divine nature, although the two natures act in unity through the unique Person of the Son.[120] Given this unity, Christ did not have to pray in order to work miracles. He worked miracles "by His own power"—that is, by the power of his Godhead.[121] Yet Christ was careful to work miracles in a way that, while displaying his divine power, did not cast doubt upon the reality of his human nature.[122] Christ's miracles, ordained as they were to the end of human salvation (even when the miracles involved inanimate substances, such as loaves), confirmed rather than obscured the salvific reality of the God-man's two natures. To show Christ's divine power, Christ's miracles touched upon the entire created realm but always had as their purpose human salvation.[123]

This chapter began by examining Aquinas's account of incarnate Wisdom. I emphasized that Christ's establishment in the fullness of grace from his conception did not impede the Holy Spirit's historical engagement in Christ's life. Rather, Christ's fullness of grace provided the Holy Spirit with the freedom, through Christ's humanity, to effect the historical embodiment of God's Wisdom in Israel. The mysteries of Christ's life leading up to his passion underscore the way in which Christ's life uniquely engages the central roles of the divinely constituted society of ancient Israel. By this means, Aquinas shows how each aspect of Jesus' ministry has an intelligible place in God's plan for human salvation through the words and deeds of Christ Jesus, who fulfills the purposes of divine Wisdom for Israel, as these purposes have been revealed in Israel's Torah. We now are ready to turn our attention to Aquinas's treatise on Christ's passion. As befits this central mystery of Christ's life, the treatise on Christ's passion will deepen the theme of Christ's threefold office by enabling us to grasp more profoundly the structure of Christ's fulfillment of the Law as the expression of divine Wisdom incarnate.

3 The Cross of Jesus Christ

Since Christ is the incarnate Word, everything that Christ does (from his coming into the world to his resurrection and ascension) has redemptive significance.[1] Nonetheless, Christ's passion represents the apogee of his redemptive work, since it is primarily here that he brings the Old Law to fulfillment. Jean-Pierre Torrell underscores in this regard Aquinas's exegesis of two biblical passages: Jesus' response to John the Baptist (Jesus' *first words* in the Gospel of Matthew), "Let it be so now: for thus it is fitting for us to fulfill all righteousness" (Mt 3:15), and Jesus' words from the cross, "It is consummated" (Jn 19:30).[2] Torrell notes that for Aquinas, "the whole life of Jesus is found situated between [these] two major acts of free submission to the Law of God."[3] Given the significance of the Gospel of Matthew for Aquinas's account of the mysteries of Christ's life,[4] it is not surprising that the fulfillment of the Torah would play a significant role in Aquinas's theology of salvation. As Donald Senior has remarked (discussing Mt 3:15) in his recent commentary on Matthew's Gospel:

> More important for Matthew are the first words of Jesus in the Gospel: "Let it be so now; for it is proper for us in this way to fulfill all righteousness" (3:15). The verb "fulfill" (*pleroo*) is a crucial concept for Matthew's theology, as its use in the formula quotations attests. Linked to "righteousness," in this verse it has the immediate sense of "carry out" or "act in accord with," but there may be

51

a deeper sense in which Matthew uses this verb here, implying a sense of "prophetic fulfillment" (Meier 1979). Jesus "brings to completion" or "brings to its intended purpose or goal" that which God has ordained. The verb is used in this sense in the formula quotations as well as in the keynote text of 5:17, "Do not think that I have come to abolish the law or the prophets; I have come not to abolish but to fulfill." The term "righteousness" (*dikaiosyne*) is another key Matthean concept (Przybylski 1980). "Righteousness" or "justice" is a divine attribute, signifying God's fidelity and right relationship to Israel. It also characterizes proper human response to God, implying faithfulness, obedience, and ethical integrity.[5]

One should expect Aquinas to engage these Matthean themes in important ways; and in fact, as will be explored in the present chapter, he does so.

Surprisingly, Hans Urs von Balthasar has faulted Aquinas's theology of salvation precisely for overlooking the significance of the Old Testament. In Balthasar's view, the key aspect of the Old Testament is its development, through figures such as Isaiah's suffering servant, Jeremiah, and Job, of the soteriological theme of "exchange of places," by which a righteous person suffers God's wrath on behalf of sinners.[6] Balthasar argues that Aquinas's account of Christ and salvation lacks an appreciation for the "exchange of places."[7] As we will see, however, Aquinas reads the Old Testament not primarily in terms of Deuteronomy's covenant curses but in terms of the positive precepts of the Mosaic Law. For Aquinas, the "exchange of places" occurs from within the positive context of Christ's fulfillment of the Mosaic Law, not from within the (purely substitutionary) context of man confronting God's righteous wrath. Aquinas does not neglect the fact that Christ, by fulfilling the Law in his passion, undergoes the fullness of the covenantal curses and thus pays the entire penalty of sin: "It is written (Lam. 1:12) on behalf of Christ's Person: O *all ye that pass by the way attend, and see if there be any sorrow like unto my sorrow.*"[8] Yet Aquinas's account of the "exchange of places" involves satisfaction, not substitution. Christ suffers for our sins but does not suffer as damned by God.[9]

This chapter will proceed in two steps. First, I will discuss Aquinas's presentation of Christ's passion as the fulfillment of the Mosaic Law and will show how this theme accounts for the material of Aquinas's treatise on Christ's passion. Second, I will argue that the precepts of the Mosaic Law—moral, ceremonial, and judicial—correspond to the three offices of ancient Israel: prophet, priest, and king. It will thus become clear that by fulfilling and transforming the law, Christ engages every aspect of the covenantal history of Israel and thus brings not only the law but also the entire history of the people to a transcendent fulfillment marked by universal forgiveness of sin and elevation to the triune life.

Christ's Passion and Israel's Law

Since Adam and Eve fell through disobedience, Christ's salvific action must be (as St. Paul says) an act of obedience. In 3, q.47, a.2, Aquinas deepens this insight. He argues that Christ's supreme act of obedience—his passion—actually fulfills the Old Law.[10] As a scriptural reference, he points to St. John's Gospel, which records Jesus' final words from the cross, "It is consummated" (Jn 19:30). Aquinas understands Christ to mean that the Old Law has finally been consummated in him.[11] Aquinas then shows briefly how Christ's perfect act of obedience, flowing from the supernatural grace that infused Christ's soul at the moment of the hypostatic union, simultaneously fulfills all three aspects of the Old Law. Since charity is the form of all the virtues, Christ's perfect charity, which he displayed "inasmuch as he suffered both out of love of the Father . . . and out of love of his neighbor," perfectly fulfilled the moral precepts of the law. Second, Christ perfectly fulfilled the ceremonial precepts (which direct man to God) in the self-sacrifice that he offered upon the cross. Finally, Aquinas employs Ps 69:4 to explain how Christ perfectly fulfilled the judicial precepts (which direct the relations of human beings to each other): "He *paid that which* He *took not away*, suffering Himself to be fastened to a tree on account of the apple which man had plucked from the tree against God's command." In other words, he, though innocent, took upon himself the suffering due to all others.

In q.47, a.2, therefore, Aquinas provides a motif that draws together the material of his treatise, which spans qq.46–49. Aquinas's treatise explores, and balances, the three ways in which Christ's passion simultaneously fulfilled the Old Law. Aquinas, of course, does not arrange his questions around the three kinds of precepts. He arranges his material in a more scientific order: q.46 concerns the passion itself; q.47, the efficient cause of the passion; and qq.48–49, the effects of the passion. Yet in each of these questions, his analysis reveals how Christ's passion is redemptive within the context established by Israel's Law.[12] Discussing Aquinas's *Commentary on the Epistle to the Hebrews* (the biblical commentary whose themes are most present here), Kenneth Hagen has remarked that for Aquinas, "The continuity of the two Testaments and the base of their comparison is *lex* and the figure of *legislator*."[13] Christ, who as God was already the "principal legislator" of the law of which Moses was the promulgator, fulfills and transforms Moses' law.[14] This perspective, present in the *Summa Theologiae* as well as in the *Commentary on the Epistle to the Hebrews*, enables Aquinas to achieve a balanced integration of Christ's charity, his sacrifice, and his suffering.

The Ceremonial Precepts

I will begin with Christ's fulfillment of the ceremonial precepts because this aspect of the Old Law has a special place in Aquinas's understanding of Christ's passion.[15] Earlier in his Christology, Aquinas had devoted an entire question to Christ's priesthood (3, q.22), underscoring the special significance of the ceremonial precepts of the Old Law. The ceremonial precepts, as Aquinas states in 1–2, q.101, a.1, are properly the determinations of the moral law "which pertain to the Divine worship," so it is not surprising that they have foremost dignity in his presentation. The ceremonial precepts, primarily those precepts instituting the sacrificial system, cultically represent the right order of man to God, but the sacrifice of animals inevitably falls short of this right order.

In contrast to the modern view of sacrificial offerings, Aquinas attributes to sacrifice a positive symbolic force.[16] In 1–2, q.102, a.3, ad 8, Aquinas notes that Christ's sacrifice is prefigured in the Old

Law by three kinds of sacrifices: burnt offerings, peace offerings, and sin offerings, each of which represent a stage of the spiritual life. Since Aquinas holds that people living under the Old Law truly participated (through the Old Law) in the New Law,[17] he can apply the later Christian distinction between the "counsels" and the "commandments" to the spiritual life of Israelites. Burnt offerings, he suggests, were intended to "show reverence to His [God's] majesty, and love of His goodness: and typified the state of perfection as regards the fulfilment of the counsels." Burnt offerings were burnt completely in order to represent the self-offering of the *whole* man. Similarly, peace offerings were offered out of thanksgiving for divine favors received, and also in supplication for new favors. Aquinas holds that this kind of sacrifice "typifies the state of those who are proficient in the observance of the commandments."

The third kind of sacrifice, the sin offering, represents (as the name implies) imperfection. Aquinas states that this kind of sacrifice "was offered to God on account of man's need for the forgiveness of sin: and this typifies the state of penitents in satisfying for sins." This sacrifice was the special duty of the priests of the Old Law.

With this background, one will understand more easily how Christ fulfills the ceremonial precepts. In 3, q.48, a.3, Aquinas asks whether Christ's passion operated by way of sacrifice. His answer explores the nature of Christ's sacrifice. The proper meaning of sacrifice, he notes, is "something done for that honor which is properly due to God, in order to appease him [*ad eum placandum*]." This definition emphasizes the reconciling aspect of sacrifice; and in this sense, Christ's sacrifice was primarily a sin offering. On the other hand, Christ's sacrifice also embodied the other two kinds of sacrifice. Aquinas cites Augustine to make clear the relationship between sacrifice as a perfect act and as a sin offering: "A true sacrifice is every good work done in order that we may cling to God in holy fellowship, yet referred to that consummation of happiness wherein we can be truly blessed." Christ's perfect charity meant that his sacrifice was both a peace offering and a burnt offering, or gift of the whole person, anticipating the "consummation of happiness"; but his sacrifice was also a sin offering, intended to enable us to regain "holy fellowship" with God. Christ's sacrifice thus draws together the three kinds of sacrifices in the Old Law. Aquinas concludes with two more citations of Augustine.[18] Augustine compares the relationship of Christ's one sacrifice to the various sacrifices of the Old Law, with the relationship of a single concept to the many words in which it may be expressed. Indeed, Christ's sacrifice not only unifies the various kinds of sacrifices of the Old Law but also unifies the priest with the victim and the one who offers with the one who receives.

Emphasizing that Christ's sacrifice unifies the various kinds of sacrifices of the Old Law leaves Aquinas with a difficult problem: if Christ's sacrifice is a "positive" sacrifice, then why is it a sacrifice of human flesh, an act explicitly forbidden in the Old Law? In the same article, therefore, he confronts this objection. He states that because the ceremonial precepts are "figures," one should expect that the reality would surpass them. Although it would have been unfitting to sacrifice human flesh under the Old Law, *Christ's* flesh is a fitting sacrifice for four reasons. As with many of his arguments from fittingness, he draws these reasons from Augustine.

First, Christ's sacrifice is ordered to the redemption of human beings, and specifically to the sacramental system. Therefore, the sacrifice of Christ's flesh is fitting, since otherwise men could not truly receive Christ in the Eucharist. Second, God took on flesh precisely in order to offer it in sacrifice; otherwise, God would not have needed to become incarnate. Third, Christ's flesh was unblemished by sin and therefore constituted a perfect offering that, when participated in through the sacraments, "had virtue to cleanse from sins." Fourth, in Christ's case the offering of human flesh was acceptable, since he himself willed in perfect charity to offer his *own* flesh.[19]

Having demonstrated that Christ's sacrifice must be seen as a positive offering, Aquinas devotes the next article (q.48, a.4) to exploring the nature of Christ's sacrifice specifically as a sin offering. As a sin offering, Christ's sacrifice operates according to the modes of redemption and satisfaction. By means of these two categories, Aquinas seeks to account for the wide variety of scriptural passages—among the texts he cites are 1 Jn 2:2, Eph 5:2, 1 Pt 1:18, Gal 3:13, Jn 8:34, Rv 1:5, and Rom 3:25—that attribute propitiatory efficacy to Christ's passion. In 1–2, q.87, he has already explained that mortal sin incurs a "debt" of eternal punishment because of the violation of the order of justice (the order by which the creature's will is conformed to the divine will)—an order that belongs intrinsically to the relationship of the rational creature to the Creator.[20] So long as man is infected by original sin, he owes this debt of punishment. Moreover, he cannot pay it of himself: "if a sin destroys the principle of the order whereby man's will is subject to God, the disorder will be such as to be considered in itself irreparable, although it is possible to repair it by the power of God."[21] Original sin imposed an ontological debt upon human nature. This corruption of human nature underscores the unity or solidarity of human nature (instantiated in individual human beings) before God, a solidarity constituted intrinsically by the order of justice. Christ's death, as the death of a sinless man, redeems or pays this debt by restoring the order of justice, which is revealed as an order of divine charity.

Christ's sacrifice can also be described as "satisfaction," which operates on the same principles as redemption. As noted above, Anselm developed the concept of satisfaction that Aquinas uses in q.48, a.2: "He properly satisfies for an offense who offers something which the offended one loves equally, or even more than he detested the offense."[22] Aquinas holds that the just penalty (or result) of the interior disorder caused by original sin is sensible pain and suffering, culminating in death.[23] To restore the soul to justice, therefore, a human being would need to undergo suffering and death as the just penalty of sin, so that the disorder "might be remedied [interiorly] by the contrary of that which caused it"—that is, by the free embrace of the penalty as it embodies God's order of justice.[24]

In this article, Aquinas notes three objections to the idea that Christ's passion brings about our salvation by way of satisfaction. The first objection argues that no one can make compensation for the sins of another. The second objection points out that since crucifying Christ, God incarnate, was the most grievous of all sins, the crucifixion could not satisfy for this new sin. The third objection holds that Christ's passion is merely one good act, which cannot balance out all sins.

Aquinas's answers reveal how he overcomes the juridical tendency of Anselm's definition by exploring the dynamics of Christ's priesthood.[25] To the first objection, he responds that all who believe in Christ participate in his passion as members of his Mystical Body. Repeating an argument made in detail in 1–2, q.87, a.7, he notes that oneness in charity enables the lover to satisfy for the beloved. The unity or solidarity of human nature before God results not only from membership in the same species but also from Christ's charity, which extends to all human beings. In light of this solidarity of human nature, Aquinas later remarks that Christ's sacrifice is "a most acceptable sacrifice to God" because "Christ's voluntary suffering was such a good act that, because of its being found in human nature, God was appeased for every offense of the human race,"[26] although this universal reconciliation has to be appropriated by each person through membership in Christ's Mystical Body by faith and charity.

To the second objection, Aquinas insists once again that Christ's sacrifice should be seen as positive, since Christ, in his human will (perfectly conformed by charity to his divine will), chose freely to satisfy for our sins. To the third, Aquinas explains that the compensation offered by Christ is not merely the suffering of a particular instance of human nature but rather the suffering of a human nature hypostatically united to the divine Person of the Logos. It is the hypostatic union that accounts for the perfect virtue of his human soul (perfected and elevated by the Holy Spirit) and that makes the suffering of his human nature more than sufficient compensation for all sins. In short, Christ's sacrifice makes satisfaction because it is the personal act of Christ as mediator and priest, whose actions are motivated by supreme charity.[27]

The Moral Precepts

In the standard reading of medieval soteriology, Anselm is famous for his theory of satisfaction and Abelard for his insistence that charity is the key to Christ's saving work. Aquinas, like other thirteenth-century theologians, argues that both are right. In this he is again following the Old Testament, which considers love to be the primary element of sacrifice, and indeed of worship.[28] Christ could not have fulfilled the ceremonial precepts without also perfectly fulfilling the moral precepts. The prophets of the Old Law had condemned the Temple sacrifices of their day as mere external forms, undertaken without charity. Aquinas, therefore, is careful to emphasize the role of charity in Christ's sacrifice.[29]

Aquinas notes that charity is the ecstatic movement of the will toward the divine good *as good*, "according as it can be apprehended by the intellect."[30] The charitable will loves the divine good for the divine good's own sake and loves all human beings insofar as they are ordered to this good. As a supernatural virtue, charity is created participation in the Holy Spirit, who is Love. No true virtue is possible without charity, since all virtue is ordered to the good, and since charity, which is ordered to the ultimate good, is necessary to direct all virtues perfectly toward the good. In this sense, charity is called the "form" of all the virtues as well as the "source of merit" for all our acts.[31]

Although it might seem that charity is the same in every person who possesses charity, in fact there are various degrees of charity, corresponding to the degree of the person's participation of the Holy Spirit. In 2–2, q.24, a.8, Aquinas notes that human charity can be called "perfect" in three ways. For present purposes, it is sufficient to examine only the highest perfection of human charity. Aquinas explains that the most perfect kind of human charity belongs to Christ and to those who are fully united to Christ in heaven. On earth, only Christ displays this most perfect charity, which requires "that a man's whole heart is always actually borne towards God."[32] The grace of the Holy Spirit, infusing the human nature united to the divine nature in the Person of the Word, provides Christ with this perfection, which enables his human will always to be in accord with his divine will. In this state of highest human charity, the person is able to "think always actually of God, and to be moved by love towards Him."

The connection that Aquinas makes here between always contemplating God and always loving him is significant. Christ possesses while on earth the most perfect charity possible for man, precisely because of his possession of the beatific vision, which consists of contemplating God always. It is this perfect charity that enables Christ to fulfill perfectly all aspects of the law. Only Christ's possession of the beatific vision enables him to love perfectly, as man, the ultimate end that his intellect fully apprehends; thus Christ can fulfill perfectly the ceremonial precepts corresponding to this ultimate end. Likewise, Christ can fulfill perfectly the judicial precepts because he suffers out of charity for each and every man, known to him (non-discursively and non-conceptually) by means of the beatific vision. As the *Catechism of the Catholic Church* puts it, "Jesus knew and loved us each and all during his life, his agony, and his Passion and gave himself up for each one of us: 'The Son of God . . . loved me and gave himself up for me.' [Gal 2:20] He has loved us all with a *human heart*."[33]

Christ's beatific vision, in short, enables him to know perfectly what he is doing, and this knowledge enables him to love perfectly both God and those whom he is reconciling to God. Since Christ knows, as man, how his acts fit into the divine plan, his acts truly express the incarnate manifestation of the love of *God*. Thus for Aquinas, as for Abelard, the person who meditates upon Christ's passion is able to "[know] thereby how much God loves him, and is thereby stirred to love Him in return, and herein lies the perfection of human salvation."[34] God's movement of love toward us inspires, by the power of the Holy Spirit, a corresponding movement in us toward God. By this love, we appropriate the reconciliation gained for us by Christ's passion. Faith alone does not cleanse from sin; only faith working through love can truly participate in Christ's passion.[35]

Aquinas thus sees Christ's passion as the most complete human expression of charity. Indeed, he argues that even the smallest details of the passion are totally infused by charity. Christ, on the cross, remained always an active lover, even as a passive victim. This activity manifested itself most evidently in his prayer for his persecutors.[36] Given Christ's ability to perform miracles, Aquinas can also hold that Christ's charity governed the very entrance of the nail into his flesh. Christ's charitable will must actually permit the infliction of the wounds of the crucifixion because Christ's "spirit had the power of preserving his fleshly nature from the infliction of any injury; and Christ's soul had this power, because it was united in unity of person with the Divine Word."[37] In short, he can truly affirm that "Christ's love was greater than his slayers' malice."[38] Although Christ's passion may seem to represent the triumph of sin, it is in fact the triumph of his charitable human will, acting as an instrument of the divine will.

In Aquinas's view, therefore, Christ's human will is empowered, by his fullness of grace, to embody at every moment of his life the love of God for all human beings. As he says in q.47, a.3, ad 3, "The

Father delivered up Christ, and Christ surrendered Himself, from charity." Thus Christ, in fulfillment of the moral precepts of the Old Law, willed his death with perfect charity—that is, with complete love for his death's object, known to him by means of the beatific perfection of his human intellect. The necessary conformity between Christ's two wills provides a basis for estimating Christ's psychological state upon the cross: his intellect remains clear and ordered to its object, since intellectual confusion always distorts the will and, indeed, actually lessens sorrow and suffering.[39]

Finally, by participating in Christ's passion as members of his Mystical Body, we are conformed to Christ to such a degree that Christ's moral perfection becomes a true example for us. In q.46, a.3, Aquinas notes that Christ's passion was the most suitable means to achieve the end of man's salvation, first because it revealed God's charity but second "because thereby He set us an example of obedience, humility, constancy, justice, and the other virtues displayed in the Passion, which are requisite for man's salvation." Christ's perfect charity does not therefore make him "superhuman"; rather, he becomes the "exemplar" cause of the holiness that is objectively the ultimate end of every human being.

The Judicial Precepts

Third and last, Christ fulfills the Old Law's judicial precepts, those that "determine" the moral precepts toward one's fellow human beings. The judicial precepts, primarily those precepts instituting the regulation of exchange and punishment for crime, are also figurative. By shaping the government of Israel, they suggest the right order that should exist between man and his fellow men, but in practice, like any human politics, they are unable to produce this right order. In a sense, I have already touched upon the fulfillment of the judicial precepts by discussing how Christ's passion operates according to the modes of "redemption" and "satisfaction." Although God could have redeemed man simply by command, God chose to restore the order of justice by the death of a sinless man— in other words, by a satisfactory sin offering. By this choice, Aquinas argues, God displays "more copious mercy" than he would have had he simply forgiven sins by fiat, since in Christ's passion, God enabled *man* to restore the order of justice.[40] Christ, as man, restores justice both between man and God and between men. "Redemption" and "satisfaction" primarily concern the former, since they are directed to God. However, in Christ's satisfactory suffering, there is also the fact that he is suffering for all men. He is related to all other men by his suffering, as the one who bears their suffering. In this way, his suffering is the fulfillment of the judicial precepts of the Old Law.[41]

The fulfillment of the judicial precepts, like the fulfillment of the ceremonial and moral precepts, could not have been fully accomplished by a mere man. In his treatise on the Old Law, Aquinas had explained that some of the judicial precepts call for severe punishment "because a greater sin, other things being equal, deserves greater punishment."[42] Since Christ suffers for all sins, it is fitting that he undergo the greatest punishment. He is able to do so because his human nature, as the human nature of the Logos, could suffer with more physical and spiritual sensitivity than other men. Therefore, although Christ's "slightest pain would have sufficed to secure man's salvation, because from His Divine Person it would have had infinite virtue,"[43] Christ fulfilled the judicial precepts by undergoing the greatest suffering. Moreover, in contrast to the limited scope of the actions of a mere man, Christ was able to fulfill the judicial precepts because he suffered for each sinner individually: while suffering our penalty, he contemplated our ultimate end and (as Head of the Mystical Body) ordered the merits of his suffering to the end of our being united with God.

I have already examined why Aquinas holds that Christ must have possessed beatific vision, even on the cross. This aspect, then, has to be balanced with the fact of Christ's supreme suffering on the cross. Although Christ suffered in his whole soul, as regards its unified *essence*,[44] Aquinas explains that when the soul is viewed in terms of its various *powers* (i.e., in terms of the objects engaged by the rational soul), Christ did not suffer in his speculative intellect, whose object is God. As noted above, Aquinas holds that, in contrast to the general human experience, the higher part of Christ's soul (i.e., his speculative intellect) "was not hindered in its proper acts by the lower" and that therefore—because of Christ's fullness of grace—"the higher part of His soul enjoyed fruition perfectly while Christ was suffering."[45] But if Christ's speculative intellect was perfectly serene, how could Christ be said to suffer? Aquinas answers that if by "suffering" one means the confusion of the speculative intellect, the obscuring or distorting of the person's deepest relationship with God, then it is true that Christ could not have suffered in this way.

According to Aquinas, Christ suffers in two ways. First, he suffers through the sensitive powers of his soul, which apprehend his bodily pain. Second, he suffers in his practical intellect by seeing what is contrary to the love of God, even while his speculative intellect continues to enjoy perfect contemplation of God. As Aquinas explains in 1, q.77, a.3, the intellect is one power, but it has two functions, which may be termed the speculative and practical intellects. The speculative intellect is concerned with the contemplation of eternal things, the practical intellect with the disposal of temporal things.[46] Aquinas uses this psychology from the *prima pars* to explore the mystery of Christ's suffering on the cross: Christ "suffered indeed as to all His lower powers; because in all the soul's lower powers, whose operations are but temporal, there was something to be found which was a source of woe to Christ."[47] In contrast, Christ's higher reason or speculative intellect could not experience sadness because its object was God, who is infinite Goodness.

In q.46, a.6, Aquinas details these two aspects of Christ's suffering. The cause of Christ's sensitive pain is evident: the wounding of his body. In contrast, Christ's "interior pain" or "sadness" must have had multiple causes. Aquinas suggests that Christ's practical intellect would have experienced acute sadness especially for the sins of humankind; for the sin of those (including his apostles) who betrayed, abandoned, or condemned him; and for his approaching death. Aquinas then argues that Christ's sensitive pain and intellectual sadness were the greatest possible on earth.[48] In this regard, he notes that the sources of Christ's pain were the greatest because the wounds of the crucifixion afflicted the most sensitive parts of the body and because Christ grieved for *all* sins.[49] Second, Christ's body and soul were perfectly made, so they possessed a greater sensitivity to suffering than any inferior body and soul would possess. Third, Christ did not allow the higher powers of his soul to soothe the sensitive pain or interior sadness experienced by the lower powers of his soul. Fourth, Christ *chose* to suffer, "and consequently He embraced the amount of pain proportionate to the magnitude of the fruit which resulted therefrom." He freely willed to endure the greatest suffering, and all classes of suffering,[50] in order to make manifest his fulfillment of the judicial precepts.

Aquinas is careful to add two caveats. First, although Christ's interior sadness is "the greatest in absolute quantity," his sadness remains governed by the "rule of reason": that is, the sadness in his lower reason is governed by his higher reason.[51] Therefore, Christ's sadness is not hopeless or estranged from the truth, so exteriorly it may not have seemed to be the greatest sadness. Interiorly, however, since his sadness is measured by his higher reason's perfect wisdom, his sadness has, of all human suffering, the greatest intensity: "this grief in Christ surpassed all grief of every contrite heart,[52] both because it flowed from a greater wisdom and charity, by which the pang of contrition is intensified, and because He grieved at the one time for all sins, according to Isa. 53:4: *Surely He hath carried our sorrows.*"[53] Perfect wisdom intensifies, rather than takes away, suffering over sin. Aquinas also points out that Christ's grief for his approaching death would, by itself, surpass every other human grief, since Christ's bodily life is that of the Son of God.

Second, Aquinas notes that to take on the penalty for our sin, Christ does not need to take on the penalty of eternal suffering, or damnation. The judicial precepts require a punishment proportionate to the sin. Since Christ bears all the sins of this world, his suffering is fittingly the greatest *of this world.* His suffering does not need to match the suffering of the damned, since their suffering pertains to the next world. As Aquinas states, "The pain of a suffering, separated soul belongs to the state of future condemnation, which exceeds every evil of this life, just as the glory of the saints surpasses every good of the present life."[54] Christ could not take on this eternal suffering, since eternal suffering consists precisely in having rejected Christ's passion.

This context stands behind Aquinas's interpretation of certain scriptural passages that, when not interpreted in light of Christ's perfect charity, confuse theologians. In q.46, a.4, ad 3, Aquinas gives his interpretation of four such passages: Dt 21:23 ("He is accursed of God that hangeth on a tree"), 2 Cor 5:21 ("Him that knew no sin, for us He hath made sin"), Gal 3:13 ("Christ hath redeemed us from the curse of the law, being made a curse for us"), and Rom 8:3 ("having the resemblance of the flesh of sin"). Following Augustine, he holds that these texts refer to Christ's having "become sin" by taking on "the penalty of sin," which is death. In this sense, Christ is "made a curse for us" because he takes upon himself the curse that fell upon Adam and Eve after their sin. In taking on the curse, Christ himself remains sinless, and his body, *of itself*, does not bear the marks of corruption that characterize bodies conceived in the state of sin.

Although Christ does not become, according to Aquinas's reading of St. Paul, the object of God's wrath to the point of damnation, God wills that Christ, as man, freely pay the penalty of sin. On this basis, Aquinas approaches another difficult text. He argues that Christ's words from the cross, "My God, my God, why hast Thou forsaken me?" (Mt 27:46), are intended to reveal that God could have shielded Christ from the passion but did not.[55] The cry of abandonment manifests the central truth of the passion: God gave his only Son into the hands of sinners, to be numbered among the guilty. As we have seen, Aquinas teaches that God did this so that the order of justice (now revealed as the order of charity) might be restored not extrinsically by divine compulsion or fiat but intrinsically by enabling *man*—Jesus of Nazareth—to fulfill the threefold law and merit beatitude.[56] Jesus receives this complete beatitude in his resurrection, which thus becomes the formal cause of our salvation.

Aquinas's treatise on the passion articulates the profound way in which Christ Jesus brings Israel's history to fulfillment. Beginning with the moral precepts of the Old Law, he shows how Christ's perfect charity grounds his fulfillment on the cross of the Old Law's ceremonial and judicial precepts, through which he reconciles all things in himself. Aquinas thereby demonstrates the *unity* of the Old Law and the New Law, even while underscoring the infinite *newness* of the New Law, by which we share in Christ's divine Spirit. Moreover, Aquinas at the same time provides a rich understanding of the relationship between nature and grace: the moral precepts of the Old Law are "natural," but they are fulfilled and elevated to the ultimate end by Christ's supreme charity, a supernatural virtue. Calvary thus represents the transcendent fulfillment not only of Sinai but also of the order of all creation in God's wise and loving plan.

Aquinas holds together these elements in a delicate balance, making manifest how Christ's passion indicates not God's wrath but God's superabundant goodness in allowing humankind (in Christ Jesus), by the exercise of free will, to possess the dignity of restoring the *imago dei* obscured by sin.

Christ as Prophet, Priest, and King

To appreciate fully Aquinas's treatise on the passion, one should also recognize that Aquinas is engaging Israel's threefold office. The theological importance of Christ's threefold office has recently been highlighted by the Methodist theologian Geoffrey Wainwright.[57] As in his earlier works, Wainwright is seeking categories that will assist in both the reunion of the churches and the revival of the classical tenets of Christian faith. In his historical section, Wainwright shows that the "threefold office" provides a unique opportunity for ecumenical theology. This way of describing the breadth of Christ's saving work dates back to Justin Martyr, Eusebius of Caesarea, and John Chrysostom and is found in Calvin, Schleiermacher, Newman, and Barth, as well as in the Catechism of Trent, *Lumen Gentium*, and the *Catechism of the Catholic Church*.[58]

In light of its historical and ecumenical significance, Wainwright defends the usefulness of considering Christ's threefold office against critics who charge that it presents a "static," ahistorical Christology. Wolfhart Pannenberg in particular has argued that the threefold office fails to convey Christ's historical movement from "humiliation" to "exaltation." In response, Wainwright seeks to show that the value of considering Christ's work in terms of the threefold office lies in its ability to demonstrate that the exalted King is the same as the slain Lamb: the way in which Christ is prophet, priest, and king in his humiliation *reveals* the way he is prophet, priest, and king in his exaltation, although the two states of "humiliation" and "exaltation" are certainly not the same.[59]

Wainwright suggests that the concept of the threefold office truly came into its own in the work of John Calvin. Although he briefly makes note of the presence of the threefold office in Aquinas's *Summa Theologiae*, he assumes that Aquinas merely alludes to it.[60]

In what follows, I will extend Wainwright's ecumenical project by exploring (as chapter 2 began to do) the profound use that Aquinas makes of Christ's threefold office. In an article tracing the development of the trilogy "prophet-king-priest" from the Old Testament through the history of Christian theology, Yves Congar has already remarked upon the importance of the threefold office for Aquinas's Christology.[61] Congar points especially to texts in Aquinas's scriptural commentaries (on the Psalms, Isaiah, the Gospel of Matthew, the Epistle to the Romans, and the Epistle to the Hebrews).[62] While acknowledging that "Thomas has not constructed a treatise on the work of Christ according to the schema of the three offices," he suggests that the theme retains a significant presence in Aquinas's systematic work, including the *Summa Theologiae*.[63] Congar's approach has recently been echoed by Jean-Pierre Torrell and has been developed, with further attention to the scriptural commentaries, by Benoît-Dominique de La Soujeole.[64]

I will propose that Aquinas's presentation of Christ's fulfillment of the law should be interpreted in light of Israel's threefold office. By means of the threefold office, Aquinas not only ties his depiction of Christ to the history of ancient Israel but also shows how Christ's preaching, sacrificial death, and lordship are intimately connected. In short, I will argue that Aquinas's treatment of Christ's threefold office continues to provide a model for uniting—in light of the history of Israel—the Incarnation of divine Wisdom and the fulfillment of Israel's Torah.

Aquinas on Christ's Threefold Office

Wainwright cannot be faulted for overlooking Aquinas's development of the theme of Christ's threefold office. Although Aquinas, in his inaugural lecture as *baccalarius biblicus* in Paris, structured his analysis of the New Testament around Christ's threefold office,[65] the *tertia pars* of the *Summa Theologiae* contains only two direct references to it as such. The first is found in a question devoted to Christ's priesthood.[66] Because of the evident difficulties surrounding the biblical affirmation that Christ is a "priest" (see Heb 4:14)—for example, Christ was not from the tribe of Levi, nor did he slay himself—Aquinas treats Christ's priesthood in a distinct question. In the same question, however, Aquinas points out that Christ, as the Head of the Mystical Body, is also "lawgiver" and "king," since the Head cannot lack the graces possessed by members of the Body.[67] Christ's threefold office, in other words, is constitutive of his role as Head of his Mystical Body, the Church.

The second reference to Christ's threefold office appears in a question devoted to the "flesh" of Christ. Christ's flesh, which comes from the Virgin Mary, has theological significance because by it Christ belongs to the people of Israel. Christ's ancestors, the progenitors of his flesh, received the covenant, the law, and the promises. Among these ancestors, Abraham and David stand out as the two to whom God made special promises about their descendants. Aquinas follows St. Paul (Gal 3:16) in holding that Christ is the promised "seed" of Abraham who will be the fulfillment of God's promises and a blessing to the nations.[68] Likewise, Christ is the one who will establish David's royal throne forever. By his flesh, therefore, Christ has a special connection to Abraham and David. This connection is confirmed, Aquinas suggests, by Christ's threefold office of "king, prophet, and priest" because in these roles Christ takes up and fulfills aspects of Abraham's and David's roles in salvation history.[69] In this way, the threefold office displays Christ's dignity as the Messiah of Israel.

The brevity of these references makes evident that the threefold office does not operate as a structuring principle in the *Summa Theologiae*. As he explains in the prologue to the *tertia pars*, Aquinas organizes his material in two parts. The first twenty-six questions discuss the principle of Christ's words and deeds—that is, "the mystery of the Incarnation itself, whereby God was made man for our salvation."[70] The remaining questions treat the words and deeds themselves—the salvific "mysteries" of Christ's life. This division reflects Aquinas's effort to give theology "scientific" form: in seeking to understand actions, one must first examine the source or principle from which the actions arise.

However, Aquinas does connect Christ's threefold office with the ability of his words and deeds to fulfill God's covenantal relationship with Israel and to extend this covenant to all the nations. The full significance of Christ's threefold office for Aquinas becomes clear only in light of Aquinas's understanding of how Christ's passion fulfills the Old Law. I will argue that Christ's roles as prophet, priest, and king correspond to Aquinas's threefold division of the Old Law into moral, ceremonial, and judicial precepts. This means simply that when Christ fulfills the threefold Old Law in his passion, he does so as prophet, priest, and king. Christ's threefold office is not for Aquinas an extrinsic way of describing Christ's saving work. Rather, it belongs to the inner intelligibility of his cross.[71]

The prophetic office consists of proclaiming God's law and foretelling the rewards that will be reaped by those who follow it. For Aquinas, Moses, who received the Old Law from God and delivered it to the people, is the greatest Old Testament prophet.[72] In describing Christ's threefold office, Aquinas uses the terms "prophet" and "lawgiver" interchangeably.[73] A prophet teaches the people how to live according to God's law, awaiting the fulfillment of God's plan of salvation. Christ is thus a prophet, and more than a prophet, because he gives (primarily by his passion) God's salvific gift of the New Law, which is the inner principle by which human beings are enabled to observe the moral precepts.

The ceremonial precepts are "determinations" of the moral precepts in regard to the relationship of man to God.[74] These precepts of the Old Law have to do with the various ceremonies by which God wills that Israel worship him. Under the Old Law, the Levitical priesthood directed this public worship. As the epistle to the Hebrews makes clear, Christ's role as priest fulfills the ceremonial precepts of the Old Law.

Finally, the judicial precepts are determinations of the moral precepts in regard to the relationships between human beings.[75] The judicial precepts of the Old Law regulated the administration of justice in Israel. The administration of justice, in both the political and the economic realms, was ultimately the responsibility of the king. Christ was crucified with the title "the King of the Jews." Christ's passion, Aquinas argues, fulfills the judicial precepts, since Christ establishes justice between human beings by undergoing more than sufficient suffering for all sins.[76] In Aquinas's view, Christ's kingship, founded upon his suffering, attains its fullness in the eschatological "kingdom of God." The kingdom will come in full when Christ, having passed just judgment upon all things, establishes for eternity the heavenly community of beatitude.[77] Christ's kingship, therefore, corresponds to (and fulfills) the judicial precepts of the Old Law.

In this way, Aquinas draws the Old Covenant's three roles of priest, prophet, and king into the heart of his reflection upon the saving work of Christ, who fulfills and perfects the Old Covenant. In all of Christ's words and deeds, although primarily in his passion, Christ's threefold role as Israel's true prophet (the one who gives the New Law of charity and reveals that man's "ultimate end" is communion with the divine Trinity), priest (the one who offers the perfect sacrificial worship to God), and king (the one who orders all things according to the justice of divine charity) is in some way manifested. Aquinas's soteriology is thus grounded in the history of God's relationship with Israel, even as it goes beyond that history. In what follows, I will seek to explore in more detail what it means, in Aquinas's view, for Christ to be priest, prophet, and king.

Before doing so, however, there remains one more introductory task. One should recall Aquinas's understanding of the structure of the Incarnation. Christ is true God and true man, but he is one Person.[78] His human nature is not an autonomous human subject, or "person," but rather subsists in the divine Person of the Word.[79] Since Christ is one subject, everything that Christ does, as man, can be attributed to his divine Person.[80] Everything that Christ does, as man, thereby has divine efficacy. On the other hand, one must be careful not to ascribe human limitations to God. God does not change; human beings do.[81] Therefore, when describing Christ as "priest, prophet, and king," one should keep in mind that these titles describe his human nature. Because of the hypostatic union, these attributes in a real sense "belong to" the divine Word as subject; but they are nonetheless attributes of Christ *as man*.[82]

Although this distinction between Christ as God and as man sometimes, for modern readers, leaves the impression that Christ's acts as man are extrinsically related to his divinity,[83] in fact Christ's human will, by which he acts as man, is profoundly united to his (eternal) divine will. Although Christ's human will moves on its own, it always moves in obedience to the inward prompting of his divine will. Aquinas thus describes Christ's human will as the living "instrument" of his divine will.[84] Christ's human will, as the will of the human nature that subsists in the divine Person, is enabled to be the perfect created "instrument" of the divine will. This means that Christ's human actions always perfectly embody the divine will to redeem humankind. Christ as man is prophet, priest, and king; yet the subject, the "person," who acts as prophet, priest, and king is the divine Word. Christ, in his human nature, enters into and reveals the true salvific meaning of Israel's threefold office. Since he is the Son of God, his human actions make present the divine power in a way that brings salvation to all people.

We are now prepared to examine in detail Aquinas's understanding of Christ's threefold office. Christ's passion certainly does not conform to what one might expect when thinking of a Levitical priest, a Davidic king, or a prophetic lawgiver. Since Christ is God incarnate, although he does not *negate* the Old Covenant models of prophet, priest, and king, he supremely transforms and elevates them. The Old Covenant models do not "determine" Christ's mode of action; Christ himself is the ultimate pattern who norms the Old Covenant models. This insight undergirds Aquinas's presentation. I will begin with Aquinas's understanding of Christ's kingship, since this role denotes the heavenly communion toward which both his priesthood and his role as prophet-lawgiver are ordered.

Christ the King

As already noted, Aquinas considers Christ's passion to be the "consummation" of his kingship. Christ's sufferings consummate his kingship because he suffers for the sins of all human beings and thereby establishes justice (since he pays the debt owed by all humankind for sin) between all human beings. As a just king, Christ reigns over a just people. Christ's passion, in other words, truly is the definitive victory of the merciful God over all injustice.

Nonetheless, each human being must choose whether to accept this gift of justification. Christ's passion truly establishes a state of reconciliation, but he does not dictate the way in which each person will participate in this order of justice. Each human being must choose how to orient him- or herself in relation to the universal reconciliation established by Christ's self-gift. Those who refuse to participate in Christ's self-gift do not thereby fall from the order of justice; rather, they simply experience the order of justice by way of the punishment of loss (the loss is that Christ has died for them, and they have rejected the gift). Those who accept the gift experience the joy of being transformed by Christ's Spirit into the image of Christ's holiness. The eschatological goal of this transformation is eternal life, in which the community of the blessed will reign with Christ by sharing in Christ's beatific communion with the Trinity.[85]

With regard to Christ's kingship, therefore, Christ's transfiguration is, as the next chapter will discuss more fully, the interpretative lens through which one should view his passion. Christ's transfiguration reveals the ultimate "end" toward which his suffering is directed: the life of glory, or the beatification of soul and body. In the life of glory, the blessed will possess the "clarity" that characterized Christ's miraculously transfigured body.[86] This "clarity" represents the fact that the beatified body shares in the spiritual holiness of the soul. The state of holiness, informing the whole person (body-soul), constitutes the "kingdom of God"—that is, the communion of the blessed with the Trinity.[87] Christ's "kingdom," in short, is not like an earthly community in which people are united by rules, common interests, force, and tolerance. Rather, Christ's kingdom is the communion of the blessed with God (and with each other in God) through the *inner* bond of charity, a bond so strong that it transforms not only the souls of the blessed but also their bodies.[88] Christ the king reigns in us, interiorly and intimately, through the power of self-giving charity.[89]

Following the order of the mysteries of Christ's life (as confessed in the articles of the Nicene Creed), Aquinas suggests that Christ's kingship is reflected preeminently in his sitting at the right hand of the Father and in his coming to judge the living and the dead. As God, Christ eternally sits at the right hand of the Father.[90] As man, Christ is raised to this dignity by the grace of the hypostatic union.[91] Sitting at the Father's right hand means abiding in the Father's eternity and sharing in the Father's rule.[92] As the Magi recognize, therefore, the newborn Christ is "born King of the Jews."[93] Aquinas makes clear, however, that this sharing in the Father's rule cannot be imagined in external terms: sharing in the Father's rule does not mean dominating others but rather consists in possessing divine beatitude.[94] For Aquinas, then, Christ's kingship is both "consummated" by his suffering *and* founded upon his possession of beatitude (in his human soul) from the moment of his birth. The fact that his soul is already beatified actually grounds the profundity of his suffering because his possession of beatitude unites his suffering with the divine plan to make all things just in Christ. In this way, his suffering consummates his beatific "kingship."

Having established the nature of Christ's kingship, Aquinas then turns to Christ's judiciary power, namely, his coming to judge the living and the dead.[95] In this regard, he first notes that judiciary power belongs to the entire Trinity but is rightly attributed to the Son.[96] It is clear, therefore, that Christ, as God, has judiciary power to judge each man's heart. But does Christ possess this judiciary power *as man*, in his humanity? Aquinas points out that judgment is a prerogative of the Head of the Mystical Body. Since Christ received the grace of headship as man, he must possess (as man) the power to judge his members.[97] Christ's headship flows from the grace of the hypostatic union, which causes his human nature, at the instant of its conception, to subsist in the divine Person of the Word. As we have seen, this unfathomable unity of Christ's human nature with God "beatifies" his soul through the activity of the Holy Spirit. In knowing the Word, Christ knows all human beings, in their inner reality, in the Word.[98] This knowledge of human hearts enables Christ, as man, to judge all human beings. His judgment is thus not an extrinsic judgment. Rather, the "judgment" refers to the ordering of all things according to his justice.[99] The blessed, as members of Christ's Mystical Body, share in his judiciary power by accepting the justice that he gives them through his passion.[100]

Christ the Prophet

Aquinas defines prophecy as the "vision of some supernatural truth as being far remote from us."[101] It follows that, of the three offices, Christ's role as prophet is the most difficult to grasp. This is so because an integral component of prophecy is lack of clear intellectual "vision," and Christ possesses from the moment of his conception the "beatific vision" of the Word and of all things in the Word.

In Aquinas's view, those who possess such beatific vision (including the blessed in heaven) "cannot be called prophets."[102] How, then, is Christ a "prophet"? Aquinas gives a complex answer. He argues that as "comprehensor"—that is, as regards his beatific knowledge—Christ is not a prophet. But as "wayfarer"—that is, as regards his infused knowledge—Christ *is* a prophet.[103]

Before proceeding, therefore, it will be necessary to review how Aquinas distinguishes beatific, infused, and acquired knowledge. Beatific knowledge (which Aquinas describes as "the knowledge of the blessed or comprehensors") is not, as is sometimes assumed, God's knowledge. Rather, beatific knowledge signifies the rational creature's intellectual "vision" of God's essence.[104] This vision *does not comprehend* God's essence, in the sense of grasping totally God's essence.[105] God is infinite and thus always infinitely exceeds the rational creature's finite intellectual grasp. Nonetheless, beatific knowledge is a true (though finite) participation in God's knowledge of himself. Aquinas explains that human beings, because they are created in the image of God, have the capacity for beatific knowledge, although they must be elevated by grace (Aquinas describes this elevation as the reception of an intellectual "light participated from the Divine Nature") to obtain such knowledge.[106] The beatific vision replaces the light of faith with the light of glory, in which the blessed see God "face-to-face."[107]

Beatific knowledge belongs to the "comprehensor," since by beatific knowledge the human being sees God directly, without mediation.[108] In contrast, infused and acquired knowledge belong to the "wayfarer," since they involve knowledge mediated by intelligible species or representations. Infused knowledge comes about when God infuses into the rational creature's intellect "intelligible species proportioned to the human mind."[109] In his discussion of prophecy, Aquinas makes clear that prophecy requires *infused* knowledge.[110] The physician who recognizes that a man with a certain disease will soon recover is *not*, Aquinas points out, a prophet.[111] Rather, such a physician is simply employing the knowledge that he has acquired from investigation and experience. Acquired knowledge, therefore, cannot be classed as prophecy, although it may indeed foretell the future. True prophecy must involve knowledge that surpasses the power of natural human reason; in other words, it must have its source in divine revelation (the infusion of the "prophetic light") rather than in the prophet's own intellectual *habitus*.[112]

Christ's office as prophet, in short, must stem from his infused knowledge, not his beatific or acquired knowledge. Given that Christ has the beatific vision from the moment of his conception, however, why would Christ need infused knowledge? As Aquinas notes in an objection, "all other knowledge compared to the beatific knowledge is like imperfect to perfect."[113] Does not the possession of perfect knowledge remove all imperfect knowledge? Aquinas's answer reveals, once again, the necessity (and difficulty) of grasping the explanatory set of terms that he is using to understand Christ's human knowing. For Christ, the possession of the beatific vision does not remove the need for infused and acquired knowledge, since as a "wayfarer" he has need of images to communicate his knowledge to his fellow human beings. Beatific knowledge consists in direct, unmediated intellectual "vision" of God. Such knowledge cannot be translated into discursive expression. In contrast, Christ's infused knowledge, "whereby He knows things in their proper nature by intelligible species proportioned to the human mind," enables him to communicate his knowledge of divine realities.[114] The intelligible species of divine realities must be infused, since they cannot be acquired by natural human reason, which operates only upon tangible realities. Aquinas holds that Christ's prophecy draws particularly upon the species infused into his imagination,[115] which explains his imaginative portrayals of spiritual realities such as heaven and hell.

Like a prophet, then, Christ receives infused knowledge about supernatural realities, and he communicates this knowledge (e.g., the mystery of the Trinity) to his fellow human beings.[116] In Aquinas's view, however, Christ is at the same time far more than a prophet. This is so primarily because Christ does not receive infused knowledge in a transitory way but rather possesses it from the beginning as "habitual" knowledge—that is, within his intellectual *habitus*.[117] Christ, therefore, does not constantly depend upon new revelations from God in order to utter new teachings. Rather, he teaches about God, and about God's plan for human salvation, with the supreme self-confidence of one who fully knows what he is speaking about.

It remains to clarify the content of Christ's teachings. As prophet, Christ teaches the New Law. Aquinas conceives of the content of the

New Law as a fulfillment, not a destruction, of the Old Law. Christ does not abolish the commandments; rather, he shows how they can be truly obeyed in light of the supernatural destiny that he reveals.[118] With his disciples and in public, Christ uses parables, preaching, and conversation as a means to reveal that he himself is the Messiah of Israel, who alone has the power to interpret and fulfill the Old Law by perfectly following it, in its literal as well as its figurative meaning. In revealing his authority and salvific mission, he reveals the trinitarian communion that he shares with his Father in the Holy Spirit, and he reveals the kingdom of God—that is, God's will to share divine life with human beings. Finally, Christ reveals that the path to perfect holiness is through sharing, by faith and charity, in his passion, because by his passion he reconciles man to God. Christ does not merely teach all these things. Rather, like many of the prophets of the Old Covenant, he demonstrates the authoritative nature of his words by performing miracles.[119]

Yet as Aquinas repeatedly points out, the true content of the New Law cannot be transmitted by mere words, or even by words confirmed by miracles.[120] The New Law is primarily the grace of the Holy Spirit.[121] Citing St. Paul, Aquinas explains that "Christ's doctrine, which is *the law of the spirit of life* (Rom. 8:2), had to be *written, not with ink, but with the Spirit of the living God; not in tables of stone, but in the fleshly tables of the heart,* as the Apostle says (2 Cor. 3:3)."[122] It follows that Christ's prophetic office is not limited to his teachings and to the miracles by which he confirms his teachings. On the contrary, Christ is most fully a prophet when he is carrying out his saving work on the cross. Christ enlightens humankind through his passion because, by suffering out of love for us, Christ enables us to receive of his fullness of grace.[123] In short, he becomes our inner teacher by giving us the grace of the Holy Spirit, which is the New Law.

Christ the Priest

By considering Christ's priesthood in a distinct question (3, q.22), Aquinas signals that he considers Christ's priesthood to be especially definitive of his saving work.[124] Certainly, the *full* breadth of that work becomes visible only when one understands Christ's kingly and prophetic offices. Nonetheless, as Christ himself suggests at his Last Supper by instituting the Eucharist, his salvific passion will be above all a priestly sacrifice.

In q.22, Aquinas first asks whether the office of priest is befitting to Christ.[125] The objections that follow point out that Christ does not seem to fit the role of priest. He belongs to the tribe of Judah rather than to the tribe of Levi. Furthermore, he is a lawgiver, which would seem to preclude him from also being a priest (since God established Moses as a lawgiver and Aaron as a priest).[126] Aquinas responds by noting that Christ is not a priest of the Old Law. Rather, he fulfills the priesthood of the Old Law by offering the perfect sacrifice, which the ceremonies of the Old Law prefigured. Therefore, he is not bound to come from the tribe of Levi, nor is he limited to a particular office.[127] Aquinas explains that priesthood consists in mediating a liturgical "exchange" of gifts between God and the people: God gives divine gifts to the people, and the people offer gifts to God out of reverence, thanksgiving, or sorrow for sin.[128] Christ, then, is the true priest. In his passion, he offers out of charity a perfect gift (his humanity), and through him God bestows divine gifts upon all humanity. Foremost among these gifts is the removal of sin.[129] Christ suffers the penalty due to each human being for sin, and through incorporation into his Mystical Body all human beings are invited to receive the grace that heals our souls of the deformations caused by sin.

Having explained the uniqueness of Christ's priesthood, however, Aquinas confronts another set of difficulties. In his passion, Christ would appear to be merely the victim, not the priest. He was arrested, sentenced, and nailed to a cross by others. How then could he have been acting as a priest? Furthermore, the Old Law prohibited the offering up of human beings in sacrifice. Does Christ, as priest, violate this prohibition?[130] Aquinas draws the basis for his answer to these questions from Augustine's *De Civitate Dei*.[131] In this work, Augustine states, "Every visible sacrifice is a sacrament, that is a sacred sign, of the invisible sacrifice" (Book 10, ch. 5). This is how the passion must be understood. An "invisible sacrifice," Aquinas notes, is the free offering of one's spirit to God. Christ's passion, therefore, was a true sacrifice because it represented the "invisible sacrifice" by which Christ freely offered himself to God for the purpose of raising humankind to God.[132] Since Christ freely chose to undergo his passion for our salvation (as the Gospels' account of Christ's "agony in the Garden" make clear), he can rightly be considered to be acting as "priest," even though he is also the sacrificial "victim." On the other hand, Aquinas also makes clear that Christ's priestly action cannot be interpreted as a suicide. Although Christ freely chose to undergo his passion, he did not crucify himself. Thus, his passion is not an act of human sacrifice in the sense forbidden by the Old Law.[133]

Aquinas takes up one more crucial issue. As we have seen, Christ's priesthood functions to bring salvation to human beings. After this salvation has been achieved, however, it might seem that Christ would no longer be a priest. The other two offices are more easily conceived as eternal: so long as the community of the blessed exists, it follows that Christ must rule as "king" and "lawgiver." Priesthood, in contrast, appears to be superfluous once the life of glory has been established. Nonetheless, Aquinas argues that Christ's priesthood is eternal. The priestly office, he points out, does not consist simply in the function of offering sacrifice. Such a conception of priesthood does not take into account the end or purpose of priesthood, which is that "those for whom the sacrifice is offered, obtain the end of the sacrifice." The end toward which Christ's sacrifice is directed is that human beings might attain beatific communion with God. This end, therefore, is *constitutive* of his priesthood. In other words, the life of glory consummates, rather than abolishes, Christ's priesthood.[134] Since the blessed receive eternal life through Christ's sacrifice, Christ's priesthood is an eternal reality; the fruits of Christ's priesthood last forever, so Christ's priesthood lasts forever. Indeed, Aquinas holds that Christ will never lose the scars from his crucifixion. He describes Christ's scars as "the trophies of his power."[135] The scars make eternally manifest that love is the form of Christ's victory.

For Aquinas, as for the New Testament, Christ's saving work means primarily his passion (the other mysteries of Christ's life are also salvific, but they take their bearings, as it were, from Christ's passion). By his passion, Christ perfectly fulfills the Old Law's moral, ceremonial, and judicial precepts in both their literal and their figurative meanings and in so doing inaugurates the New Law. As we have seen, the three offices correspond to the three kinds of precepts. It follows that if one wishes to grasp what fulfilling the moral, ceremonial, and judicial precepts truly signifies, one needs to explore Aquinas's understanding of Christ's three offices. The second half of this chapter, therefore, focused upon distinguishing the aspects of Christ's saving work that each office reveals.

I have emphasized the distinctiveness of each office. It may be appropriate, then, to conclude the chapter by affirming the unity of Christ's work. The concept of Christ's threefold office enables Aquinas to compose an account that reflects equally Christ's (historical) status as the Messiah of Israel and his (eschatological) status as Lord of the Church. The distinctions that characterize the threefold office cannot be reified, as if Christ were performing three different works. Rather, each office points to *one* reality: the engagement of Christ's salvific love in reconciliation. As prophet, he gives humankind the interior law of love that is the grace of the Holy Spirit. As priest, he reconciles humankind to God by offering himself as a holy sacrifice. As king, he reconciles human beings to each other by suffering for all. In this way, he perfectly fulfills and transforms Israel's Torah.[136]

PART 2

The Fulfillment
of Israel's Temple

4 To the Image of the Firstborn Son

Since Aquinas did not compose a treatise on Israel's Temple (in contrast to his treatise on the Mosaic Law, which includes the laws relating to Israel's *cultus*), it could seem in the chapters that follow that I am exaggerating the importance of the Temple in Aquinas's theology of salvation. However, as argued above, Aquinas's use of scriptural themes in the *Summa Theologiae* is more subtle and profound than is generally recognized. In his study of the place and function of Scripture in Aquinas's theology, Wilhelmus Valkenberg has remarked that "Aquinas's theory on the relation between Scripture and theology, and his commentaries on Scripture have been studied extensively, but . . . his actual practice of using Scripture in his systematic theology has not been studied yet."[1] This pattern of research has tended to obscure the fact that one should expect to find the mature fruit of Aquinas's biblical interpretation in his *systematic* works.

With this point in mind, I will begin my study of Christ's fulfillment of the Temple, as in the introductory chapter on Christ's fulfillment of the law, by means of a dialogue with a Jewish scholar whose work spans the fields of biblical exegesis and theology. The work of Jon D. Levenson provides insight into the architectonic pattern of Torah and Temple in the theology of the Old Testament. In light of Levenson's work, the way in which Aquinas's interpretation of ancient Israel's Temple plays a central role in his understanding of the salvation accomplished by Christ will become more clear.

A Jewish Approach to Torah and Temple:
Levenson's *Sinai and Zion*

Levenson begins with the proposition that "a discussion of the two great mountain traditions, that of Sinai and that of Zion, can clarify the ideas which gave Israelite religion and all later forms of Judaism, including the Judaism of our day, their characteristic shape and their phenomenal durability."[2] The "mountain traditions" to which Levenson refers are the two covenants associated, respectively, with the giving of the Torah and with the construction of the Temple: the covenant that God makes with the people of Israel (mediated by Moses) at Sinai and the covenant that God makes with King David at Jerusalem (Zion). In the biblical account, the first covenant marks the giving of the Torah to Israel. While recognizing that these laws may have been developed over time rather than revealed all at once by God at Sinai,[3] Levenson seeks to probe the theological meaning of the fact that Israel, as a people, understood herself to be related to God (covenant being a concrete mode of intimate relation to God) by *laws*. Laws presume a lawgiver or an authority behind the laws, so Israel's relationship to God was seen as one of subject to ruler.[4] On the other hand, Israel's relationship to God was not dryly legalistic in the modern sense, as when God is imagined as a distant and arbitrary judge. Rather, God, as covenantal partner, lawgiver, and ruler, enters into the very fabric of Israel's history.[5] In response, Israel "comes into the fuller knowledge of God" by obeying the laws (*mitsvot*) of the Torah.[6] Obeying the laws is Israel's means of embodying her intimate (covenantal) relationship with God.[7] Since all the laws are "personal commandments" given by God, the laws make present in history God's personal love for Israel, by which God shapes her life in a manner pleasing to himself.[8] Levenson concludes, "Thus, observance of the Mosaic Torah is the opposite of an obstacle to a loving and intimate relationship with God. It is the vehicle and the sign of just that relationship."[9] By observing the Torah, the ancient Israelite enabled all aspects of his or her life to express God's covenantal love. In Levenson's view, no further form of "soteriology" is needed.[10]

If Sinai were not followed by Zion, God would be related to Israel simply through the covenantal event on Sinai and its continual reaffirmation through observance of God's Torah. God would relate to human beings fundamentally through the gift of law. This relationship is an intimate one, yet it also preserves God's otherness or freedom.[11] God the transcendent lawgiver is not bound by an idolatrous cult that would reduce him to human proportions. Yet Sinai is *not* the only covenant. God also enters into a covenant with King David, in which God unconditionally agrees to preserve the Davidic dynasty. Furthermore, he places his "name" upon the temple constructed by David's son Solomon.

The Davidic covenant would seem to destroy the balance achieved by the covenant at Sinai. God, it would seem, no longer relates to Israel as transcendent ruler and lawgiver. Instead, God attaches himself, as if he were a merely local deity, to a particular dynastic line and to the temple controlled by that dynastic line. As Levenson points out, the Temple "was a royal sanctuary, close to the king's palace, with which it shared a destiny."[12] The people no longer relate to God simply by obeying his law; rather, as if God were confined to human proportions, the people relate to God by visiting his Temple, where he "dwells." Faced with this apparent contradiction between Sinai and Zion, Levenson interprets the Davidic covenant through the lens provided by 1 Kgs 8:27, in which Solomon, presiding over the dedication of the Temple, proclaims, "Will God indeed dwell on the earth? Even heaven and the highest heaven cannot contain you, much less this house that I have built!" He interprets 1 Kgs 8 not only in its historical and biblical context but also in light of his study of "mythic" symbolism, which draws heavily upon the work of Mircea Eliade. Thus, he not only seeks out the meaning intended by the author of 1 Kgs 8,[13] but also, as a Jewish theologian, engages the biblical text in further theological questioning, inspired by the patterns that Eliade has uncovered in world religions.

Through phenomenological research in the field of comparative religion, Eliade identified the myth of a "cosmic mountain" in a variety of cultures.[14] Although Levenson suggests that the parallelism identified by Eliade may be "overstated," he argues that the significance that the Davidic covenant (identified with the city of Jerusalem and the Temple) came to possess in Israel's religion should be understood in light of the myth of the "cosmic mountain."[15] The "cosmic mountain" is considered to be the "navel" of the world, the meeting place of heaven and earth, the paradisal realm of sacred (nonlinear, liturgical) time. Levenson admits that such ideas in relation to Zion are found more prominently in rabbinic literature than in the biblical texts. Such texts as 1 Kgs 8, however, contain the basic idea of the cosmic mountain: "As the junction between heaven and earth, Zion, the Temple mount, is a preeminent locus of communication between God and man."[16] As 1 Kgs 8 makes clear, this preeminence does not mean that people have to go physically to Jerusalem in order to communicate with God. Rather, Jerusalem and the Temple form a "conduit through which messages pass from earth to heaven, no matter where, in a geographical sense, they originated."[17] God does not dwell anthropomorphically in the Temple. Rather, by placing his "name" there, God enables all people to pray to him through the mediation of Zion, even while demonstrating that he transcends the local limitations associated with the building itself.[18]

On the basis of 1 Kgs 8 and similar texts found in the Psalms and Deuteronomy, Levenson goes on to state, "The fact is that the Temple and the world, God's localization and his ubiquity, are not *generally* perceived in the Hebrew Bible as standing in tension."[19] As a "microcosm" or epitome of the universe, and as the point of juncture between heaven and earth, the Temple bridges God's transcendence and his immanence. The presence of God in and through the Temple (which, as a microcosm, epitomizes God's presence in the world/cosmos) manifests God's transcendent, heavenly "presence." Levenson concludes, therefore, that "Mount Zion, the Temple on it, and the city around it are a symbol of transcendence, a symbol in Paul Tillich's sense of the word, something 'which participates in that to which it points.'"[20] God relates to human beings through the Temple, not because God is contained anthropomorphically in the Temple, but because the Temple, as the true "cosmic mountain," participates in and manifests God's transcendent "presence." For this reason, prayer will be mediated by the Temple independent of one's physical relation to the Temple, and even independent of whether the Temple remains standing in Jerusalem. Finally, Levenson points out that the holiness of the Temple cannot be separated from the holiness of those with whom God relates through the Temple. Law and Temple, Sinai and Zion, necessarily complement each other. Exegeting Psalm 24, Levenson remarks,

"The ethical tradition . . . celebrates the order and lawfulness of man, through which he qualifies for entry into the presence of God in the palace he has won. . . . The Temple represents the victory of God and the ethical ascent of man. The cosmic center is also the moral center."[21] The true "cosmic mountain" requires a people who have been *formed by the Torah,* so that they might truly be able to participate, in all the details of their lives, in God's transcendent "presence."

Levenson then addresses the nature of postbiblical Judaism, which has had to come to terms with the seemingly permanent destruction of the Temple and its liturgy. In postbiblical Judaism, the identification of the Temple as the true "cosmic mountain" takes on an even greater eschatological significance. The Israelite's longing to ascend to the Temple and dwell there (see Psalm 27) already expressed, even before the destruction of the Temple, an eschatological hope.[22] This hope is only intensified by the physical destruction of the Temple and the gradual acceptance of this destruction as a lasting reality. The "cosmic mountain" thus continues to embody God's relationship to his people in modern Judaism.

Aquinas's Exegesis

This analysis of Levenson's approach to the nature and meaning of God's relationship to the Temple should help us to understand Thomas Aquinas's approach to the same issue. In certain ways, it is misleading to compare Levenson and Aquinas. As a medieval theologian, Aquinas does not consider the text from a historical-critical perspective. Although he is interested in understanding the meaning that the text had for the ancient Israelites, he does not seek to reconstruct the history of the composition of the text or suppose that there may ultimately be contradictory perspectives included in the final version of the text. Similarly, he knows little about the Near Eastern context, other than aspects that are mentioned in the biblical text itself or are noted by Moses Maimonides in his *Guide for the Perplexed.* Levenson, in contrast, displays a thorough training in and knowledge of such historical-critical methods and results, and he situates these results within the comparative framework provided by Eliade's research into mythic symbolism.

Furthermore, Aquinas writes not only as a medieval but also as a Christian theologian, so he brings to the text a different outlook on ancient Israel's history and a different set of theological questions than does Levenson from a Jewish perspective.[23] Levenson refers to "the Christian concept of an 'economy of salvation' which enables one to inherit the status of Israel without the obligation to fulfill the Mosaic law. . . . Once the total plan has been made known, the law, good in its own time, becomes obsolete and even a hindrance to appreciation of the new revelatory plan."[24] In a certain sense, this summary of Christian "supersessionism" applies to Aquinas's approach. Aquinas considers the law to be good "in its own time," and he argues that Christ's passion makes the judicial and ceremonial precepts of the Torah obsolete. Indeed, he considers the Epistle to the Hebrews to have been written specifically "against the errors of those converts from Judaism who wanted to preserve the legal observances along with the Gospel, as though Christ's grace were not sufficient for salvation."[25] He holds that for Christians, continued observance of the now-obsolete laws constitutes a hindrance to "appreciation of the new revelatory plan."[26]

On the other hand, Aquinas does not imagine an "economy of salvation" in which Christians no longer observe the Mosaic Law. As we have seen, in contrast to linear supersessionism, Aquinas holds that Christians continue to observe the Mosaic Law, but no longer in its old form. As he states in elucidating the "mystical sense" of Heb 9:19, "The book of the Law is sprinkled [with blood and water], because the passion of Christ fulfilled the Law: 'It is consummated' (Jn 19:30); 'I have not come to destroy the law, but to fulfill it' (Mt 5:17)."[27] Being united by faith, hope, and charity with Christ means fulfilling the Mosaic Law in its perfect form and meriting (by grace) eternal life with and in Christ. Aquinas's view that one can continue to fulfill the laws, but now according to the new meaning and fullness that Christ gives them, might seem to be relativizing the laws by "spiritualizing" them. Yet far from "spiritualizing" the laws, Christ's passion—and human beings' participation in Christ's passion through the sacraments and through the life of charity—gives a radically *embodied* fullness to the laws.

Aquinas's interpretation of the theological significance of God's relationship to the Temple is thus shaped by his christological reading of the Old Testament.[28] This fact alone might seem to invalidate any real comparison with Levenson's work. Among scholars who employ the historical-critical method, the notion of a threefold "spiritual sense" of Scripture, on which basis Aquinas and other Christian theologians have found references to Christ and the Church in the Old Testament, has little credibility. Baruch Halpern eloquently states the historians' complaint against a "christological" or "spiritual" reading of the Old Testament:

> The confessional use of the Bible is fundamentally antihistorical. It makes of the Scripture a sort of map, a single, synchronic system in which the part illuminates the whole, in which it does not matter that different parts of the map come from divergent perspectives and different periods. . . . Worshipers do not read the Bible with an intrinsic interest in human events. Like the prophet, or psalmist, or, in Acts, the saint, they seek behind the events a single, unifying cause that lends them meaning, and makes the historical differences among them irrelevant. In history, the *faith*ful seek the permanent, the ahistorical; in time, they quest for timelessness; in reality, in the concrete, they seek Spirit, the insubstantial. Confessional reading levels historical differences—among the authors in the Bible and between those authors and church tradition—because its interests are life present (in the identity of a community of believers) and eternal.[29]

In response to this common criticism, I must first note that one cannot (nor would one wish to) defend all methods or examples of the "confessional use of the Bible." Yet if one focuses upon the example of Aquinas, it would seem that Halpern misunderstands what the "confessional" reader of the Bible is trying to do. First of all, Halpern seems to think that to expect to find a unified meaning in history is an "antihistorical" approach. In reply, Aquinas would almost certainly point out that such a view of history as *necessarily* lacking a unified meaning is itself "antihistorical": that is, it would seem *a priori* to rule out God's providence.[30] Aquinas argues that God (from eternity, his eternal "present") creates because he has an end in view; otherwise, since no one acts without a goal, God would not have created. Since God is God, moreover, we can assume that

God's plan is efficacious. Thus, we can expect—and we certainly cannot rule out—that history has a unified meaning. Moreover, if God reveals that Christ is the key to history, then we can expect to find implicit references to Christ throughout history (and particularly in God's relationship to Israel). Drawing upon Augustine's *De Doctrina Christiana*, Aquinas explains, "The author of Holy Writ [*sacrae Scripturae*] is God, in whose power it is to signify his meaning, not by words only (as man can also do), but also by things themselves [*res ipsas*]."[31] It may well be of the very nature of history, in short, that "the part illuminates the whole," to use Halpern's phrase.

Second, Halpern argues that confessionalists "do not read the Bible with an intrinsic interest in human events." As noted above, it is true that Aquinas does not approach the biblical text critically, in the sense that he does not analyze the genesis of the text or suppose that the text contains various strands of redaction that may actually contradict each other.[32] But it would not be true to suggest that Aquinas had no interest in the human events, in all their particularity, that make up the biblical narrative. On the contrary, Aquinas sought to understand, as best he could, given the available sources, the history of ancient Israel as it was experienced by ancient Israelites, not simply as it prefigured Christ and the Church. In Aquinas's view, the opposition that Halpern identifies between attention to the "historical" sense and attention to the "spiritual" or "confessional" sense is a false opposition. Since God signifies his meaning through historical realities, one must come to know the historical realities in themselves before one can grasp their possible spiritual significance in the divine plan. Aquinas argues that the historical sense of the biblical text—that is, the realities signified directly by the words (not simply "historical" realities, but also, for example, the reference of parables)—always grounds the spiritual sense, in which the words indirectly signify further spiritual realities.[33] Lacking knowledge of the historical sense of the text, one has no basis to speculate about possible spiritual senses. In his theological analysis of the Mosaic Law, therefore, Aquinas always carefully explores what the particular law or precept might have meant for the ancient Israelites before proposing possible ways in which the precept, in the divine plan, may prefigure aspects of the life of Christ or of the Church.

In short, Aquinas's "confessional" approach does not, *pace* the criticism expressed by Halpern, seek to negate history. Even though Aquinas is a medieval Christian theologian, therefore, his work remains capable of being brought into dialogue with the work of modern scholars, such as Levenson, who are well versed in historical criticism. In attempting to draw out the meaning of ancient Israel's religion, Aquinas and Levenson both focus upon the covenants of Sinai and Zion and seek to understand these covenants in their biblical context. Levenson reads the covenants of Sinai and Zion in light of comparative religion and the experience of the Jewish people during the period after the final destruction of the Temple and the loss of the land. Aquinas reads the covenants of Sinai and Zion in light of the life of Christ and the development of the Church. Given Aquinas's extensive theological analysis of the constituent elements of the Mosaic Law, one might conclude that Aquinas pays attention only to the Torah and neglects the other aspects of ancient Israel's religion. In fact, however, I will argue that Aquinas's understanding of the theology of the Old Testament is very much in accord with Levenson's emphasis upon the two covenants.[34] For both, fulfillment of the Temple in liturgy (the heavenly Jerusalem, the kingdom of God) requires fulfillment of the Torah in justice. The two are ultimately one.

Aquinas on the Temple

While a number of scholars have written about Aquinas's lengthy analysis of the Mosaic Law,[35] his approach to the theme of God's relationship to the Temple (and particularly the theological claim made in 1 Kgs 8:27) has received much less attention. Since Aquinas makes relatively few comments about the Temple, scholars have not noticed how his view of the Temple complements his analysis of the Torah. Just as Levenson demonstrates the interplay between Sinai and Zion, so also Aquinas shows how the fulfillment of the Torah (the New Law) is also the fulfillment of the Temple (the indwelling Holy Spirit/Trinity). He begins by examining Israel's understanding of the Temple.[36] Like Levenson, he identifies 1 Kgs 8 as a theological commentary upon the Temple. By quoting 1 Kgs 8:27, 29–30, he sets before the reader of the *Summa* the two key elements of the passage: first, the affirmation that God infinitely transcends the Temple (8:27), and second, the fact that God has nonetheless chosen to place his "name" there (8:30).[37] On this basis, he concludes that Israel, as represented by the Temple-theology of 1 Kgs 8, did not build the Temple to bring God physically closer. In Aquinas's view, St. Paul was simply being a faithful Jew, not a "spiritualizer," when he argued that "God who made the world and all things therein, the Lord of heaven and earth, dwelleth not in temples made by hands" (Acts 17:24).[38] The theological reason for the building of the Temple, Aquinas suggests, is found in the meaning that 1 Kgs 8 attaches to God's "name." He proposes that the promise that God's "name" would dwell in the Temple meant that the liturgy of the Temple (i.e., the prayers of the people who revere the Temple) would manifest God.

In short, the significance of the Temple in the religion of Israel was that it manifested true worship. The Temple was a place of unique communication between God and humankind because it was a place of true worship. In contrast to Levenson, Aquinas concentrates not on the mythic symbolism of Zion but on Zion as a place of opposition to *idolatry*. The poetic images that the psalmists and prophets use to speak about Zion are, in his view, imaginative (and profound) ways of speaking about the glory of true worship. In the context of a world burdened by idolatry, the Temple's intimate association with God's "name" consists in true worship. God relates to the Temple not anthropomorphically, by taking up residence in a building, but liturgically, in that the Temple, through the actions of those who reverence it, embodies true worship. By establishing (as soon as Israel had achieved enough social stability to finance and defend a Temple) one location for the sacrificial liturgy, God ensured that Israel's (official) worship would conform to his instructions.[39]

For Aquinas, true worship inevitably means worship that is implicitly ordered to the trinitarian worship in which Christ, through his passion, enables us to share. Aquinas understands "implicit" to mean completely unknown. As soon as the reality is in any way known, it has become to that extent "explicit." It follows that, in Aquinas's view, all true worship of God (by those who do not know Christ), after sin, shares implicitly in Christ's worship. This is so because, in God's plan, Christ is the one who, by taking away the obstruction of sin, enables human beings to share in the heavenly liturgy. As Aquinas notes with regard to pious Gentiles, "If, however, some of them were saved without receiving any revelation, they were not saved without faith in a Mediator, for, though they did not believe in Him explicitly, they did, nevertheless, have implicit faith through believing in Divine providence."[40] This use of "implicit" preserves the particularity of the non-Christian worship, since it does not argue that non-Christians "really" intend to be worshipping Christ.[41] Rather, non-Christians whose worship is not idolatrous really do not know Christ. Nonetheless, in God's plan, their worship is mediated by Christ as the one mediator of worship of the triune God.

The spiritual sense, when applied to the Temple, is intended to give play to the implicit relationship of Israel's worship to the redemptive and mediating work of Christ. Since God prepares Israel as the people among whom the Messiah would be born, ancient Israel's worship prefigures Christ in a unique and definitive way. Even so, few Israelites had anything beyond implicit faith in Christ. Aquinas holds that the priests, who were educated in the law and knew the prophecies, may have had some explicit knowledge of the inner meaning of the animal sacrifices that they offered. The people, on the other hand, did not recognize that the animal sacrifices prefigured anything. Yet by their sincere participation in the sacrificial liturgy, the people manifested implicit faith.[42] Aquinas argues that participation in the sacrificial liturgy of the Temple constituted a special form of implicit sharing in Christ's worship because even the Temple's implements of worship (such as the candlestick and the altars of holocausts) were, in God's plan, fitting prefigurements of Christ.[43] Along these lines, Aquinas suggests that the spiritual meaning of the consecration of the tabernacle and its vessels was to prefigure the sanctification, by the Holy Spirit, of the "living tabernacle," the Mystical Body of Christ.[44]

The New Law mediated by Christ, Aquinas holds, is the grace of the Holy Spirit.[45] The Holy Spirit sanctifies each believer who, by faith and charity (and, if available, the sacraments of the Church), shares in the passion of Christ. In attributing the work of spiritual regeneration to the Holy Spirit, he explains that the Spirit-filled person is conformed to Christ: "it is necessary that our spiritual regeneration come about through that by which we are made like the true Son; and this comes about by our having his Spirit."[46] Israel's Torah and Temple are thus fulfilled by the New Law. The Spirit who makes the person a temple of God conforms him or her to the Son, who fulfills all justice. Since "faith comes by hearing" (Rom 10:17), no one receives the grace of the Holy Spirit as a mere individual.[47] The grace of the Holy Spirit joins the believer to the "Mystical Body" of believers, united by faith and charity. Thus Aquinas's soteriological vision, like Levenson's,[48] is based upon Torah and Temple, although Aquinas interprets these aspects of Israel's religion in light of Christ.

The Virgin Mary

The significance of the Temple in Aquinas's doctrine of salvation helps to explain the placement within the *Summa* of his theological reflection upon the Virgin Mary. It has not been sufficiently noticed that Aquinas includes the series of questions regarding the Virgin Mary at the center of his soteriological treatise in the *tertia pars* of the *Summa*.[49] For Aquinas, Christ's saving work is never cut off or isolated from its beneficiaries, as if Christ objectively redeemed human beings and then, at a later time, human beings were found who subjectively appropriated this redemption. Rather, as Aquinas's interpretation of 1 Kgs 8 suggests, whenever human beings manifest God's "name" by holy worship, this practice embodies a degree of proleptic participation in the effects of Christ's saving work, even before the actual passion and resurrection of Christ. The Virgin Mary is the preeminent example of such participation. God promised that his "name" would dwell in the Temple; the Virgin Mary receives the promise that the child that she will conceive by the power of the Holy Spirit "will be called holy, the Son of God" (Lk 1:35). Recognizing this parallel, Aquinas argues that the images of God's presence in the Temple and of the Temple's holiness prefigure not only the incarnate Son but also the Virgin Mary's graced relationship with her Son in the Spirit. Thus, adopting the Septuagint translation, he reads Ps 46:4, "The most High has sanctified his tabernacle," as an image (in accordance with his understanding of the spiritual sense) of the Virgin Mary's sanctification by the Holy Spirit.[50] Likewise, following the interpretation of St. Augustine, Aquinas suggests that the closed gate that Ezekiel sees in his vision of the restored Temple (Ez 44:2) signifies, when read according to the spiritual sense, Mary's virginity.[51] In short, the Virgin Mary, full of the grace of the Holy Spirit, is the new "temple" chosen by God to receive the incarnate Son of God in her womb.

In accord with the frequent images of the Temple's holiness in the Old Testament (images whose richness is exposed by Levenson), Aquinas holds that God must have made the temple that housed his incarnate Son worthy of receiving God incarnate.[52] God's "name" dwelt in Israel's Temple because the Temple was the place where the holy sacrificial liturgy, which God had instructed Israel to perform, manifested God's "name." It follows that, in Aquinas's view, God's presence can abide only in a place that, like Israel's Temple in its ideal state, is characterized by holy actions—in other words, liturgy (the Greek *leitourgia* means, in the New Testament, both public cultic service and acts showing forth Christian charity). Therefore, the Virgin Mary, as the temple that received God's incarnate presence, must have been holy in her actions, which flowed from her sanctified soul. As Aquinas points out, in reference to Christ as Wisdom incarnate in the womb of the Virgin Mary, "Wisdom will not enter into a malicious soul, nor dwell in a body subject to sins" (Wis 1:4).[53] Sin is opposed to God, so it was fitting that the mother of God incarnate, whose womb served as a physical temple in which the Holy Spirit conceived the human nature of Christ,[54] also in a spiritual way shared in the blessings brought by Christ—namely the sanctifying presence in her soul of the Holy Spirit.

Levenson describes Israel's Temple as "a place of electrifying holiness" that, as "the world in essence" through which "God relates simultaneously to the entire cosmos," serves as "the conduit through which messages pass from earth to heaven."[55] This description captures equally well Aquinas's understanding of the Virgin Mary, whom he understands as the fulfillment of the profound symbolism of the Temple. For Aquinas, the Virgin Mary becomes the "conduit" of God's Word because of her great holiness, which is itself a gift of God. Moreover, he suggests that the Virgin Mary, in her "yes" to God at the Annunciation, answers for the whole created order that will be redeemed by Christ. He explains that the Annunciation was necessary, not simply to inform Mary of what was to come, but also because the Incarnation constitutes "a certain spiritual wedlock between the Son of God and human nature."[56] As an event analogous to marriage, the Incarnation required the consent of the betrothed, so "the Virgin's consent was besought in lieu of that of the entire human nature."[57] This marriage, whose bridal chamber was the Virgin's womb, is made public when the Christ unites his disciples to himself by faith and is consummated "when the bride, i.e., the Church, is led into the resting place of the groom, i.e., into the glory of heaven."[58]

The Virgin Mary is thus representative of the salvation of the entire Mystical Body. Commenting on the mystical sense of Jn 2:2, Aquinas notes that "the mother of Jesus, the Blessed Virgin, is present in spiritual marriages as the one who arranges the marriage, because it is through her intercession that one is joined to Christ through grace."[59] He recognizes that the symbolism of the Temple is fulfilled not only by Mary individually but also by the whole Church that is gathered by the Holy Spirit through Mary's graced "yes."[60] Mary's perfect obedience manifests the charitable justice that, in fulfilling the Torah, fulfills the Temple. As Aquinas remarks, Mary "instructs the servants [us], 'Do whatever he tells you,' in which, indeed, consists the perfection of all justice. For perfect justice consists in obeying Christ in all things: 'We will do all that the Lord commanded us' (Ex 29:35)."[61]

Christ's Transfiguration and Resurrection

If the Virgin Mary (and the Church) specially embody what it means for human beings to participate in the triune life by holiness, Christ himself is the most perfect fulfillment of Israel's Temple. Christ is the ultimate source for understanding the Trinity's indwelling, since Christ mediates this indwelling to all other human beings.[62] Trinitarian indwelling cannot, of course, be understood as the Trinity moving spatially. Rather, the missions of Son and Spirit indwelling human beings describe a movement of the rational creature, who attains (by sanctifying grace) each of the Persons of the Trinity as the object or term of his or her knowing and loving. This experiential union with the Trinity comes about through the mediation of Christ, who, insofar as we are conformed to his image by his Holy Spirit, leads us to his Father.[63] As St. Bonaventure remarks, "since Jesus Christ was the highest and supreme *worshipper* of all, it was He who first commanded that this truth [that God is Trinity] be preached clearly and openly throughout the entire world."[64] Christ's transfiguration and resurrection reveal what the gift of trinitarian indwelling ultimately means for Christ's "members." Therefore, the present chapter is the place to examine these two mysteries of Christ's life in detail. I will suggest that the glory manifested by the transfigured and risen Christ shapes the worshipping community into a people whose suffering (the vocation of those who share in Christ's reconciling justice, his fulfillment of Torah) already is experienced in light of the bodily glorification that trinitarian indwelling (fulfillment of Temple) brings.

In contrast to the position of contemporary theologians who argue that the eternal triune life involves an analogous form of suffering,[65] Aquinas's reflection upon the Temple indicates that suffering does not provide an analogy for the state of *glory*, even though suffering characterizes the life of the righteous in the fallen world. In exploring the mystery of the Incarnation, Aquinas adopts the principle that "the human nature assumed by the Word of God is ennobled [*meliorata*], but the Word of God is not changed, as Augustine says (Q.83, q.73)."[66] For Aquinas, *kenosis* as descriptive of the Incarnation signifies not an intradivine drama of the Father's "abandonment" of the Son but rather God's gracious will, manifesting his goodness, to save humankind by assuming a human nature to the subsistence of the Word. Aquinas interprets the transfiguration and resurrection as indicative of the reality that Christ's suffering overcomes all suffering. God in Christ achieves the salvation of his poor, who suffer on earth. Sharing in this salvation means eternal "clarity," or spiritual fullness, of soul and body.[67]

Aquinas on Christ's Transfiguration

Aquinas grounds his view of the transfiguration upon his consideration of what the fulfillment of God's covenantal relationship with Israel entails. The key aspect of this fulfillment is the formation of the "new Israel," or the worshipping community explicitly centered upon Israel's Messiah. This community, the Mystical Body of Christ, is the true Temple. The purpose of Christ's transfiguration, Aquinas suggests, is to further the process of shaping this Messianic community, which has its ultimate origin in Christ's suffering. For this reason, Christ must reveal not only his future suffering but also the end or goal of his suffering to his disciples, who will need to follow his path of suffering in order to reach the end that Christ's sacrifice enables them to attain. As Aquinas describes the Christian life, "hard and rough is the road, heavy [*laboriosum*] the going, but delightful [*iucundus*] the end."[68] The transfiguration displays the "delightful" nature of this end. He holds that the transfiguration, like Christ's other miracles, is intended to reveal the spiritual fruits that will result from Christ's "Passover." He states, "Now in order that anyone go straight along a road, he must have some knowledge of the end: thus an archer will not shoot the arrow straight unless he first see the target."[69] The "target" in this case is the glory displayed by Christ's transfigured body. Aquinas emphasizes that the disciple, who in this life must be configured to Christ's suffering body on the cross, will in the kingdom of God be configured to Christ's glorious body.[70] In this regard, he cites the Vulgate's translation of Phil 3:21, "*Reformabit corpus humilitatis nostrae, configuratum corpori claritatis suae.*"[71] In the first article of his question on Christ's transfiguration, Aquinas makes clear that the transfiguration signifies the future state of glory in which the present state of suffering or "handing oneself over"—as Christ, preparing for his passion, is about to do—will be replaced by sharing in the glory of the active fullness of knowing and loving (itself another form of self-giving) that constitutes the triune life.

In the same article, Aquinas inquires why Christ chose "clarity" to signify the future state. As described by the Gospel of Matthew, which Aquinas cites in the *sed contra*, Christ "was transfigured before them; his face shone like the sun and his clothes became white as light" (Mt 17:2). Why, Aquinas asks, did Christ not choose another attribute of glorified bodies?[72] Aquinas reasons that in fact Christ did at other times miraculously display, to a certain degree, the other three qualities that glorified bodies, to judge from the postresurrection accounts, exhibit; for example, Christ's walking on water displays "agility," and the infant Christ passing through the closed womb of the Virgin displays "subtlety" (just as the resurrected Christ passed through the locked doors of the upper room).[73] On the other hand, Aquinas points out, "Of those four gifts, clarity alone is a quality of the very person in himself; whereas the other three are not perceptible, save in some action or movement, or in some passion."[74] Christ chose to be miraculously transfigured in order to indicate to his disciples that the state of glory transforms the *whole* person, not simply the *activities* of the person.[75] The worship to which Christians are called is a gathering not of functionaries but of persons.

Aquinas then asks whether Christ's transfiguration represented a real instance of what might be called "heaven on earth." Citing the authority of Jerome, Chrysostom, and Damascene, he holds that the transfiguration was indeed an instance of heaven on earth. Christ's passion was preceded by a real revelation to his disciples of the end, which is none other than heaven or the state of glory. The disciples truly are witnesses to the "clarity" of the state of glory in earthly space and time. This is possible, Aquinas notes, because Christ's Godhead had already, through the hypostatic union, glorified Christ's soul, which in accord with its union with the Godhead even on earth receives the fullness of grace in a uniquely intimate way, exceeding the perfection attained by the blessed saints in heaven. Because of his divinity, Christ had the power to cause (miraculously) this glory to overflow into and transfigure his body; but Christ chose not to do this except in the case of the transfiguration.[76]

While insisting that the disciples truly saw the end embodied miraculously, however, Aquinas makes an important distinction. Christ's transfiguration was a miracle. Therefore, his transfiguration was not a *full* instance of glorification. Aquinas states, "The clarity which Christ assumed in His transfiguration was the clarity of glory as to its essence, but not as to its mode of being."[77] In the state of glory, the bodies of the blessed will possess clarity immanently, as part of their new being; they will not need constant miracles to sustain or replenish their clarity. In short, Christ miraculously revealed to his disciples the clarity of glory, but nonetheless he cannot be said to have possessed a "glorified body" during his transfiguration. Christ's body was still mortal, and of itself Christ's body possessed neither clarity nor any of the other gifts of the glorified state.[78]

It follows that Christ's transfiguration both manifested the end to the new community *and* signaled that the full revelation of the end awaited the Paschal events. Aquinas emphasizes this dynamic aspect, which enables the transfiguration truly to reveal the end without thereby downplaying the necessity of the path of *suffering* that, not only in the case of the disciples but also in the case of Christ, leads to attainment of the end of bodily glorification. He also suggests that Christ's transfiguration does not simply establish Christ as an individual exemplar of what the end of glorification will mean for the human body. Rather, appropriating the interpretation of Gregory the Great, Aquinas proposes that the refulgence of Christ's clothing, distinguished from the shining of Christ's face, "signified the future clarity of the saints, which will be surpassed by that of Christ, just as the brightness of the snow is surpassed by that of the sun."[79] Christ's transfiguration reveals not merely the clarity that will be possessed by a beatified individual but indeed the spiritual and bodily glory of the whole Mystical Body, Head and members. In Gregory's words, cited by Aquinas, Christ's "garments signify the righteous, because He will unite them to Himself."[80] In support of this view, Aquinas adduces a text from Isaiah, "Thou shalt be clothed with all these as with an ornament" (Is 49:18). The transfigured Christ's clarity displays the movement from suffering to glory that characterizes the eucharistic worship.

Having made this connection to the Mystical Body of Christ, Aquinas explores the significance of the *witnesses* of the transfiguration. He begins by noting that the Mystical Body, although constituted by the salvific mission of Christ, includes people who lived before Christ: "Now men are brought to the glory of eternal beatitude by Christ,—not only those who lived after Him, but also those who preceded Him."[81] Aquinas is not denying the "discontinuity" brought by Christ. He recognizes that human beings are saved only through the mediation of Christ, whose passion, as superabundant satisfaction, removed the impediments of sin that otherwise obstruct the mission of the Holy Spirit. On the other hand, attention to God's plan suggests that those who are enabled by God (through the grace of Christ) to participate interiorly in the preparation for the coming of Christ belong proleptically to Christ's Mystical Body. The Mystical Body is not the negation of Israel but rather is Israel's messianic fulfillment. By pointing to Christ, the faithful of Israel implicitly share in the promised fulfillment. Aquinas, therefore, identifies the transfiguration as an event for Israel, even as it shapes the "new" Israel (i.e., the visible community centered on the Messiah). Drawing upon patristic sources such as Chrysostom and Hilary, Aquinas affirms that it is fitting for Moses and Elijah to be present at Christ's transfiguration because in this way Christ shows that his glory and his upcoming passion, far from cutting him off from the law and the prophets, magnificently fulfill what they had foretold.[82] The presence of Peter, James, and John—the leaders of the disciples—likewise demonstrates that the end manifested by Christ's transfiguration is the focal point that joins Israel, which in God's plan prefigures Christ, with the Church, which presents him to the world through Word and sacrament. This (often hidden) unity of Christ's Mystical Body through the course of history undergirds the symbolism of the liturgy.

Aquinas's consideration in article 3 of the function of the witnesses leads naturally to the topic of the next (and final) article, which treats the Father's testimony that "this is my beloved Son, with whom I am well pleased; listen to him" (Mt 17:5). In his discussion of these words, Aquinas again emphasizes the way in which Christ's transfiguration signals the fulfillment of Israel in Christ's Mystical Body, now made visible in the eucharistic Church.[83] For Aquinas, the Father's words bear upon the "adoption" of the sons (and daughters) of God in the Son. Aquinas recalls that the Father uttered similar words at Christ's baptism. He then notes that Christ's baptism signifies the state of grace, while Christ's transfiguration signifies the state of glory. The transfiguration thus represents the final stage by which the adoption of sons in the Son occurs. Aquinas explains, "The adoption of the sons of God is through a certain conformity of image to the natural Son of God. Now this takes place in two ways: first, by the grace of the wayfarer, which is imperfect conformity; secondly, by glory, which is perfect conformity, according to 1 Jn 3:2."[84] Although the disciples now live by the gifts of grace, most prominently faith, hope, and charity, the Father's words at Christ's transfiguration indicate that the disciples (and the faithful of Israel, represented by Moses and Elijah) will in eternal life be conformed more perfectly to the mystery of the Word's generation and will indeed come to share, in the flesh, the glory of the triune life.

Like all the mysteries of Christ's life, therefore, the transfiguration is a trinitarian event. Comparing the event of Christ's transfiguration with that of Christ's baptism, Aquinas suggests that "also in the transfiguration, which is the mystery of the second regeneration [i.e., the state of glory], the whole Trinity appears—the Father in the voice, the Son in the man, the Holy Ghost in the bright cloud."[85] This interpretation reiterates the point that Christ's transfiguration is not merely an event that manifests Christ's dignity; rather, the transfiguration is fundamentally about the formation of the new Israel, characterized by the experience of trinitarian indwelling, which will culminate in the heavenly Jerusalem. In Christ, the communion of believers (worshippers) will move from grace to glory. Aquinas characterizes this movement as a movement away from suffering: "just as in baptism He [the Holy Spirit] confers innocence, signified by the simplicity of the dove, so in the resurrection will He give His elect the clarity of glory and refreshment from all sorts of evil, which are signified by a bright cloud."[86] Refreshment from evil means truly sharing, in the essence and the powers of the soul, in the triune life. The highest activities of the blessed will be transformed by the Holy Spirit, so that what the blessed do, the Holy Spirit does in them.

This refreshment will enable the rational creature to be fully in act, in a way infinitely beyond the natural capacities of the creature, yet in a way that completely perfects the creature and removes the creature from the suffering caused by the privation that evil is. Aquinas recognizes that this "refreshment" of glory "surpasses in excellence the sense and faculty of all mortal beings."[87] This fact explains why the disciples, hearing the Father's words, fell prostrate in fear. Yet Aquinas concludes his treatment of the transfiguration by reminding the reader that "men are healed of this frailty by Christ when He brings them into glory. And this is signified by what He says to them: *Arise, and fear not.*"[88] Christ's transfiguration, in short, manifests the movement by which the communion of saints—the true Temple, the Mystical Body of the Messiah—is brought to eternal fulfillment in worship.

Aquinas on Christ's Resurrection

Only in light of Aquinas's approach to Christ's transfiguration can his treatment of Christ's resurrection be understood.[89] The same themes appear: the relationship of suffering to glory, the meaning expressed by Christ's body, and the function of the witnesses. On the other hand, whereas the transfiguration merely pointed to the future glory, the resurrection is God's *victory*, in Christ, for the salvation of all. Aquinas sees the resurrection as the triumph of God's justice on behalf of the lowly, as had been promised by the Old Testament. At the beginning of his treatment of Christ's resurrection, Aquinas states that Christ's resurrection is fitting "[f]irst of all, for the commendation of Divine Justice, to which it belongs to exalt them who humble themselves for God's sake, according to Lk 1:52: *He hath put down the mighty from their seat, and hath exalted the humble.*"[90] This quotation from Mary's Magnificat makes clear that the resurrection is not only Christ's triumph but (in Christ) the triumph of all Israel, understood as the community of the just.

The preceding question, on Christ's descent into hell after his death, sounds the same note of triumph.[91] Before Christ, every person upon dying entered hell because all were subject to the penalty of original sin. Among these persons, there were varying degrees of guilt. Aquinas holds that some souls, having received the grace of Christ in anticipation of his coming, already possessed the virtues of faith, hope, and love and had been sanctified in their earthly lives (before the coming of Christ) to the point where they owed the penalty only of original sin, not of personal sin. Aquinas describes these souls as the "saints" of the Old Testament. Other souls also possessed these virtues but were undergoing necessary purgation for their personal sins. Aquinas recognizes, therefore, not only a "hell of the lost" (i.e., the unrepentant) but also a "hell of the just" and a purgatorial hell.[92] These distinctions are based upon Aquinas's principle that "[t]he name of hell stands for an evil of penalty, and not for an evil of guilt."[93] Given this principle, it is possible for Christ's soul to descend into hell because although guiltless, Christ "came to bear our penalty in order to free us from penalty, according to Is 53:4: *Surely He hath borne our infirmities and carried our sorrows.*"[94] Bearing our penalty means enduring death, and death means the separation of the soul from the body. Aquinas specifies that Christ's soul "descended into each of the hells" but abode among, and enlightened, only the souls of the just (who owed the penalty of original sin).[95] To the souls of the lost, who rejected him and suffer in hell the penalty of this loss, Christ displayed his glory to their shame; to the souls of those in purgatory, Christ's glory spurred their hope.[96]

With regard to the souls in purgatory and the souls of the just, Aquinas suggests that Christ's descent into hell functioned *sacramentally*, since those who lived before Christ were not able to be joined intimately to Christ's passion by the sacraments of the Church. Instead, therefore, the souls in purgatory and the souls of the just received the application of the healing power of Christ's passion, which functions as a "universal cause" of salvation, by means of the particular action of Christ's descent into hell. Aquinas states that "as the power of the Passion is applied to the living [after Christ] through the sacraments which make us like unto Christ's Passion, so likewise it is applied to the dead through His descent into hell."[97] In this way, Christ's descent into hell causes his resurrection to be not only his triumph but also the triumph of the souls of the just, now united sacramentally to his passion. By descending into hell, Christ delivers the souls of the saints of the Old Testament from hell (through the power of his passion) and admits them to the glory of the beatific vision.[98] Aquinas cites Zec 9:11, "Thou also by the blood of Thy testament hast sent forth Thy prisoners out of the pit, wherein is no water."[99] Although Aquinas posits that the liberated souls do not ascend from hell so long as Christ's soul remains there, nonetheless they are immediately glorified, "because His presence was part of the fulness of their glory."[100] Christ's resurrection, then, truly marks the (liturgical, sacramental) triumph of Israel, led by the Messiah — even though the bodily resurrection of the saints awaits the general resurrection at the end of time.

As in the case of the transfiguration, Aquinas emphasizes that this triumph is a movement from suffering to its opposite, glory. Christ's passion, for Aquinas, is representative of the immanent life of the Trinity insofar as Christ's passion is a manifestation of God's superabundant life of charity. Aquinas recognizes that Christ's passion, viewed in itself, was the enduring of "evils [*malis*]."[101] He refuses to idealize suffering: suffering, except as an earthly manifestation of charity, is in no way an analogous form of glory. In short, it is the resurrected Christ who reveals the state of glory, although the crucified Christ is the means or path by which we gain entrance to this state. Citing Rom 4:25 ("He was delivered up for our sins, and rose again for our justification"), Aquinas states that Christ's passion delivers us from evil, while Christ's resurrection advances us towards good.[102] The reality of Christ's resurrection fortifies our faith, hope, and charity. To distinguish the Head from the members, Christ's bodily resurrection comes before that of the rest of human beings.[103]

While glory is the opposite of suffering, Christ's glorified body retains its scars from the crucifixion. Aquinas argues that Christ's open scars represent the rewards of suffering, not suffering per se. Quoting Bede, he states that Christ retains his open scars "as an everlasting trophy of His victory."[104] They signify his victory over sin and death by his passion and mark him as the one priestly mediator for all eternity.[105] Similarly, Aquinas follows Augustine's suggestion that traces of the martyrs' scars may remain in their glorified bodies.[106] Such scars represent not primarily the corruption of the body but rather the spiritual triumph of the person whose faith, hope, and charity hold firm in the face of violent attacks upon his or her bodily existence. This kind of scar, therefore, belongs to the spiritual dignity of the glorified body, in contrast to other kinds of scars or deformities. With regard to Christ, he notes, "The scars that remained in Christ's body belong neither to corruption nor defect, but to the greater increase of glory, inasmuch as they are the trophies of His power; and a special comeliness will appear in the places scarred by the wounds."[107] Christ's glorified body will radiate even more beautifully at the locations of his scars because his scars—as the physical testimony to his sacrificial mediation—are the true glory of his body. Insofar as the marks of suffering indicate spiritual triumph, it is fitting that such marks remain even after the conditions of suffering are eternally past. In this way, the body enters fully into the spiritual glorification of the person. Christ's resurrection expresses the full meaning of his bodily life by glorifying his body with its scars from his passion.

After his resurrection, Christ showed himself not to all but only to those to whom he wished to reveal himself. Drawing upon Pseudo-Dionysius's conception of hierarchy, Aquinas explains that divine revelation proceeds by the immediate revelation of divine realities "by God to higher persons, through whom they are imparted to others."[108] These higher persons, in this case, were angels and Christ's Israelite disciples and followers, male and female. The good news thus flowed from the angels to Israel to the Gentiles, from the spiritually higher to the lower."[109] Except in unique cases, such as that of Paul, burning charity is the requirement for seeing (whether in the flesh or in the spirit) Christ after his resurrection.

The new Israel looks forward to sharing in the Messiah's glory. Aquinas notes that Christ appeared to the disciples, but did not stay with them, in order to make clear that he had risen to glory, not to a continuation of earthly life.[110] As we have seen, grace flows from Christ's Godhead to his human nature, and his humanity serves as the instrument by which God restores and perfects humankind. Since bodily resurrection is a gift of divine grace, Christ's resurrection is the efficient and exemplar cause of our resurrection—efficient in regard to the causality of Christ's Godhead working through his human nature, exemplar as the model. Aquinas explains that "just as all other things which Christ did and endured in His humanity are profitable to our salvation through the power of the Godhead, as already stated (q.48, a.6), so also is Christ's Resurrection the efficient cause of ours, through the Divine power whose office it is to quicken the dead; and this power by its presence is in touch with all places and times; and such virtual contact suffices for its efficiency."[111] This does not mean that glory is the destiny of every person. Christ's resurrection is *properly* said to be the exemplar cause only of the resurrection of the just, for only they will rise to the state of glory.[112] This is especially evident in the case of the souls of the resurrected persons because only righteous souls, who have received beatitude, can be said to be conformed to or raised by Christ.[113]

By identifying the affinity of Aquinas's approach with Levenson's (despite the obvious and equally important differences), I have sought to shed light on the significance of Aquinas's interpretation of the Temple. Neither theologian is attempting to impose an overarching "biblical theology" that would ignore the historical reality, or particularity, of ancient Israel. Instead, both theologians, despite their differences in confession and method, desire to grasp the meaning (in God's plan) of ancient Israel's historical development. Both are convinced, in answer to Solomon's question, that God will indeed dwell on the earth. For Levenson, this means understanding the Temple as the true "cosmic mountain," in relation to which holiness (Torah) is enacted. For Aquinas, it means understanding trinitarian indwelling in worshippers and the resulting "overflow" of the soul's sanctification into the body. Without negating the terrible reality of suffering, Christ's transfiguration and resurrection manifest that the suffering of God's poor participates in God's *victory*, through Christ's suffering, over evil. The history of suffering becomes intelligible in the spiritual and bodily glorification of the Mystical Body, Head and members.

5 Israel, the Church, and the Mystical Body of Christ

The previous chapter was more evocative than illus-
trative of what kinds of actions share in Christ's fulfillment
of the Temple. We saw that the fulfillment of the Temple
requires "electrifying holiness" and that the eschatologically fulfilled Temple will be the gathering of resurrected
and glorified human beings in Christ. When Aquinas turns
to illustrating how believers participate in Christ's threefold fulfillment of the law and thereby share in Christ's fulfillment of the Temple, he does so in two ways. The first
way is through his extraordinarily detailed account of the
virtues in the *secunda-secundae*. The second way is through
his account of the sacraments. Just as Christ's humanity is the
"instrument" of his divinity, the sacraments are the "instruments" that convey the power of Christ's passion to human
beings. Together, the virtues and the sacraments reveal how
one fulfills Torah and Temple in Christ.

This dual approach poses a problem for more limited
studies such as this one. Emphasizing the sacraments in
describing the Mystical Body as the fulfillment of Israel's
Temple risks seeming to spiritualize away the embodied fulfillment of the Torah, which is, after all, enacted by Christ
upon a cross. On the other hand, if one focuses on detailing
the particular virtues that Christians must possess, one risks
misrepresenting Aquinas's account of the Mystical Body.
After Christ, the sacraments (specifically baptism) normally
precede and inititiate the full life of virtue, and the sacraments sustain the life of virtue. Thus, the sacraments have a

certain logical priority over the virtues. Moreover, this priority is augmented by the fact that the *telos* of Christian life is perfect charity expressed as perfect worship. The life of virtue (ultimately perfect charity) finds its consummation in perfect worship of God. Although charity is the bond that unites the members of the Mystical Body with Christ, Aquinas's discussion of the Mystical Body revolves around the progressive states of worship (from the Old Law to the New Law to the state of glory).

To follow Aquinas in spelling out the virtuous life (within the context of the various states of life) would be another project—related to, but not the same as, my effort to explore the covenantal pattern of Aquinas's account of salvation. In describing the Mystical Body, this chapter will therefore focus upon Aquinas's understanding of the sacraments. For the most part, I will assume that the reader will keep in mind what has already been said about the embodied fulfillment of the Torah that is required for fulfillment of the Temple. One cannot emphasize too strongly that Aquinas's account of the Church, rooted in his theology of Christ's passion, recognizes and requires the distinctiveness of Christian life in the world. In this vein, Frederick Bauerschmidt has recently remarked, "What if moving to join Christ 'outside the camp' is the way in which the church practices a political *theologia viatorum?* If we begin to think in this way, then we can begin to see that the church constituted by God as a community of pilgrims is not only politically 'relevant,' but is in fact *itself* a 'politics,' a historically situated tradition within which the good is pursued."[1] As we have seen, moving to join Christ "outside the camp" means participating in Christ's offices as prophet, priest, and king. For Aquinas, of course, "outside the camp" does not mean setting up an *alternative* "positive law" or necessarily refusing to participate in the existing system of positive law. While the Church may well be described as a "politics," this could not for Aquinas be taken to suggest that the Church's divine law replaces or abrogates the structures of positive law that sustain human communities in ways different from, though ultimately ordered to, the Church's mission.[2]

Although the Church's constitution is differentiated from Israel's, it seems clear the "politics" which constitutes the Mystical Body as the visible Church cannot be deduced from outside God's covenants with Israel. Commenting on George Lindbeck's call for a "people-of-God" ecclesiology based upon a return to Israel's story, Scott Bader-Saye has proposed that "the demise of the last remnants of Christendom in the West and the repudiation of anti-Judaism combine to present a unique opportunity to recover the significance of Israel for ecclesiology."[3] In dialogue with Jewish and Christian theologians, Bader-Saye's *Church and Israel after Christendom: The Politics of Election* demonstrates that the Church's self-understanding cannot ignore that of Israel, precisely because the Church is called to be Israel fulfilled (in Bader-Saye's terms, a people who live in the graced freedom of *election*).

In arguing that Aquinas conceives of the Church as the fulfillment of the Temple, I will seek to develop Bader-Saye's insight further in a Catholic direction. Bader-Saye holds that the early Church, including the patristic period, gravitated toward a gnostic rather than Jewish ecclesiology: "early Christian theology spiritualized and individualized election, detaching it from corporate, bodily existence and reformulating it on the basis of spirit and belief. That is to say, election fell prey to a gnostic redescription. No longer a communal claim about the formation of a people in this world, election became information about individual salvation in the next world."[4] Bader-Saye's anti-Constantinian view that "[t]he church . . . having shed its Jewish historical context, allowed itself to be grafted into the history of nation and empire" is his justification for narrating Church history in a typically modern way: he jumps directly from Eusebius—whose perspective he presents as representative of patristic ecclesiology—to "the birth of modern political liberalism," leaving out the medievals entirely.[5] Yet Bader-Saye's work, by drawing attention to the ecclesiological significance of people of Israel, indicates the path necessary for an accurate appropriation of Aquinas's perspective.[6] As a messianic people, the people of God attain their full status as the Body of Christ: the latter reality in no way revokes the earlier covenants.[7]

Following the biblical witness, Aquinas identifies four "states" in man's *reditus* to God: the state before the law, the state of the Old Law, the state of the New Law, and the state of glory.[8] The first three "states" are ordered to the fourth and therefore are intended to prepare human beings for the perfect worship of God. The Temple, and the community of Israel organized (by the Torah) around the Temple, prefigures such perfect worship: in this sense Aquinas notes that "it is true to say that Christ was sacrificed, even in the figures of the Old Testament: hence it is stated in the Apocalypse (13:8): *Whose names are not written in the Book of Life of the Lamb, which was slain from the beginning of the world.*"[9] Christ's Mystical Body is the fulfillment of the Temple because the members of the Mystical Body are united to the perfect worship that Christ, in his passion (as man), offers the triune God.

It follows that although the visible Church, as the community of the New Law (and thus as the Mystical Body on earth), is distinct from Israel, it is nonetheless related, through Christ, to the community of the Mosaic Law. To understand the full significance of Christ's Mystical Body as a liturgical communion, therefore, one needs to examine the form of the community of Israel.[10] For Aquinas, salvation history consists of the perfecting of the worship of God, which will culminate in eternal beatitude.[11] By requiring the perfection of the entire community, Israel's status as God's "bride" and "tabernacle" (a status that the prophets recognized had been granted but not yet fulfilled) signifies the *unity* of human beings in the worship of God — the unity of perfect *communio*.[12]

Aquinas's Understanding of History: Divine Pedagogy and Divine Law

Aquinas does not approach history in the same way that a modern historian would. Modern historiography focuses upon great events, leaders, and the social fabric of everyday life; in contrast, Aquinas, while aware of such things, sees history as primarily the unfolding of humankind's relationship with God. While not minimizing the significance of historical change, he does not conceive of this history of humankind's relationship with God in evolutionary terms. On the contrary, as we have seen, he holds that in all times and places there have been people who have believed, at least implicitly, in Christ and have thus been sharers in the New Law, which is the grace of the Holy Spirit.[13] His understanding of implicit faith includes, in places where the biblical revelation is unknown, those people who believed "in Divine providence, since they believed that God would deliver mankind in whatever way was pleasing to Him."[14] Sharing in the New Law, therefore, does not depend upon having the good fortune to live at a certain place or time. At every time and place, some people do good and others evil.[15]

On the other hand, Aquinas recognizes that the condition of human beings, both in their relationship to God and in their relationships with one another, has indeed changed dramatically over the course of human history.[16] Since God made all things good, it follows that he created the first man and woman in a state of justice or right order in relation to God and to each other (a state that was sustained by grace).[17] But the first human beings quickly lost this justice by choosing finite goods over God. Human beings became unjust or disordered not only in their relation to God and to each other but also internally. Because the sense appetites no longer obeyed the intellect, man increasingly "fell under the influence of his sensual impulses."[18] Hampered by these disordered appetites, the process of reasoning was obscured, and idolatry and other sins prevailed.[19]

At this point, God revealed to Abraham, by utterly "gratuitous election," the covenantal promises that would reverse the state of darkness.[20] Having revealed his intention to bless all peoples through Abraham, God proceeded to gather a people under the leadership of Moses and to give them a written law that not only made clear the elements of justice (both between human beings and God among human beings) but also prefigured the way in which true justice would be perfectly fulfilled and elevated to the level of supernatural communion. For Aquinas, justice is the dynamic foundation of all community and friendship, including communion and friendship with God, who is infinite Goodness. The purpose of all laws, Aquinas holds, is to make human beings good or virtuous.[21] Put another way, "every law aims at establishing friendship, either between man and man, or between man and God."[22] As God's covenant with Abraham suggests, the written law given to Israel does not aim merely at friendship between human beings. Citing Lv 19:2, Aquinas points out that God wills to draw Israel into a deeper communion with himself: "You shall be holy, for I am holy."[23] Holiness is true worship of God, who is holy. The written law thus served as a "pedagogue" by which Israel was taught the components of justice in relation to God and to fellow human beings in order to be raised to communion with God.

Second, however, the written law served as a pedagogue by demonstrating that, given the state of sin, human beings *could not* perfectly follow the written law, even though they could recognize its righteousness.[24] In this way, the written law taught Israel to look for a "Messiah" who would fulfill the written law, both in its literal commands and in its figurative significance (most evident in its ceremonial precepts). Associated with the coming Messiah was the idea that the written law would become an inner law so that it could be perfectly obeyed.[25] Through Christ's passion, the justification promised by the written law was fulfilled.[26] We have seen that Christ's passion, as the supreme act of his love, reestablishes justice between humanity and God and among human beings as condign satisfaction for all the wounds caused by sin. Christ, whose humanity is infused by the fullness of the grace of the Holy Spirit, shares this grace, as Head, with all those for whom he has died. Through his saving work, therefore, he gives the New Law—the grace of the Holy Spirit—which enables all people to participate interiorly, by "living" faith and the sacraments of faith, in Christ's righteous worship. Joined to Christ, the incarnate Son of God, by his Holy Spirit, believers are raised with him to become adopted "sons" of God, destined to enjoy beatific communion in Christ with the Trinity.[27]

In short, Aquinas holds both that in all times and places some people are joined to Christ by faith and charity *and* that the divine pedagogy of the Old Law and the explicit proclamation of the New Law (which flows from Christ's passion) radically improved the human race. Certainly the Gentiles who had not heard of the divine revelation could be saved by implicit faith in a redeemer. However, Aquinas notes that one of the precepts of the law specified that Gentiles who were willing to be circumcised and to observe the law should be allowed to join the people of Israel. He explains that the law directed people to salvation "more perfectly and more securely" than could the Gentiles' reliance on providence, as grasped by the natural law.[28] This was so because the Old Law not only forbade and punished idolatry but also "disposed" its adherents to Christ through its ceremonies and prophecies.[29] He states that the Jews were highly exalted over the Gentile nations: "The more a man is united to God, the better his state becomes: wherefore the more the Jewish people were bound to the worship of God, the greater their excellence over other peoples."[30] The key to human excellence is right worship. If the Old Law had such a beneficial effect, then it makes sense that the proclamation of the New Law would also bring enormous spiritual blessings to the world because of the proclamation of the good news and the institution of the sacramental worship through which believers are united to Christ's passion and thereby receive the grace of the Holy Spirit. Aquinas conceives of the state of the New Law (the period beginning after Christ's passion) as marked by the Holy Spirit being given "abundantly" throughout the world.[31]

Israel: Community in Relation to God

We have seen that, for Aquinas, divine law is a pedagogy whose purpose is to form a holy community that embodies true worship. However, if this is so, why do the community of Israel and the community of the Church differ markedly in appearance? Why does God, as it were, devote so much effort to building up the community of Israel if he then wills to start "anew" in building up the community of the Church? More specifically, how is the community of the Church related, in God's plan, to the community of Israel? To answer these questions, I will examine in more detail Aquinas's understanding of the nature of the community of Israel. I should emphasize that my approach will not address the subject of Jewish-Christian relations— that is, the issues surrounding the fact that the two communities have continued to exist side by side. My intention, rather, is to trace Aquinas's systematic conception of the kind of community that biblical Israel is, in hopes of gaining insight into his conception of the kind of community that the Church is. When referring to Israel, therefore, I have in mind Israel as constituted by the law (not "Israel" as a modern nation-state or as communities in the diaspora, for whom many of the judicial and ceremonial precepts, most notably those regarding sacrifices, are no longer possible to fulfill).

Discussing the judicial precepts of the Old Law, Aquinas refers to Nm 24:5, "How beautiful are thy tabernacles, O Jacob, and thy tents, O Israel." In Aquinas's view, this verse signifies that Israel exemplifies "the beautiful ordering of a people."[32] The people of Israel, he holds, cannot be understood simply in the way that we understand other states. Other states are constituted by human law; Israel is constituted by divine law. This does not mean, of course, that Israel's law deals only with the people's relationship to God and not with their relationships with each other. Rather, Aquinas explains that "just as the precepts of human law direct man in his relations to the human community, so the precepts of the divine law direct man in his relations to a community or commonwealth [*communitatem seu rempublicam*] of men under God."[33] The divinely revealed law of Israel, therefore, has precepts regarding relations both to God and to human beings. Israel's precepts regarding relations to human beings, however, are distinguished from the precepts of mere human law in that divine law always places relations to human beings in the context of relations to God.

The distinction becomes clear in the examples that Aquinas gives. The laws found in Deuteronomy and Leviticus regarding property and exchange, he recognizes, would not please proponents of business as usual, who look at things merely from the viewpoint of human law. Aquinas cites a number of texts, including "Going into thy neighbor's vineyard, thou mayest eat as many grapes as thou pleasest" (Dt 23:24); "He to whom anything is owing from his friend or neighbor or brother, cannot demand it again, because it is the year of remission of the Lord" (Dt 15:2); and "When thou shalt demand of thy neighbor any thing that he oweth thee, thou shalt not go into his house to take away a pledge" (Dt 14:10).[34] What orchardist would like the idea that his neighbors could simply stroll in and eat their fill? As the objection goes on to point out, is this not tantamount to robbery? Likewise, does not the Jubilee year ("the year of remission of the Lord") put an impossible strain upon the principles of exchange? And what banker would ever loan anything without having access to something else as security?

Aquinas responds to these objections by pointing out the distinctiveness of divine law. Since the purpose of divine law is to promote charity (love for God and love for neighbor[35]) rather than merely to promote "the temporal tranquillity of the state,"[36] the Old Law's precepts regarding relations with human beings will necessarily reflect the divine pedagogy. In Aquinas's view, therefore, the precept that permits people to eat from the produce of their neighbors does not encourage stealing but rather attempts "to accustom men to give of their own to others readily."[37] Divine law does not contradict human law (as would happen, for example, if divine law were to condone stealing), but it goes beyond human law in order to teach people to treat each other not merely according to what is fair but according to what is charitable. The same holds for the precepts that involve loans and exchange. In this case, the divine law tilts the balance in favor of those who are borrowers. Divine law does this not to punish lenders but to encourage the practice of being always "ready to come to one another's assistance."[38] The divine law thus reminds people that the purpose of lending is, fundamentally, to help others, not to make a profit off them. Human law, while not unjust in itself, establishes precepts about economic relationships solely in order to promote a stable social order, which depends upon the citizenry possessing a certain level of virtue. In contrast, divine law formulates precepts about economic relationships with the primary goal of establishing practices that promote the end of *charity*.

Israel, therefore, is elevated above other peoples by its reception of divine law, which is ordered to charity. However, Aquinas never loses sight of the equally important reality that Israel could not, of itself, perfectly obey the law and that Israel awaited a Messiah who would bear Israel's sins and whose coming would be associated with the instilling of God's law in human hearts. Israel's law, in short, points beyond itself to a future event, which will embody the consummation of charity. Aquinas explains that charity—a participation in God's own love—cannot be given by a written law but only by God himself. The end of divine law must involve the indwelling of God in the human heart.[39] Thus for Israel's law to be fulfilled, it must simultaneously be transformed into an inner law. Israel's law is not its own end; rather, it awaits a fulfillment that will transform it.

For Aquinas, the fact that Israel's law is not its own end explains the nature of the community of Israel. Israel receives a "special sanctification"[40] above other peoples not merely because Israel is constituted by divine law but also because the *end* toward which the community of Israel is striving is the fulfillment of the divine law.[41] Since the divine law that Israel receives can never be isolated in God's plan from its fulfillment, Aquinas is able to hold that the community of Israel is exalted primarily because of Christ. He states that "God vouchsafed [*exhibuit*] both the Law and other special boons [*beneficia*] to that people, on account of the promise made to their fathers that Christ should be born of them."[42] When the Messiah fulfills the divine law, therefore, the community of Israel will also be brought to fulfillment in the person of the Messiah. Indeed, since "a law is nothing more than a dictate of reason in the ruler by whom his subjects are governed,"[43] the law is in the ruler and by participation in those who are ruled.[44] The Messiah, as the true ruler of Israel, fulfills the law not as an isolated individual but rather as the embodiment of the community.

In sum, the community of Israel is, in God's plan, built up *for Christ*.[45] The fact that God willed to become incarnate for our salvation meant that the God-man must be born within a certain nation or people. Having chosen to restore and perfect human beings from the side of human beings rather than by divine command, God prepared for himself a people whose laws would, if fulfilled in both their literal and their figurative sense, reestablish justice between God and humanity and among human beings. God gave the people of Israel a divine law so that the incarnate Son of God might, as a member of this people, perfectly fulfill its law (in this way fulfilling his responsibility, as a member of a people, both to be obedient to the people's law and to be obedient, as a man, to God[46]) *and* thereby restore the whole world to justice. Our salvation in Christ, therefore, cannot be truly understood outside the context of the law that constituted Israel as a holy community. Israel's community attains its end or goal in Christ's passion; at the same time, the Church, whose community is constituted by sacramental participation in Christ's passion, has her beginning. Christ's passion is the point where the two communities unite: Israel, through her divinely revealed law, informing the shape of the Messiah's saving work, and the Church deriving her constitution (the New Law) from the fulfillment of the law by the Messiah's saving work.

The Church: Uniting All Things in Christ

To this point, I have sought to show that the community of Israel is relevant to understanding the Mystical Body because Christ, in his salvific passion, represents and fulfills the structure of the community of Israel. However, I must now change direction and ask why, if Israel is a divinely ordained community ordered to friendship with God, God willed to establish a markedly different community (the Church) after Christ's passion. Why did God not simply extend Israel's constitution to the nations?

The answer to this question follows from the nature of Christ's representation of the people of Israel in his passion. When Christ fulfills the law, he does so not as an autonomous individual but as a member of the people that is constituted by the law. On the other hand, the whole community does not fulfill the law; rather, *Christ* perfectly fulfills the law for his fellow human beings, who are unable to accomplish this work themselves. Justification, therefore, consists in being united to Christ's fulfillment of the law.[47] Moreover, Christ's fulfillment of the law is not a merely literal accomplishment, as if all Christ did was follow the letter of the law.[48] Although Christ's passion is a sacrifice, it goes far beyond the sacrifices of the law that prefigured it. Likewise, although Christ's passion fulfills the judicial precepts because Christ freely wills to endure for us the just penalty of our sins, his suffering for all sinners goes far beyond what the judicial precepts themselves envision.[49] When Christ (divine Wisdom incarnate) fulfills the law, he reveals its divine meaning. Christ's passion explicitly reveals that the ultimate end of the law is found not in the ceremonial and judicial precepts themselves (although these provide a certain order toward God) but in friendship with the divine Persons through the God-man Jesus Christ, who has fulfilled the precepts of the law for us.[50] Instead of being ordered to God through an exterior law, human beings will now be ordered to God through profound interior union (by faith, hope, and charity and the sacraments of faith) with Christ, who, as the God-man, is the true mediator between God and man. Aquinas can thus describe Christ as "our wisest and greatest friend."[51] Since Christ's Person is divine, friendship with the man Christ entails intimate friendship with God. This friendship is the fulfillment of Torah and Temple: Christ invites all human beings to share with him the eternal liturgy that is the triune life.

Friendship with Christ is something different, therefore, from membership in the community that prepared for Christ. Although Christ's saving work cannot properly be interpreted outside the context of Israel's law, Christ, in fulfilling the law, revealed the deeper meaning of the precepts that built up Israel as a particular community. Israel's *cultus* was taken up (and transformed) in Christ's self-sacrifice; Israel's judicial system was taken up into Christ's suffering. In place of the sacrificial system that structured the worship of Israel, the new communal worship—the "new Israel"—must embody union with Christ's sacrifice, whose perfection is expressed by Augustine's remark that in the New Law, "the same one true Mediator reconciling us with God through the peace-sacrifice might continue to be one with Him to whom He offered it, might be one with them for whom He offered it, and might Himself be the offerer and what He offered."[52] Likewise, the new community cannot be constituted by judicial precepts that pertain only to one people because, by suffering for the sins of all people, Christ breaks down the juridical division between Jews and Gentiles in relation to God and thus, fundamentally, in relation to each other.[53]

What, then, is to be the constitution of the new community? As we have seen, Christ, by fulfilling the law, restores and perfects our communion with God and with each other. Christ's passion promises the most intimate possible communion not only because Christ makes us just (justice being the foundation of true community) but also because in Christ human nature is hypostatically united with the divine Person of the Word. The passion of the Messiah, therefore, reveals that the community of Israel, in its deepest expression, was intended to prefigure and to dispose human beings for profound communion with the Trinity.

This communion of the rational creature with the triune God—a communion that is perfect *worship*—can be brought about only by the elevation and transformation of the human being through the grace of the Holy Spirit. Christ, at the moment of his Incarnation, received the fullness of grace both on account of the union of his human nature with the divine Person of the Son and on account of his mission to bestow the life of grace upon others.[54] Aquinas explains that the grace of the Holy Spirit, which qualifies the essence of the soul, is the source of all the infused or supernatural virtues, which enable the powers of the soul to attain the supernatural end of beatitude.[55] Grace shaped all of Christ's actions, making them perfect expressions of charity, which is the form of all the virtues. Christ's fulfillment of the law was possible only because of his fullness of grace, since only his perfect charity makes sense of his sacrifice and suffering. For this reason, Aquinas holds that all grace is mediated by Christ, the one mediator between God and human beings. When we receive the grace of the Holy Spirit, we are enabled to participate in Christ's fulfillment of the law, by which he merits bodily resurrection.[56] Cooperating with grace, we become just through the works that grace enables us to perform. The source of our justification, ultimately, is not our own works but Christ's meritorious justice,[57] which we share in by grace.

Communion with Christ, therefore, means sharing in his grace. It is this sharing that we signify when we speak of being "in Christ." Since grace is (as a "quality" of the soul that has received the Holy Spirit) a spiritual reality, communion with Christ is primarily a spiritual reality. The community of Israel was based on the written law; in contrast, the new community in Christ is based on the inner communion established by the grace of the Holy Spirit, which infuses the virtues of faith, hope, and charity by which we are united to Christ's saving work. Since Christ himself is the mediator of this grace, he is said to possess *gratia capitalis*, the grace of headship; since our communion with Christ profoundly unites us in the bonds of charity, the community that is formed is likened, as regards its intimate unity, to a Mystical Body.[58] This emphasis on spiritual communion might seem to make any visible community superfluous. Certainly, it relativizes visible communion, since membership in the Mystical Body depends ultimately upon possession of charity. Those on earth who do not have charity, whatever their status in the visible communion, are in fact only potential, not actual, members of the Mystical Body.[59] As Aquinas states, the New Law is primarily an interior law, since the New Law "is chiefly the grace itself of the

Holy Ghost, which is given to those who believe in Christ."[60] It might seem, therefore, that the concept of the Mystical Body actually neglects the significance of our bodies.

In fact, however, Aquinas decisively rejects the concept of a purely invisible Mystical Body. He does so by analyzing the way believers are included in the Mystical Body through worship. In both Israel and the Church, inclusion in the Mystical Body is achieved through the spiritual realities of faith and charity, but these spiritual realities cannot be cut off from corresponding physical "signs" or sacraments—Israel's Temple and its fulfillment in the Church's sacramental structure and worship.[61] Aquinas repeatedly invokes the principle that after sin, "the condition of human nature . . . is such that it has to be led by things corporeal and sensible to things spiritual and intelligible."[62] The sacraments of the Old Law were therefore necessary to signify the future coming of Christ; likewise, the New Law requires sacraments that signify Christ's past Incarnation and passion.[63] In this regard, Aquinas cites Augustine's remark that "[i]t is impossible to keep men together in one religious denomination [*nomen religionis*], whether true or false, except they be united by means of visible signs or sacraments."[64] Community, to be true, cannot be invisible.

It follows that both the sacraments of the Old Law and the sacraments of the New Law are described by Aquinas as "signs in protestation of the faith whereby man is justified."[65] On the other hand, Aquinas radically differentiates the sacraments of the New Law from those of the Old Law.[66] As we have seen, the Old Law outlines the mode of justification, but it does not of itself provide the inner principle (the grace of the Holy Spirit) that justifies. Similarly, then, the sacraments of the Old Law do not confer the inner principle of justification.[67] Instead, the sacraments of the Old Law are "visible signs" that enable the people of Israel to confess their "faith in the future coming of a Saviour."[68] This faith, of course, is implicit: Aquinas notes that the people of Israel express faith in the future coming of Christ not directly but by "using these figures [the sacraments of the Old Law] to the honor of God."[69] Since confession of faith is a necessary part of faith,[70] the sacraments of the Old Law belong integrally to the movement of faith. While the sacraments of the Old Law do not cause grace, they nonetheless have a necessary role in embodying the inclusion, by faith and charity, of the holy men and women of Israel in the Mystical Body.

Since the New Law is primarily the grace of the Holy Spirit, the sacraments of the New Law must contain and cause grace. The sacraments of the New Law "contain" grace because they possess an "instrumental power of bringing about the sacramental effects,"[71] namely, restoring and perfecting the soul.[72] The sacraments have this power, Aquinas explains, because they are related in the manner of a "separate instrument" to the "united instrument" that is Christ's humanity. Christ's passion is the instrument by which God delivers us from sins; the sacraments, in turn, derive their power from Christ's passion, since the grace of the Holy Spirit flows to us from the saving work of Christ, which removes the obstacle of sin.[73] In light of the instrumental power of the sacraments of the New Law, Aquinas holds that these sacraments (specifically those of initiation, and above all baptism) directly *cause* incorporation into Christ's Mystical Body.[74] In the state of the New Law, under normal circumstances, baptism *causes* the movement of grace that justifies the believer by setting up within him the supernatural life of faith. Aquinas also notes that the sacraments of the New Law cause "a certain Divine assistance in obtaining the end of the sacrament."[75] Thus, sacramental grace is not superfluous even in the person who already has habitual grace, the infused virtues, and the gifts of the Holy Spirit.

The sacraments of the New Law, therefore, not only embody believers' profession of faith in Christ but also actually cause and assist believers' life in Christ. The corporeal elements of the sacraments are received bodily and have the spiritual effect of incorporating us into Christ's Mystical Body by filling us with the grace of the Holy Spirit. They have this spiritual effect because they are instruments of the incarnate Word, who gives his Spirit through them.[76] Aquinas describes the reality of incorporation into the Mystical Body in terms of the imprinting of a "character."[77] By causing the grace of the Holy Spirit to transform the recipient in a permanent way, the sacraments of baptism, confirmation, and ordination "mark" or "seal" the recipient in the image or "character" of Christ.[78] The natural *imago dei* in us becomes, Aquinas suggests, permanently Christic, thereby enabling believers to participate in the worship established by Christ's passion.[79] This participation is a sharing in Christ's priesthood. Through baptism and confirmation, believers share in Christ's priesthood passively, by being enabled to receive fully the divine gifts; through ordination, believers share in Christ's priesthood actively, by being enabled to bestow the divine gifts on others.[80] In short, these sacraments, by giving us a permanent power to share in the worship that Christ offers on the cross "in Spirit and truth" (Jn 4:23–24), prepare us for the properly ordered communion of body and soul (in worship) that will characterize the members of the Mystical Body in eternal life.

When understood correctly, moreover, worship ("in spirit and truth," Jn 4:23–24) provides the key to understanding why the Church on earth—despite the fact that the New Law is primarily the grace of the Holy Spirit justifying us interiorly—must be a *visible* communion. Christ institutes the sacraments to enable us fully to participate in and receive the grace of the Holy Spirit through his salvific act of sacrificial worship on the cross. As we have seen, all the sacraments derive their efficacy from Christ's passion. The sacraments only have spiritual power because Christ, as God, institutes and works through them.[81] It follows that the greatest sacrament is the Eucharist,[82] even though the Eucharist is not necessary for salvation in the way that baptism, under normal circumstances in the state of the New Law, is necessary.[83] Aquinas considers the Eucharist the greatest sacrament for three reasons: the Eucharist contains Christ substantially rather than simply sharing in Christ's power instrumentally, the other sacraments are ordered to the proper reception of the Eucharist, and the Eucharist is the pinnacle of all liturgical acts.[84]

Aquinas draws a profound connection between Christ's passion, his Mystical Body, and the Eucharist.[85] By the Eucharist, Christ, who has died for all people, draws believers into the most intimate friendship with himself. The Eucharist *is* Christ "under the sacramental species": as Aquinas states, "we eat Christ," who nourishes us spiritually.[86] The Eucharist is the sacrament that most profoundly signifies Christ's Mystical Body, composed of all those who are friends of Christ by charity.[87] In this regard, Aquinas notes that it was fitting that Christ instituted the sacrament of the Eucharist on the eve of his passion "because last words, chiefly such as are spoken by departing friends, are committed most deeply to memory; since then especially affection for friends is more enkindled, and the things which affect us most are impressed the deepest in the soul."[88] In receiving the Eucharist, the very body, blood, and divinity of Christ crucified for our salvation, believers come to embody, through the sacramental action, the intimate friendship or communion with Christ that expresses most perfectly their new existence as members of Christ's Mystical Body.

The liturgy of the Eucharist thus makes fully present the reality of communion that is the Mystical Body.[89] Aquinas here goes beyond Scott Bader-Saye's claim that the "Eucharist . . . becomes the place where God's corporeal election of Israel is extended to the Gentiles."[90] For Bader-Saye, the key to the Eucharist is that, through consuming Christ's Jewish flesh, Gentiles enter into God's covenant with Jews according to the flesh. In contrast, for Aquinas, the Eucharist's significance lies in the fact that the risen Christ, through his real presence in the Eucharist, shares with all believers the justice gained by his passion. The Eucharist is a "sacrifice," Aquinas explains, not merely because it represents Christ's sacrifice, but also because of its effect: "by this sacrament, we are made partakers of the fruit of our Lord's Passion."[91] We are incorporated into the sacrifice that Christ made upon the cross and thereby share in the forgiveness of sins and outpouring of the Holy Spirit that his sacrificial love brought about for humankind. Christ's passion, not the consumption of Jewish flesh, provides the crucial link between Mosaic Law and New Law (the grace of the Holy Spirit).[92]

For Aquinas, in short, the sacraments create a visible community whose purpose is to mediate participation in Christ's passion. As suggested by Augustine's remark that human beings cannot be kept together in one religion without "visible signs or sacraments,"[93] unity of faith, in our earthly life, is grounded on sacramental unity. Aquinas affirms that the Church "is built on faith and the sacraments of faith."[94] Whereas in heaven we will no longer need the sacraments or the visible Church, on earth the Word and His Spirit are mediated to human beings by visible signs. For this reason, the "character" imprinted by the sacrament of orders (fully participated in by the bishops) bestows on the recipient not only the power to perform the sacraments but also the power to proclaim fully the (scriptural) Word by articulating the true content of faith.[95] This power is a gift of the Holy Spirit, since the Holy Spirit gives sacramental grace. In Aquinas's view, therefore, the governing of the Church by the Holy Spirit of her Head and the governing of the Church by the hierarchy do not conflict, despite the inevitable failings of the human beings who are called to lead the Church. The Church, as the Mystical Body on earth, is the community of the Holy Spirit.[96] In this sense, the Church is fundamentally an interior communion. Yet the Holy Spirit preserves the Church's unity of faith through the visible ministry of bishops, led by the bishop of Rome.[97]

By examining Aquinas's understanding of Israel and the Church, I have sought to demonstrate that for Aquinas the Mystical Body of Christ is the fulfilled Temple, the visible locus of true worship. As the fulfilled Temple, the Church is a community of worshippers characterized by the indwelling of the Trinity in believers through the mediation of Christ, present in sacrament (preeminently the Eucharist) and in word. Aquinas makes clear that the teachings of the Church — teachings affirmed by the bishops in accord with their sacramental authority — belong to the sacramental economy, which has as its ultimate end beatific communion with the Trinity. Just as Israel's covenantal relationship with God cannot be detached from the specificity of Israel's laws and Temple, so also the Church's sacramental embodiment of the new covenant in Christ's passion cannot be detached from the specificity of the Church's doctrine. Aquinas does not detach faith from the sacraments of faith: even implicit faith is ordered to sacramental consummation. To proclaim the good news of the radical *communio* of charity gained by Christ's passion, a visible community is needed that embodies the spiritual unity of the Mystical Body. Such a community, foreshadowed by Israel, is the Church, constituted by faith and the sacraments of faith. This community of proclamation and worship, ordained to the beatific vision, shares in Christ's fulfillment of the Torah and thereby, as Christ's Mystical Body, fulfills Israel's Temple.

6 The Heavenly Jerusalem

As *Sacrosanctum Concilium*, the constitution on the sacred liturgy promulgated by the Second Vatican Council, teaches, "In the earthly liturgy we share a foretaste of that heavenly liturgy which is celebrated in the Holy City of Jerusalem toward which we journey as pilgrims, where Christ is sitting at the right hand of God, Minister of the sanctuary and of the true tabernacle."[1] The heavenly liturgy, in relation to which the Church's earthly liturgy (as a real sharing in Christ's saving work) provides a true "foretaste," is thus described—as it is in the New Testament—in terms drawn from the Old Testament, such as "Jerusalem," "sanctuary," and "tabernacle." These terms bring out the continuity between the Old and New Laws: both are fulfilled in the heavenly liturgy. As we have seen, Aquinas reads both Testaments in light of this anagogical sense, which identifies in both Testaments figures of the state of glory.[2] In this regard, he acknowledges his debt to Pseudo-Dionysius, who states that "the New Law itself is a figure of future glory."[3]

This dynamic order of both the Old and New Laws toward the heavenly liturgy is central to Aquinas's account of law. His description of this order, in an article dealing with the ceremonial precepts of the Old Law, is worth quoting here in full:

All the ceremonial precepts of the Old Law were ordained to the worship of God, as stated above (q.101, aa.1,2). Now external worship should be in proportion to the internal worship, which consists in faith, hope, and charity. Consequently exterior worship had to be subject to variations according to the variations in the internal worship, in which a threefold state may be distinguished. One state was in respect of faith and hope, both in heavenly goods, and in the means of obtaining them,—in both of these considered as things to come. Such was the state of faith and hope in the Old Law.—Another state of the interior worship is that in which we have faith and hope in heavenly goods as things to come; but in the means of obtaining heavenly goods, as in things present or past. Such is the state of the New Law.—The third state is that in which both are possessed as present; wherein nothing is believed in as lacking, nothing hoped for as being yet to come. Such is the state of the Blessed. In this state of the Blessed, then, nothing in regard to the worship of God will be figurative; there will be naught but *thanksgiving and voice of praise* (Isa. 51:3). Hence it is written concerning the city of the Blessed (Rev. 21:22): *I saw no temple therein: for the Lord God Almighty is the temple thereof, and the Lamb.* Proportionately, therefore, the ceremonies of the first-mentioned state which fore-shadowed the second and third states, had need to cease at the advent of the second state [the New Law]; and other ceremonies had to be introduced which would be in keeping with the state of divine worship for that particular time, wherein heavenly goods are a thing of the future, but the Divine favors whereby we obtain the heavenly boons are a thing of the present.[4]

The Old Law's ceremonial precepts, Aquinas goes on to state, last forever in the sense that they are taken up into the reality—ultimately the heavenly liturgy—which they foreshadow.[5] Aquinas thus shows that the covenant with Israel lasts forever. Aquinas's conception of salvation, however, ends with neither Temple nor Church: rather, as already noted, it ends with communion, in the Mystical Body of Israel's Messiah, with God in the heavenly liturgy, the perfect worship and praise described by the prophet Isaiah.[6]

The *Summa Theologiae* is an unfinished work. Aquinas had intended to conclude the *tertia pars* with a discussion of the state of glory, but he died before he could begin this task. A few months before his death (around the age of fifty), Aquinas stopped work on the *Summa*, declaring that he could write no more. In comparison with the mystery of the divine realities revealed by Christ, he felt, all that he had written was mere "straw."[7] Perhaps fittingly, Aquinas's mature reflection upon the state of glory awaited his own entrance into that blessed state.

In his *Commentary on the Sentences*, Aquinas had already treated the topics that he would have included in the *Summa*'s analysis of the state of glory. As Otto Pesch remarks, "the list, at least, of questions and of themes of the treatise on eschatology had been established since the beginnings of the scholastic period."[8] Although he would have modified, in his mature work, the positions that he had taken twenty years earlier in his *Commentary on the Sentences*, nonetheless the latter work provides insight into what Aquinas would have said in the *Summa*. On the basis of material from the *Commentary on the Sentences*, Raynald of Piperno completed the *tertia pars* after Aquinas's death by the addition of supplementary questions.[9] The value of this supplement should not be underestimated, if only because it reminds us that Aquinas did address the topic of the state of glory, if not in his last work.[10] A case can thus be made for employing the *Commentary on the Sentences* as a means of bringing our own study to completion. However, I will use this resource cautiously. In this regard, I have benefited from the work of Simon Tugwell, who has shown that Aquinas changed his mind after the *Commentary on the Sentences* on the issue of the separated soul's perfect beatitude.[11]

At this point, it may be helpful to review the structure of my study. I have argued that Aquinas conceives of human salvation in terms of law and liturgy, Torah and Temple. Law and liturgy are ultimately one. As indicated by the ceremonial precepts, perfect fulfillment of the law—perfect holiness—is manifested by perfect worship, the true liturgy of praise. Jesus of Nazareth, the Messiah of Israel, takes up and transforms Israel's Torah and Temple by his saving work, culminating in his Paschal mystery of suffering, death, and resurrection. As the Son of God, Jesus' fulfillment of Torah and Temple is such that all human beings are enabled to share in the grace of the Holy Spirit that flows through his meritorious actions. This eucharistic sharing is modeled preeminently by the

Virgin Mary and follows the pattern established by Christ in his path from suffering to glorification. As sharers in Christ's Paschal mystery, believers are incorporated into Christ's Mystical Body, in which human worship attains real communion with the divine Trinity. The interior transformation caused by this communion brings about, more and more fully, the transformation of the sinner into a holy "temple of the Holy Spirit" who is able, in Christ, to be holy (fulfilling the law) and to worship the Trinity with perfect praise (fulfilling the Temple).

Given this background, this chapter will probe the nature of eternal life. Without denying that eye has not seen nor ear heard "what God has prepared for those who love him" (1 Cor 2:9), the theologian must take on this task. Medieval reflection upon the state of glory has at times been dismissed as the product of dualistic views of the human person, which result in lack of regard for human history. In their recent *Hope against Hope: Christian Eschatology at the Turn of the Millennium*, Richard Bauckham and Trevor Hart remark, "There is little doubt that other-worldly preoccupation has often sapped the strength of a proper concern for the here and now within Christianity."[12] Blaming Platonic philosophy, as well as misreadings of St. Paul, for an "other-worldliness" that has diminished Christian theological respect for the body, Bauckham and Hart argue that "the persistence among Christians of belief in an 'immortal soul' which is separable from and survives the body, being in effect 'the bit which really matters', is adequate testimony to this fact"[13]—that is, to the baneful influence of Platonic "other-worldliness." I hope to show, on the contrary, that Aquinas's eschatology (with his understanding of the spiritual soul) indicates, not a flight from history, but the liturgical consummation of history.[14]

As Otto Pesch has argued, Aquinas's questions regarding the state of glory not only express concerns still present today but also flow directly from the seriousness with which he treats Scripture's testimony to eternal life.[15] I will propose that Aquinas's emphasis on the establishment (in the "new creation" in Christ) of *harmony and justice* in the cosmos and in humankind reveals that the beatific vision fulfills in the most immediate and intimate way possible the history of Israel's Torah and Temple. The sacramental system through which the Church receives Christ will be replaced, in the state of glory, by direct communion. Sacraments and ecclesial structure will no longer be needed, for the Mystical Body itself will be the perfect Temple.

The Resurrection of the Body

In seeking the intelligibility of the resurrection of the body, Aquinas extends his reflection upon the reality of the Mystical Body of Christ. As noted above, Israel's Temple signifies, in Aquinas's view, the new creation brought about by the indwelling of the Holy Spirit in believers. The new creation will be brought to fulfillment, Aquinas suggests, only when the entire created order is established in rest. Aquinas states that "the resurrection of human bodies will be delayed until the end of the world when the heavenly movement will cease."[16] In part, this conclusion reflects his medieval cosmology: he holds the view that the "higher bodies" or "heavenly movements" of the stars exert an influence upon the "lower bodies," and he argues that it would be unfitting for the lower bodies to be brought to rest before the higher bodies, which influence them, have attained rest.[17] However, this conclusion should also be interpreted liturgically. If the new creation is to be conformed *as a whole* to Christ (which the perfection of the Temple requires), then it makes sense that all bodies, higher and lower, should be transformed at once. The material creation is thus seen to possess a "liturgical" unity. Aquinas explains that by affirming that "all shall rise together," one affirms that, in the words of the gloss on Heb 11:39, "through all rejoicing each one might rejoice the more."[18] This rejoicing is the *liturgy* offered by the consummated Temple.[19]

The consummation that will be brought about by the bodily resurrection at the end of time (which will correspond to the new creation of the entire cosmos) will not be an evolutionary event; rather, it will be a revelation of the Mystical Body of Christ. The cosmos will not simply blossom forth in new creation. On the contrary, Aquinas suggests, Christ himself will work the resurrection by his presence. At the end of time, the Mystical Body—as the fulfillment of Israel's Temple—will be consummated by the God-man's direct presence. Just as Israel's Temple was to be the dwelling place of God's name, so

Christ's presence will enliven the new creation or heavenly liturgy, where (as the book of Revelation says) God himself and the Lamb will *be* the Temple. Interpreting 1 Thes 4:15, "The Lord Himself will come down from heaven . . . with the trumpet of God; and the dead who are in Christ shall rise," Aquinas explains that "the visible presence of God is called His voice, because as soon as He appears all nature will obey His command in restoring human bodies" and thus Christ's "voice" is signified by the trumpet.[20] The God-man's presence, appearing at the end of the world and initiating the general judgment of humankind, will call forth the new creation. Christ's trumpet, Aquinas states, will mark the beginning of "the feast of everlasting solemnity," the heavenly liturgy.[21]

It remains to ask what the significance of the resurrection of the body is in light of the final state of the human soul. All creatures naturally desire happiness (beatitude), but happiness cannot be obtained in this life due to the fragility and incompleteness that mark even a person's happiest moments. Therefore, happiness ultimately depends upon the resurrection of the body, since the separated soul, as the "form" of the body, is perfected only when it is once again united to the body.[22] God wills that his creatures not be frustrated in the desires that flow from their nature, although God does not will necessarily that each rational creature obtain *supernatural* perfection, since this is a free transformation of the creature and does not correspond to any natural dynamism. Aquinas comments, "All, both good and wicked, are conformed to Christ, while living in this life, as regards things pertaining to the nature of the species, but not as regards matters pertaining to grace. Hence all will be conformed to Him in the restoration of natural life, but not in the likeness of glory, except the good alone."[23] On this view, the resurrection of the bodies of the damned—that is, the souls who reject Christ—should be understood in light of God's goodness. After original sin, God alone can restore human beings to immortality, and God does this (instrumentally) through Christ's resurrection.[24]

Aquinas also shows that the damned are related to the final consummation of all things in Christ by noting that Christ is the Head of all humankind. The Mystical Body of Christ is not a partial reality but encompasses all human beings in some way. On the other hand, as Aquinas puts it, "Christ is the Head of all men, but diversely."[25]

All human beings are, in their earthly lives, united to Christ as Head in actuality or in potentiality. Some of those who are united to Christ in potentiality, however, will never "be reduced to act."[26] While Christ suffers for all men and reconciles all men to God, not all accept the salvation that he offers. Such persons, when they die, are permanently separated from the Mystical Body—which is a communion constituted by charity—because they no longer have the opportunity to conform their wills to Christ's charity.[27] This conclusion undergirds the seriousness of history. At the general judgment, the damned will know that Christ is God, but they will not see God's essence, since this vision follows upon faith and charity.[28]

The damned, who are cut off from the Mystical Body on account of their evil wills, remain related to that Body through the justice of the judgment rendered by Christ and the saints. As the judge (who judges by the measuring rod of charity), Christ sums up all things in relation to his charity. Christ is Head of all humankind not only as savior but also as judge.[29] All the saints will judge, in the sense of consenting to Christ's judgment, but some will receive a more distinct role in the judgment.[30] In communicating his judgment, Aquinas suggests, Christ will be aided especially by the saints whose lives have conformed them most fully to justice.[31] As Aquinas points out, Christ, as man, merited exaltation to the right hand of God (signifying judiciary power) by his definitive act of humility, his passion.[32] Because of their humble charity, the saints are able to judge the damned with perfect justice. Thus, the awareness of the suffering of the damned does not impede the beatitude of the saints because they love each creature in accord with its degree of goodness—that is, in accord with the creature's degree of participation in God's divine Being.[33]

Aquinas's discussion of the resurrection of the bodies of the saints focuses, by contrast, on the state of the glorified body, which (in order to share fully in the worship offered by the glorified soul) will be conformed to the qualities possessed by Christ's resurrected body. Just as Jesus risen is the same man who was born in Nazareth and died on the cross, the resurrected bodies will be "the selfsame body,"[34] yet they will not possess the defects caused by original sin, such as imperfect development, chronic disease, or decrepitude.[35] God will restore human bodies to how they would have been without original sin. This will not mean that all bodies will look alike;

rather, each body will reach its natural perfection.[36] Moreover, the bodies of the blessed will be not only restored but also perfected. The bodies of the blessed (like Christ's glorified body) will be perfected by four qualities: impassibility, subtlety, agility, and clarity. Each of these qualities removes impediments to the body's truly participating in the glorified soul's everlasting worship.

Impassibility, which was possessed by human beings in the state of original justice, signifies that the body will be perfectly ruled by the soul. Aquinas argues that through the restoration of due order, God will govern the soul, and the soul will govern the body. In the state of glory, this order will be perfected so as to be incorruptible. The soul's governance of the body means that the body will no longer be subject to disordered passions and physical corruption, although the body will retain sensation.[37] Indeed, Aquinas holds that all the senses will be perfectly in act, in conformity with the glory of the soul.[38] In short, the glorified body, no less than the glorified soul, will participate eternally in the heavenly liturgy, without fear of falling away.[39] In eternal life, physical signs of virtue (e.g., the wounds received by Christ) may remain as beautiful marks of spiritual victory, but they will no longer retain the aspect of corruptibility or invite further decay. Aquinas is careful to add that injuries received by martyrs to parts of the body necessary for bodily perfection (such as having one's head cut off) will be completely restored.[40]

The other qualities—subtlety, agility, and clarity—express the fact that the body is glorified. Transformed by the supernaturally perfected soul, the glorified body is a new creation. Aquinas cites 1 Cor 15:44: "It is sown a corruptible body, it shall rise a spiritual, i.e. a spirit-like, body."[41] "Subtlety" signifies the ability of the body to penetrate. As Aquinas explains, this ability to penetrate does *not* mean that glorified bodies take on the power of spiritual substances and no longer occupy any space.[42] Rather, the penetration of glorified bodies enables them to move together in harmony, without causing disturbance or friction, because bodies will be entirely subject to their souls as their form. There will be no crowding in the divine liturgy of heaven, no matter how many resurrected human beings are present.

Agility refers to the fact that the soul is united to the body as its mover, as well as its form.[43] The glorified body, therefore, will perfectly reflect its glorified soul's spiritual movements of praise. The praise offered bodily by the blessed in heaven will not be laborious or burdensome, and so they will not tire out and need to rest. Although the soul's beatific communion with God will be unchanging, Aquinas affirms that the blessed in heaven will not be still but will move bodily. First, such movement will glorify God by demonstrating the harmonious power of the blessed. Second, such movement will increase the perfection of the beatific vision (which in a strict sense is perfect already in the separated souls). Aquinas states that the saints' "vision may be refreshed by the beauty of the variety of creatures, in which God's wisdom will shine forth with great evidence: for sense can only perceive that which is present, although glorified bodies can perceive from a greater distance than non-glorified bodies."[44] Movement will thereby enable the saints to see, with their bodily eyes, the full panorama of the glory of God's material creation.

In order to indicate the fittingness of the saints' clarity (as well as agility), Aquinas cites Wis 3:7, "The just shall shine, and shall run to and fro like sparks among the reeds."[45] Aquinas notes that when the body is reunited to the soul and shares in its glorification, "clarity which in the soul is spiritual is received into the body as corporeal."[46] This clarity will not erase the body's natural color but will make the body resplendent, in proportion to the soul's degree of charity.[47] Like Christ's transfigured body, the glorified bodies of the saints will be more resplendent than the sun, but this light will not be blinding when looked at directly.[48]

In short, drawing upon the biblical witness to Christ's transfigured and resurrected body, and carefully preserving the corporeality of the glorified body, Aquinas sketches a powerful vision of the bodily communion of the saints within the consummated Mystical Body of Christ. Marked by harmony, movement, and light, this communion will truly fulfill the promise of Israel's Temple.

The New Creation

The intelligibility of the resurrection of the body, Aquinas suggests, requires also that the entire material creation be made new. The cosmos is not simply a useful canister for human development, which God discards once the goal has been achieved. In defending

this position, Aquinas cites the biblical testimony to the transformation of the cosmos: "It is written (Isa. 65:17): *Behold I create new
heavens and a new earth, and the former things shall not be in remem-
brance;* and (Rev. 21:1): *I saw a new heaven and a new earth. For the
first heaven and the first earth was gone.*"[49] He goes on to argue that
the dwelling place and the one who dwells there are related intrinsically because the former was made for the latter; therefore, when
the one is transformed, the other will be too. On the basis of the
axiom that "likeness is the reason [*ratio*] of love," he points out that
humankind, as a "*minor mundus*" or microcosm, "loves the whole
world [*universum*] naturally and consequently desires its good."[50]
The resurrection of the body makes sense only in the context of the
transformation of the entire material creation, to which the body
belongs. In loving themselves, human beings properly love the entire
cosmos. It is fitting that God transform the entire material creation
together.

However, what is the purpose of this transformed cosmos? In
humankind's present state, Aquinas argues, the cosmos is necessary
both for humankind's material sustenance and for enabling humankind naturally to know through visible things the invisible things
of God. It would seem that neither of these tasks would be relevant
in the state of glory, since glorified human beings no longer need
food and clothes and since they will know God by beatific vision.
Aquinas explains that the beatific vision elevates and perfects the
rational soul but leaves the senses unperfected. Although the bliss
of the beatific vision is perfect, still "the carnal eye [i.e., the sense of
sight] will be unable to attain to this vision of the Essence; wherefore that it may be fittingly comforted in the vision of God, it will
see the Godhead in Its corporeal effects, wherein manifest proofs of
the Divine majesty will appear, especially in Christ's flesh, and sec-
ondarily in the bodies of the blessed, and afterwards all in other
bodies."[51] The body, as well as the soul, will be truly taken up into
the state of glory. As bodily creatures (rational animals, as Alasdair
MacIntyre has reminded us),[52] human beings will rejoice in seeing,
with their own eyes, Christ and the other saints. Human beings will
also rejoice in the wondrous beauty of the transformed world, just as
in this life people enjoy seeing beautiful vistas. Indicating the relationship between humankind and the world, in which the latter

serves the former, Aquinas states that "man merited that this glory should be bestowed on the whole universe, in so far as this conduces to man's increase of glory. Thus a man merits to be clothed in more splendid robes, which splendor the robes nowise merited themselves."[53] The state of glory will be suffused by those delights of the body that express the soul's blessedness.

On the other hand, the transformed cosmos will not simply be a prettier version of itself, although the stars and the elements will be more resplendent so as to testify even more clearly to the glory of their Creator.[54] The movements of the stars and planets, like the movement of begetting and corruption, will cease because these movements belonged to the way in which God sustained the vitality of creation as it moved toward its goal.[55] In an age in which pets, trees, and endangered species often receive more care and attention than impoverished human beings—and when ethicists such as Peter Singer decry "specieism"—Aquinas's view that plants and animals will not remain in the transformed cosmos is especially challenging. Admittedly, the reasons he gives for the preservation of stars and the elements but not of plants and animals are rooted in his medieval cosmology, which considered the stars to be incorruptible.[56] Aquinas's basic point is that there is no purpose for all, or even some (this would pose the problem of which ones), plants and animals to live forever.[57] Since they do not have rational souls, they cannot sin, be redeemed by Christ, or enjoy the beatific vision. Were they to share in eternal life, this would mean that they would either go through the same motions endlessly—something that one would not wish for oneself—or they would have nothing to do, their goals of generation, growth, and self-maintenance having been achieved. Since Scripture says nothing of their resurrection (resurrection being reserved to human beings, in accord with the formal causality of Christ), Aquinas concludes that plants and animals will participate in the transformed cosmos as elements rather than as resurrected living creatures. Against this view, one could argue that human appreciation for the beauty of vegetative life, and the bonds that humans form with other animals, suggest that plants and animals will belong to the new creation. Only in glory will we know fully what God intends for the material creation. Aquinas's approach, however, provides a model for theological engagement with Scripture's testimony that the entire creation will be renewed at Christ's second coming. He affirms both the unity and goodness of all the material creation and the priority of humankind.

The Beatific Vision

Through the beatific vision, the faculties that separate human beings from other animals—the ability to know and love God, and all things in relation to God—are transformed, elevated, and perfected. The beatific vision constitutes the ultimate sacrifice of praise. Human knowing and loving will be taken into the knowing and loving that characterize the life of the divine Persons. Human beings will thus participate in the dynamic communion of the divine Persons and will truly "see" (by intellectual vision) the essence of God, which subsists in the divine Persons.[58] This experience, while anticipated in the sacramental liturgy whereby the Church receives communion in the God-man (and tasted briefly by souls in rapture), will go infinitely beyond the liturgy of the present state. Aquinas repeatedly returns to the Johannine passages, "We shall see Him as He is" (1 Jn 2:2) and "This is eternal life, that they may know Thee the only true God" (Jn 17:3).[59]

Much of Aquinas's discussion of the beatific vision explores the vision's profound intimacy as true friendship with God. The analogy of vision, Aquinas recognizes, can be misleading here. When we see corporeal things, their likeness is present in our mind but not their essence. God cannot be seen in this way because no corporeal likeness can convey the incorporeal.[60] Moreover, no human concept can convey God's essence for two reasons. First, the essence of God is his existence, which is not true for any created form (and thus cannot be grasped in a human concept). Second, as Aquinas states, "the divine essence is uncircumscribed, and contains in itself supereminently whatever can be signified or understood by the created intellect. Now this cannot in any way be represented by any created likeness; for every created form is determined according to some aspect of wisdom, or of power, or of being itself, or of some like thing."[61] No concept can grasp God's essence because the concept is limited, while God is unlimited.

Aquinas draws the necessary conclusion that if we say that the beatific vision takes place through a created concept, then the vision cannot be a true vision of God. Instead, God joins himself to the created intellect in an inexpressibly intimate fashion: "the divine essence is united to the created intellect, as the object actually understood, making the intellect in act by and of itself."[62] The interior presence of God transforms, elevates, and perfects the human intellect to "see" God, who makes himself (unmediated by any concept) the direct object of the intellectual vision of the glorified soul. The soul shares immediately in God's essence or intelligible Word. Yet, since only the infinite can exhaustively grasp the infinite, God is properly said to be "incomprehensible" even for the blessed. In this regard, Aquinas affirms, "God is called incomprehensible not because anything of Him is not seen; but because He is not seen as perfectly as He is capable of being seen."[63] In the worship that characterizes the state of glory, therefore, God is known yet remains a mystery.

The interior presence of God in the soul causes grace. Drawing upon the medieval axiom that whatever is known is known according to the mode of the knower, Aquinas explains that if "the mode of anything's being exceeds the mode of the knower, it must result that the knowledge of that object is above the nature of the knower."[64] To know *ipsum esse subsistens*, pure act, is natural to God alone. Grace — which is consummated in glory — describes the way in which God "unites Himself to the created intellect, as an object made intelligible to it"—that is, as an intelligible form.[65] Since grace is a true transformation of the creature's soul, it is (as it exists in the creature) *created*, although it is the work of the uncreated Trinity.[66] By grace, in other words, the creature does not *become* the Creator but rather becomes a "new creation," enabled to participate in the divine liturgy.

It might be asked, however, whether grace thus constitutes a medium between the soul and God, so that the soul does not really attain direct knowledge of God. Aquinas here distinguishes between the light of the intellect and its intelligible forms: "this light [the light of grace elevating the intellect] is to be described not as a medium in which God is seen, but as one by which He is seen; and such a medium does not take away the immediate vision of God."[67] Since the beatific vision comes about through the elevating of the intellect accomplished by grace (which, Aquinas remarks, gives the intellect "a kind of *deiformity*"[68]), it is also worth noting that those persons of higher natural intelligence are not privileged in the beatific vision. The light of glory (the consummation of the light of grace) is given by God to human beings without regard to the power, or lack of power, of their natural intellects. Instead, Aquinas holds, "he will have a fuller participation of the light of glory who has more charity; because where there is the greater charity, there is the more desire; and desire in a certain degree makes the one desiring apt and prepared to receive the object desired."[69] The saints are distinguished by their charity. Thus the divine liturgy enjoyed by the saints is not simply an exercise of the intellect but also an exercise of the will.[70]

Finally, the beatific vision enjoyed by the individual takes place within the context of the Mystical Body of Christ. Since Christ is eternally priest, he remains the source of the light of glory that enlightens the consummated Mystical Body. Those who enjoy the beatific vision do so as adopted sons in the Son.[71] Aquinas explains that "they will need consummation through Christ Himself, on whom their glory depends, as is written (Rev. 21:23): *The glory of God hath enlightened it*—that is, the city of the Saints—*and the Lamb is the lamp thereof.*"[72] The God-man remains the source of the light of glory that enlightens the consummated Mystical Body. Although spiritual adoption, as an effect in creatures, is the work of the whole Trinity, human beings are adopted through Christ: "By adoption we are made the brethren of Christ, as having with Him the same Father: Who, nevertheless, is His Father in one way, and ours in another." The grace of the Holy Spirit conforms us to Christ as exemplar.[73] In short, the missions of the Son and of the Spirit are united in building the perfect Temple.

Even in the state of glory, therefore, Christ remains the one mediator between God and humankind.[74] In Aquinas's theology, the Incarnation of the Son of God never becomes superfluous. The state of glory, in which each saint receives the wondrous gift of the intellectual vision of God, is the consummation of Christ's work, through the Holy Spirit, of reconciling all things in heaven and on earth. In this way, the links between the Old Law (Torah and Temple), the New

Law (the preaching and sacramental worship of the Church, Christ's visible Mystical Body), and the state of glory are never severed. The divine liturgy of praise that is the state of glory does not negate either the Old or the New Covenant. Instead, both are fulfilled by the perfect holiness and perfect worship enjoyed by the glorified human beings and angels in harmony with the renewed cosmos.

Conclusion

The end that God wills for humankind is beautifully expressed in the encyclical *Mystici Corporis:* "In that celestial vision it will be granted to the eyes of the human mind strengthened by the light of glory, to contemplate the Father, the Son, and the Holy Spirit in an utterly ineffable manner, to assist throughout eternity at the processions of the Divine Persons, and to rejoice with a happiness like to that with which the holy and undivided Trinity is happy."[1] As we have seen, human beings attain this end by faith, implicit or explicit, in the God-man, Jesus of Nazareth, the Messiah of Israel who reconciles God and humankind by the obedience of his cross.

This claim, which must be made by Christian theologians, should not be mistaken for a sectarian desire to impose an exterior uniformity upon humankind or to constrict human ends. As A. N. Williams has recently emphasized, what is at stake is nothing less than deification.[2] By fulfilling Israel's Torah and Temple, Christ enables humankind—by the interior movement of the grace of the Holy Spirit, mediated sacramentally—to merit beatitude, eternal sharing in the divine life, through lives that are holy sacrifices of praise. United with Christ in the communion of his Mystical Body, human beings become a new creation. The Holy Spirit transforms human beings interiorly so that they may—in conformity with Christ's life, death, and resurrection—embody charity and justice toward God and neighbor and receive the perfection of charity that is eternal life. Far from

141

constricting the human person, Christian theology, as envisioned by Aquinas, ponders the revealed path of humankind's embodied movement toward God, whose infinite love enables the saint, in the consummated Mystical Body of Christ, to enjoy eternally communion in God's triune life

God's covenant with his people Israel, therefore, is not revoked but fulfilled by the promised Messiah. In fulfilling Israel's Torah and Temple, the Messiah himself becomes the perfect embodiment of Torah and Temple, which are thus radically transformed. All human beings are called to participate, through the grace of the Holy Spirit mediated by the sacraments that are a true sharing in Christ's Paschal mystery, in the fulfillment accomplished by Christ. In this study, I have proposed that Aquinas's account of salvation hinges upon Christ's fulfillment (and transformation) of law and liturgy, Torah and Temple. As I have also suggested, Aquinas's account of salvation is therefore closer to contemporary biblical exegesis than are many modern Christian soteriologies, since Aquinas understands salvation firmly within the context of God's activity in Israel. In this regard, it may be useful to compare Aquinas's account with N. T. Wright's description of St. Paul's understanding of salvation:

The promised end of exile had arrived, but in a mysterious and unexpected fashion. Everything else followed from this. The renewed people of God *was* the new temple (failure to appreciate the huge significance of the temple within first-century Judaism has led to a gross downplaying of the "temple" theme within Pauline ecclesiology and for that matter soteriology). . . . For Jews of his day (and many other days), Torah was at one and the same time the charter of the people of God and the full and final revelation of God himself. If, then, Jesus has taken on this double role, it is no surprise to find him taking on precisely the role of Torah in Paul's understanding of the plan of the one God. It is though the Torah was made in order that, one day, the anointed representative of God's people should come to do and be what Torah apparently was and did, only this time to do it successfully and to be it fully. . . . As both God and the people of God are redefined [by Jesus's fulfillment], so the reaffirmation of Torah takes on the form of radical redefinition. No longer can the Torah keep the people of God as a single ethnic or geo-graphical unit, with all the taboos that maintain such a system. It must now become—and, in the plan of God, has now become—the new charter for the renewed people.[3]

Like Wright, Aquinas in his account of salvation develops the significance of Torah and Temple, but he goes beyond Wright by formulating a theology of history that seeks to investigate sapientially, through insight into the integral *wisdom* of God's plan, the activity of the triune God who is Creator and Redeemer. This theological approach enables Aquinas to draw connections between the created order, Israel's covenantal election, and the missions of the Son and Spirit that exegetes, who rely upon the textual narrative in its cultural context, cannot easily make.

In the first section (chapters 1–3), I showed that Aquinas, drawing upon an analogous understanding of law and upon reflection on Christ's status as Wisdom incarnate, interprets Christ's passion in light of the three kinds of precepts of the Torah and of the three "offices" of ancient Israel. Christ's passion thus fulfills all justice and constitutes perfect worship of the Trinity. The second section (chapters 4–6) showed how Christ's perfect worship also fulfills Israel's Temple. Christ's passion mediates grace—the indwelling of the Trinity that makes the person a "new creation"—to all human beings who (implicitly or explicitly) believe in him. Joined to Christ's perfect worship, through which he merited bodily glorification, believers constitute a Temple of praise that will be perfected in the state of glory. This communion, on earth, requires the proclamation of the good news and the liturgy of the sacraments (and thus the visible Church), but it is ordered to the perfection that will be the beatific vision of the Trinity.

As Aquinas presents it, *sacra doctrina* is the effort, by means of faith seeking understanding, to articulate the "whole" of the mystery of salvation as it appears to God and the blessed, for whom each aspect of the historical economy of salvation reveals God's infinite wisdom and love, the truth, goodness, and beauty of God's plan. To appreciate God's will to save human beings through Christ, one must understand why God wills that the Son enter into human history in the particular context that he did and how this context (Israel as shaped covenantally by Torah, Temple, and the three "offices") sheds light on the significance of Jesus. God wills that Jesus be a Jew, the Messiah of Israel, who brings Israel's history to fulfillment. This context informs Aquinas's systematic reflection upon Christ's saving work, even as Aquinas draws upon sophisticated theoretical categories that aid him in his sapiential task. In the words of Wilhelmus Valkenberg, "The importance of Scripture is evident not only in explicit quotations from Scripture, but also, and even more so, in implicit quotations, allusions and the use of biblical concepts and language."[4]

By arguing that Aquinas envisions salvation in terms of law and liturgy, I have sought to shed light on the scriptural as well as theoretical dimensions of *sacra doctrina* as expounded by Aquinas. It may be appropriate to close by indicating an awareness of the limitations of this study, limitations that do not belong to the *Summa Theologiae*. First, an adequate treatment of salvation should discuss in detail the God who saves. By beginning with a treatise on the triune God, the *Summa Theologiae* emphasizes that salvation is fundamentally the work of a personal God and that salvation itself is coming to know and love this God. A contemporary Thomist theology, therefore, could not stop with Aquinas's account of Christ's saving work but would need also to explore his trinitarian theology. Second, further work would also need to present a detailed picture of the manner in which human beings participate in Christ's fulfillment of Torah and Temple. As we have seen, charity is the key to Aquinas's account. Due to my focus on Christ's saving work, I have not detailed Aquinas's description of the virtuous life, for which charity provides the "form."[5] Charity is modeled by Christ as prophet, priest, and king, but in his disciples these offices are fleshed out in different ways, according to vocation and circumstance. To describe the working out of charity in those who are joined to Christ, one would need to examine how the communion of adopted sons and daughters in the Son embodies the practice of justice and love in the world. Virtue and law are not opposed here: by fulfilling the "divine law" through charity, one both fulfills and surpasses the "natural law" of the human creature. Such Thomistic moral theology has born fruit already in the work of persons influenced by Aquinas's thought, such as St. Catherine of Siena, Bartolomé de Las Casas, St. Ignatius of Loyola, and many others.

The present study, in short, belongs within a larger project, one that would reflect the breadth of the *Summa Theologiae*. Even so, however, the insights of the study may stand on their own. I have proposed that Aquinas's account of salvation is structured upon the fulfillment of Torah and Temple, law and liturgy—and that this pattern of redemption, as elucidated by Aquinas, should play a vital part in the contemporary debate. Just as Aquinas's virtue theory once needed to be retrieved from casuistical distortion and neglect, so likewise Aquinas's full account of salvation now needs to be retrieved in light of its rich christological integration of the various aspects of the economy of salvation. Aquinas's theology remains a path into the heart of the Christian mysteries because of his remarkable insight—the result, as Jean-Pierre Torrell has reminded us, of his graced life of prayer—into the truth, goodness, and beauty of the divine plan of creation, redemption, and deification.

Notes

Introduction

1. Jean-Pierre Torrell, O. P., *Le Christ en ses mystères* (Paris: Desclée, 1999), 307.

2. As Wilhelmus Valkenberg has remarked, "Thanks to the growing awareness of the Jewish roots of the Christian tradition, we might be tempted to discard any christological interpretation of the Old Testament. But it is precisely in the interreligious dialogue with Jews and Muslims that Christians discover that the person of Christ is of crucial importance to their faith." He goes on to state that "Christians must therefore acknowledge the plurality of Jewish and Christian interpretations of *Tenakh* and the Old Testament. In this respect, the relation between Jews and Christians should be characterized by both connectedness between the divergent interpretations and a respectful distance from the other interpretation." See Wilhelmus G. B. M. Valkenberg, *Words of the Living God: Place and Function of Holy Scripture in the Theology of St. Thomas Aquinas* (Leuven: Peeters, 2000), 4–5. This approach informs the present study, which seeks to learn from Jewish interpretations of Scripture, while affirming that Jesus is the promised Messiah from whom salvation comes.

3. One thinks of the work of M.-J. Lagrange, O. P., Roger Guindon, O. M. I., Ceslaus Spicq, O. P., and Marie-Dominique Chenu, O. P. All of these authors, through their written works and their students, significantly influenced the present generation of Thomistic theologians. By contrast, certain other neoscholastic theologians mistakenly tried to fit Aquinas's use of Scripture into the mold of neoscholastic positive theology. On this point, see Valkenberg, *Words of the Living God*, 44–48, as well as 187, n. 152.

4. Marie-Dominique Chenu, O. P., *Toward Understanding St. Thomas*, trans. A.-M. Landry, O. P. and D. Hughes, O. P. (Chicago: Henry Regnery, 1964): 322. See, more recently, John Boyle's description of the *Summa Theologiae* as "a guide to understanding Scripture bringing to bear all that revelation and human science have to offer" (John F. Boyle, "St. Thomas Aquinas and Sacred Scripture," *Pro Ecclesia* 4 [1995]: 103). The leading contemporary Thomistic theologians—including Jean-Pierre Torrell, O. P., Servais Pinckaers, O. P., Otto Hermann Pesch, and Leo Elders, S. V. D.— have followed Chenu's lead and made similar comments. Pesch has under-scored "the complete seriousness and absolute veneration with which the medieval theologians approach the word of Scripture. . . . It imposes the absolute path for the thought of the theologian" (Otto Hermann Pesch, *Thomas von Aquin: Grenze und Grösse mittelalterlicher Theologie* [Mainz: Matthias-Grünewald-Verlag, 1988], 193).

5. The *Summa Theologiae's* scriptural character has been shown quantitatively (in comparison with the *Commentary on the Sentences*) by Valkenberg in *Words of the Living God*.

6. To borrow Thomas Hibbs's acute characterization of Aquinas's *Summa contra Gentiles*, in *Dialectic and Narrative in Aquinas* (Notre Dame, IN: University of Notre Dame Press, 1995).

7. Torrell, *Le Christ en ses mystères*. See also Gerd Lohaus, *Die Geheimnisse des Lebens Jesu in der Summa theologiae des heiligen Thomas von Aquin* (Freiburg: Herder, 1985) and Bernard Catão, *Salut et rédemption chez S. Thomas d'Aquin* (Paris: Aubier, 1965); other important studies include Joseph Wawrykow, *God's Grace and Human Action: "Merit" in the Theology of Thomas Aquinas* (Notre Dame, IN: University of Notre Dame Press, 1995) and Romanus Cessario, O. P., *The Godly Image: Christ and Salvation in Catholic Thought from Anselm to Aquinas* (Petersham, MA: St. Bede's Publications, 1990).

8. A recent article by D. Bentley Hart, entitled "A Gift Exceeding Every Debt: An Eastern Orthodox Appreciation of Anselm's *Cur Deus Homo*" (*Pro Ecclesia* 7 [1998]: 333–349), makes the important argument that *Cur Deus Homo* does not mark a fundamental division between Western and Eastern soteriology.

9. Anselm of Canterbury, *Why God Became Man*, trans. Joseph M. Colleran (New York: Magi Books, 1969). These questions are found in Book 1, ch. 5–6 (pp. 69–71).

10. See Guy Mansini, O. S. B., "St. Anselm, *Satisfactio*, and the Rule of St. Benedict," *Revue Bénédictine* 97 (1987): 101–121. Mansini demolishes the earlier theory that the term originated in Germanic feudal arrangements.

11. On the ultimate end for which God created rational creatures, see Anselm of Canterbury, *Why God Became Man*, Book 2, ch. 1 (p. 120); on the impossibility of God forgiving sin by "fiat," see Book 1, ch. 15 (p. 91).

12. Ibid., Book 1, ch. 19 (p. 104).

13. Ibid., Book 1, ch. 11 (pp. 84–85).

14. Ibid., Book 1, ch. 23 (p. 112).

15. Ibid., Book 1, ch. 11 (p. 84). Anselm rules out the anthropomorphic notion that God suffers an injury or change. Rather, human beings are debased in two ways: first by not subjecting their wills to God's will and second by turning away from God and thus "insulting" their Creator.

16. On these points, see especially ibid., Book 2, ch. 14 (p. 140), ch. 18 (p. 156), and ch. 19 (p. 160).

17. See Richard E. Weingart, *The Logic of Divine Love: A Critical Analysis of the Soteriology of Peter Abailard* (Oxford: Clarendon Press, 1970), especially 89–91.

18. As Abelard states, "Indeed, how cruel and wicked it seems that anyone should demand the blood of an innocent person as the price for anything, or that it should in any way please him that an innocent man should be slain—still less that God should consider the death of his Son so agreeable that by it he should be reconciled to the whole world!" (Peter Abelard, *Opera Theologica*, vol. 1, *Commentaria in Epistolam Pauli ad Romanos* and *Apologia contra Bernardum*, ed. Eligius M. Buytaert, O. F. M., Corpus Christianorum 11 [Turnhout: Brepols, 1969]: 117).

19. Bernard of Clairvaux, *Life and Works of St. Bernard*, vol. 2, trans. and ed. Dom John Mabillon, O. S. B., and Samuel J. Eales (London: Burns & Oates, 1889–1896), Letter CXC, p. 580 (ch. 6).

20. According to Bernard, Abelard's rejection of an order of justice wrongly implies that Christ's suffering "was done merely that He might give man by His life and teaching a rule of life, and by His suffering and death might set before him a goal of charity" (ibid., Letter CXC, p. 583). If Christ's passion served only to teach man and directs him toward his goal, Bernard asks, "Where, then, is redemption? There come from Christ, as he [Abelard] deigns to confess, merely illumination and enkindling to love. Whence come redemption and liberation?" (589).

21. Ibid., Letter CXC, p. 581. Bernard uses Anselm's terminology of *satisfactio* and *satisfecit*, thereby signaling his approval of Anselm's work. On the other hand, Bernard does not, unlike Anselm, attempt to explore in detail the meaning of *satisfaction*, except as a way of defending the causal efficacy of Christ's suffering in achieving our salvation. Bernard's use of the Mystical Body goes beyond Anselm's rather extrinsic depiction of how Christ applies his merits to other human beings.

22. Brian O. McDermott, S. J., *Word Become Flesh* (Collegeville, MN: Liturgical Press, 1993), 223. I do not mean to single out McDermott's work. Similar conclusions are found in every recent introduction to Christology.

23. M.-D. Chenu, O. P., *Nature, Man, and Society in the Twelfth Century: Essays on New Theological Perspectives in the Latin West*, ed. and trans. Jerome Taylor and Lester K. Little (1968; reprint, Toronto: University of Toronto Press, 1997), 147.

24. Ibid., 148. Indeed, Chenu claims that many twelfth-century theologians went too far in their appreciation of the Old Testament, so that "one might say that the Old exercised a Judaizing influence upon the interpretation of the New" (148). Chenu's critique is clearly aimed also at the pre–Vatican II Roman Catholic Church.

25. On the latter topic, see Manlio Bellomo, *The Common Legal Past of Europe, 1000–1800*, 2nd ed., trans. Lydia G. Cochrane (Washington, DC: Catholic University of America Press, 1995). Bellomo focuses on the period between 1000 and 1400.

26. See Beryl Smalley, "William of Auvergne, John of La Rochelle and St. Thomas Aquinas on the Old Law," in *St. Thomas Aquinas: Commemorative Studies*, ed. Armand A. Maurer, C. S. B., vol. 2 (Toronto: Pontifical Institute of Medieval Studies, 1974), 11–71; John F. Boyle, "The Twofold Division of St. Thomas's Christology in the Tertia pars," *Thomist* 60 (1996): 441–443; see also Valkenberg, *Words of the Living God*, 196–197.

27. In his *Guide for the Perplexed*, Maimonides divides the Mosaic Law into fourteen classes of laws or precepts. However, in case this division seems unwieldy, he adds, "As is well known, the precepts are also divided into two classes, viz., precepts concerning the relation between man and God, and precepts concerning the relation between man and man." See Moses Maimonides, *The Guide for the Perplexed*, trans. (from the original Arabic text) M. Friedlander, 2nd ed. (New York: Dover, 1956), 331.

28. Alexander of Hales, *Summa Theologica seu "Summa Fratris Alexandri"* (Florence: Collegium S. Bonaventurae, 1924–1948), Book 3, Pars 2, Inquisitio 3, Tractate 1, Quaestio 2, Caput 2, Article 1 (p. 390); cf. Book 3, Pars 2, Inquisitio 3, Tractate 1, Quaestio 1, Caput 1 (Solutio) (pp. 367–368). See also the discussion in Quaestio 2, Caput 1 (pp. 386–387), where the author explains that the Mosaic Law can be taken to refer to the whole Old Testament but can also mean simply the legal precepts.

29. Ibid., Book 3, Part 2, Inquisitio 3, Tractate 1, Question 3, Caput 1–2 (p. 395f).

30. Ibid., Book 3, Part 2, Inquisitio 3, Tractate 1, Quaestio 3, Caput 1 (p. 396).

31. Ibid. (pp. 396–397).

32. Ibid. In response to an objection, the author cites the authority of the *Glossa Ordinaria* for his answer (p. 398). The Gloss had interpreted Mt 5:17, "*Christus Legem implevit, quia exteriores Legis figuras solvens impevit veritatem interiorem.*" Clearly the Glossator has in mind especially the ceremonial precepts.

33. Ibid.

34. Ibid. (p. 400).

35. At various points, Aquinas uses the Latin terms *consummare, implere*, and *adimplere*.

36. The Old Testament is made for Christ, not vice versa. Commenting on Jn 19, where Jesus is presented as fulfilling the Scripture (Old Testament) by his passion, Aquinas states that "things were written in the Old Testament because they would be fulfilled by Christ. If we say that Christ acted because the scriptures foretold it, it would follow that the New Testament existed for the sake of the Old Testament and for its fulfillment, although the opposite is true" (*Commentary on the Gospel of John*, Part II, trans. James A. Weisheipl, O. P. and Fabian R. Larcher, O. P. [Petersham, MA: St. Bede's Publications, 1999], Chapter 19, Lecture 5, p. 577).

37. The *Summa contra Gentiles* (completed 1264–1265) follows the pattern of the *Commentary on the Sentences* by discussing the Old Testament only with regard to the sacraments, and then very briefly (SCG IV, ch. 57). Discussing Christ's obedience in his passion, the *Summa contra Gentiles* states simply, "God's commandment to men deals with the works of virtue; and the more perfectly one carries out an act of virtue, the more he is obedient to God. Among the other virtues, charity is the outstanding one to which all the other are referred. Christ, then, when He fulfilled the act of charity most perfectly was most obedient to God. For there is no act of charity more perfect than the one by which a man bears even death for another" (SCG IV, ch. 55, ad 14).

38. The former is the view of Michel Corbin in *Le chemin de la théologie chez Thomas d'Aquin* (Paris: Beauchesne, 1972); the latter is the view of Valkenberg, *Words of the Living God* (188). Admittedly, Valkenberg at times associates himself more closely with Corbin's thesis.

39. See, e.g., *Commentary on the Gospel of John*, Part II, Chapter 19, Lecture 5 (pp. 576–577), and *Catena Aurea*, vol. 1, *St. Matthew*, trans. Mark Pattison (Albany, NY: Preserving Christian Publications, 1995 [1842]), 170. (Although Aquinas commented on the Gospel of Matthew, his treatment of Mt 5:17 is lost.) The *Catena Aurea* demonstrates that the key patristic source for Aquinas's theology of fulfillment is Augustine's *Contra Faustum*, Book 19, to which his debt is enormous, although his thought develops rather than merely recapitulates Augustine's.

40. *Opera Omnia*, vol. 13, *Expositio in Omnes S. Pauli Epistolas* (Parma, 1852–1873; reprint, New York: Musurgia Publishers, 1949), and *In Epistolam ad Romanos*, Caput 3, Lectio 4, in *S. Thomae Aquinatis Opera Ominia*, ed. Robert Busa, S. J., vol. 5 (Stuttgart: Frommann-Holzboog, 1980).

41. Ibid., Caput 11, Lectio 4. The Vulgate reads, "*Sine poenitentia enim sunt dona et vocatio Dei.*" Aquinas argues that *vocatio* here refers to the *electio* of the Jews, which is the permanent covenant. St. Paul in this passage argues that by opposing the Gospel the Jewish people have sinned. However, he adds that all have sinned ("God has consigned all men to disobedience"; Rom 11:32). As we will see, Aquinas thinks that the Jewish leaders, but not the Jewish people as a whole, were culpable (along with Judas and Pilate, representative of Christ's disciples and the Gentiles, respectively) for the sin of condemning Jesus to death (*Summa Theologiae* 3, q.47, aa.5–6). Far from scapegoating the Jewish people, Aquinas emphasizes that Jesus suffered at the hands of every kind of person (3, q.47, a.5). On the other hand, Aquinas argues that insofar as Jewish persons (or Gentile persons) consciously refuse to accept the Messiah, "they have submitted themselves to perpetual subjection," since only Christ frees humankind from subjection to sin (*Commentary on the Gospel of St. John*, Part II, Chapter 19, Lecture 3, p. 564).

42. On Aquinas's treatment of justification in the context of St. Paul's concern, in Romans and Galatians, to distinguish faith in Christ from works of the law, see Otto Hermann Pesch, *Theologie der Rechtfertigung bei Martin Luther und Thomas von Aquin: Versuch eines systematisch-theologischen Dialogs*, 2nd ed. (Mainz: Matthias-Grünewald-Verlag, 1985). Justification is in and through Christ, not through our vain efforts to fulfill the law on our own.

43. E.g., Psalm 119, a lengthy celebration of devotion to the precepts of the Mosaic Law, and Psalm 27: "One thing have I asked of the Lord, that will I seek after; that I may dwell in the house of the Lord all the days of my life, to behold the beauty of the Lord, and to inquire in his temple" (Ps 27:4). Numerous other psalms could be cited.

44. Jon D. Levenson, *Sinai and Zion: An Entry into the Jewish Bible* (San Francisco: Harper & Row, 1985).

45. Luke Timothy Johnson, *Living Jesus: Learning the Heart of the Gospel* (New York: HarperCollins, 1999), 154. Matthew's Gospel, no less than John's, presents a wisdom-Christology, where Jesus is seen as Wisdom incarnate who fulfills the law and the prophecies.

46. Richard B. Hays, "Response to Robert Wilken, 'In Dominico Eloquio,'" *Communio* 25 (1998): 522.

47. On this topic, see Peter J. Leithart, "Marcionism, Postliberalism, and Social Christianity," *Pro Ecclesia* 8 (1999): 85–97, especially 85–88;

see also Bruce Marshall, "Christ and the Cultures: The Jewish people and Christian Theology," in *The Cambridge Companion to Christian Doctrine*, ed. Colin E. Gunton (Cambridge: Cambridge University Press, 1997), 81–100. Marshall notes that Schleiermacher should not be considered a supersessionist, since he never granted the "election" of Israel.

48. Friedrich Schleiermacher, *The Christian Faith*, translation of the German 2nd ed. (Edinburgh: T.&T. Clark, 1989), 61, 115. Bultmann and Harnack held the same opinion.

49. Schleiermacher, *The Christian Faith*, 107.

50. For Aquinas's view of Judaism and the Jews, a topic that lies largely outside the scope of this book, see Jean-Pierre Torrell, O.P., "Ecclesia Iudaeorum: Quelques jugements positifs de saint Thomas d'Aquin à l'égard des Juifs et du judaïsme," in *Les philosophies morales et politiques au Moyen Âge*, ed. B. Carlos Bazán, Eduardo Andújar, and Léonard G. Sbrocchi (Ottawa: Société Internationale pour l'Étude de la Philosophie Médiévale, 1995), 1732–1741; cf. John Y. B. Hood, *Aquinas and the Jews* (Philadelphia: University of Pennsylvania Press, 1995), especially 106–108. As Torrell shows, nuance is necessary when assessing Aquinas's view of Judaism and the Jews, since harshly negative judgments are often presented side by side with positive judgments or placed in a context that clarifies Aquinas's intention. Commenting on St. John's account of the cleansing of the Temple, for example, Aquinas holds that "the priests of the Old Testament, who had been established to care for divine matters, gave free rein to avarice" (*Commentary on the Gospel of John*, Part I, trans. James A. Weishelpl and Fabian R. Larcher [Albany, NY: Magi Books, 1980], Chapter 2, Lecture 2 [p. 165]). Reading further, however, one discovers that Aquinas proceeds to skewer the Christian bishops of his day for simony and negligence. It is the *Christian* priests who are found to be often "so eager for and occupied with temporal gain that they neglect the spiritual welfare of their subjects" (ibid., p. 166). Although Aquinas opposed usury and accepted the discriminatory laws against Jews prevalent in all medieval Christian and Muslim nations, he rejected violence against Jews (including forced baptism), opposed the view of influential earlier medieval theologians such as Robert Grosseteste that Jews were heretics, and in many areas followed the theological insights of the medieval Jewish theologian Moses Maimonides. While it would be wrong to suggest that Aquinas's theology, insofar as it approves of discriminatory practices (the "subjection" of the Jews), provides a model for contemporary Jewish-Christian relations, it would be equally unfair to tar Aquinas theologically with the "supersessionist" brush — or so I will argue.

51. Valkenberg, *Words of the Living God*, 60.

52. Robert Grosseteste, *De Cessatione Legalium*, ed. Richard C. Dales and Edward B. King (London: Oxford University Press, 1986). See also Lee M. Friedman, *Robert Grosseteste and the Jews* (Cambridge, MA: Harvard University Press, 1934); for further historical background, see Steven T. Katz, *The Holocaust in Historical Context*, vol. 1, *The Holocaust and Mass Death before the Modern Age* (Oxford: Oxford University Press, 1994).

53. In *Sacramental Realism* (Chicago: Midwest Theological Forum, 1998), Colman E. O'Neill, O. P., critiques this dichotomy: "Theology should never, in fact, isolate Christ from believers; nor should it isolate believers from Christ. That neo-scholasticism, to look no further than recent Catholic thought, could construct, within the context of its Christology, a theory relating to 'objective redemption' is an example of the kind of artificial isolation we are thinking of. 'Objective redemption' was intended to signify the work done by Christ on earth in so far as it won salvation for all; it was then asked how this is conveyed to individuals" (39).

54. *Summa Theologiae*, 3, q.48, a.1, *sed contra*.

55. A valuable study addressing this topic is J. A. DiNoia, O. P., *The Diversity of Religions: A Christian Perspective* (Washington, DC: Catholic University of America Press, 1992).

56. Servais Pinckaers, O. P., *The Sources of Christian Ethics*, 3rd ed., trans. Sr. Mary Thomas Noble, O. P. (Washington, DC: Catholic University of America Press, 1995), xix. In his foreword to the English translation of this work, Romanus Cessario, O. P., sums up Pinckaers's approach and shows it to be a model for all Thomistic theology: "Father Pinckaers has argued consistently, before and since the Second Vatican Council, that St. Thomas must be read and interpreted anew. He must be seen not through the eyes of his commentators but from the vantage point of his forebears in the history of thought. We must know Aquinas's sources. In this book, Father Pinckaers illuminates those sources. He invites us to go even further back than the Fathers of the Church—back to the Gospel itself, with its whole moral context. This sacred instruction, Father Pinckaers contends, will supply the basis for our theological reflection. . . . Aquinas himself repeatedly invites us to return to the Word of God, that Word expressive beyond all words, and to explore every available resource of theology, philosophy, and science. He encourages dialogue with a variety of traditions, within the Church and outside of it. Far from inducing a fortress mentality in which one would seek refuge in a Thomistic system, an authentic engagement with Aquinas fosters the solidity and openness needed for ongoing theological enterprise. Finally, Father Pinckaers considers that a genuine esteem for St. Thomas will deepen our appreciation of the Fathers of the Church and

of the authentic theologians of any age" (xi). This approach to Aquinas's theology differs somewhat from that of Otto Pesch, who emphasizes Aquinas's medieval otherness and thus runs the risk of turning Thomistic theology into a primarily historical rather than systematic enterprise.

57. In Valkenberg's words, although "theological reasoning is constantly nourished by Scripture and related to Scripture," nonetheless "Scripture is not the only source for theology, because sacra doctrina does not only imply the notion of Scripture, but the notion of scientific reasoning as well" (Valkenberg, *Words of the Living God*, 10). For an excellent account of the "intellectual habituation" that acquiring theological *scientia* requires, see John I. Jenkins, *Knowledge and Faith in Thomas Aquinas* (Cambridge: Cambridge University Press, 1979).

1 Divine Law and Divine Pedagogy

1. The respondents are Eugene Borowitz, David B. Burrell, C. S. C., Ellen T. Charry, Paula Fredriksen, George Lindbeck, David Novak, and Peter Ochs, whose "Epilogue" summarizes the views of the participants and offers his own insights. I should mention that David Burrell briefly draws a distinction between *fulfillment* and *displacement* that, although Burrell does not here cite Aquinas, guides Aquinas's treatment as well.

2. Wyschogrod's interest in Aquinas's treatment of the Mosaic Law stems in part from his view that Aquinas's approach is representative of the "traditional" Christian approach, but we should also note that Wyschogrod finds in Aquinas a rare Christian theologian who takes time to discuss the various precepts of the Mosaic Law in detail.

3. Michael Wyschogrod, "Letter to a Friend," *Modern Theology* 11 (1995): 168.

4. Ibid., 169. The reference is to *Nostra Aetate* #4. This document is sometimes misread (though not by Wyschogrod) as denying that Jesus Christ fulfilled the covenants with Israel. In fact, *Nostra Aetate* is clear *both* that Christ fulfilled the covenants and that the covenants have never been revoked: "the church believes that Christ our peace reconciled Jews and gentiles and made us both one in himself through the cross," and yet "the Jews still remain very dear to God, whose gift and call are without regret" in Norman Tanner, S. J., *Decrees of the Ecumenical Councils*, vol. 2 [Washington, DC: Georgetown University Press, 1990], #4, p. 970. *Lumen Gentium* #16 makes the same point (ibid., p. 861).

5. Wyschogrod, "Letter to a Friend," 171.

6. Michael Wyschogrod, "A Jewish Reading of St. Thomas Aquinas on the Old Law," in *Understanding Scripture*, ed. Clemens Thoma and Michael Wyschogrod (New York: Paulist Press, 1987), 125–138.

7. Wyschogrod, "Letter to a Friend," 170. Regarding the notion of a "traditional view," Richard Schenk's warning is instructive: "Whereas there is a broader knowledge of the controversial history of Christological questions on the Incarnation, the ways in which medieval views of Christ varied and vacillated with parallel changes and ambiguities in the theology of non-Christian religions have received comparatively little attention" (Richard Schenk, O. P., "Christ, Christianity, and Non-Christian Religions: Their Interrelation in the Theology of Robert Kilwardby," in *Christ among the Medieval Dominicans*, ed. Kent Emery, Jr., and Joseph P. Wawrykow [Notre Dame, IN: University of Notre Dame Press, 1998], 346). See also W. G. B. M. Valkenberg, "How to Talk to Strangers: Aquinas and Interreligious Dialogue," *Jaarboek of the Thomas Instituut te Utrecht* 16 (1997): 9–47.

8. Wyschogrod, "A Jewish Reading," 125–126.

9. Ibid., 136.

10. Ibid., 137.

11. *Summa Theologiae*, 1–2, q.90. As Ulrich Kühn has shown in *Via caritatis: Theologie des Gesetzes bei Thomas von Aquin* (Göttingen: Vandenhoeck & Ruprecht, 1965), the category of law provides the framework through which Aquinas systematizes the narrative of salvation history. For a fuller discussion of Aquinas's view of law (a detailed discussion goes beyond the scope of this work), see two masterful commentaries on Aquinas's treatise: Otto Hermann Pesch, *Das Gesetz: Kommentar zu* Summa Theologiae *I-II 90–105*, Deutsche Thomas Edition, vol. 13 (Heidelberg: Graz, 1977) and Jean Tonneau, O. P., translation, notes, and appendices to *Somme théologique: La loi ancienne*, by Thomas Aquinas, 2 vols. (Paris: Desclée, 1971). J. P. M. van der Ploeg, O. P., in "Le traité de saint Thomas de la loi ancienne," in *Lex et Libertas*, Studi Tomistici 30, ed. Leo Elders and K. Hedwig (Vatican City: Libreria Editrice Vaticana, 1987), 185–199, has criticized Aquinas for emphasizing law over covenant and reason over will. This criticism does not take into account the Old Testament's own association of Torah with Wisdom, as well as the fact that the precepts are seen as covenant stipulations.

12. 1–2, q.90, a.1.

13. This participation in the eternal law is known as "natural law." See 1–2, q.91, aa.1,2. The concept of participation plays a crucial role in Aquinas's theology, including (as we will see) his account of the relationship of the Old and New Laws. For recent discussion of Aquinas's adaptation of this

Platonic concept, see John F. Wippel, "Thomas Aquinas and Participation," in *Studies in Medieval Philosophy*, ed. John F. Wippel (Washington, DC: Catholic University of America Press, 1987), 117–158, and Rudi A. te Velde, *Participation and Substantiality in Thomas Aquinas* (Leiden: E. J. Brill, 1995).

14. 1–2, q.90, a.2; see 1–2, q.3, a.1.

15. 1–2, q.92, a.1.

16. 1–2, q.90, aa.3,4.

17. Aquinas holds that human beings have a natural inclination to the true and the good. This natural inclination can be obscured (as it is in the wicked) but cannot be obliterated. See also 1–2, q.93, a.6.

18. Aquinas recounts this history in 1–2, q.91, a.6, and many other places.

19. The best recent examination of Aquinas's account of original sin is Marie Leblanc, O. S. B., "Le péché originel dans la pensée de S. Thomas," *Revue Thomiste* 93 (1993): 567–600. Given the bounds of our study, we cannot here delve into the complexities of Aquinas's account.

20. Following St. Paul, Aquinas finds in God's covenant with Abraham a foreshadowing of the completion of this covenant in one of Abraham's descendents, who will be God's (supernatural) blessing to all peoples. See 1–2, q.98, a.4.

21. 1–2, q.91, a.4, ad 1.

22. 1–2, q.98, a.1. It is important to notice that Aquinas thinks that the Old Law is good in itself, not "merely" as an anticipation of Christ, although Aquinas does not think that the Old Law is sufficient in itself to accomplish the ends which it proposes. On Aquinas's development of the concept of nature (and human nature), see Jan A. Aertsen, *Nature and Creature: St. Thomas Aquinas's Way of Thought*, trans. H. D. Morton (Leiden: E. J. Brill, 1988), and Walter H. Principe, C. S. B., "'The Truth of Human Nature' According to Thomas Aquinas: Theology and Science in Interaction," in *Philosophy and the God of Abraham*, ed. R. James Long (Toronto: Pontifical Institute of Mediaeval Studies, 1991), 161–177.

23. Ibid.

24. 1–2, q.98, a.2.

25. The figurative or "spiritual" sense of Scripture is threefold: allegorical, moral, and anagogical (1, q.1, a.10). For further discussion of how the figurative sense informs Aquinas's view of salvation history, see Marc Aillet, *Lire la Bible avec S. Thomas: Le passage de la littera à la res dans la Somme Théologique* (Fribourg: Éditions Universitaires, 1993), especially 278–312. In his scriptural commentaries, Aquinas generally refers simply to the mystical sense broadly understood.

26. For this insight, see the superb article by Colman E. O'Neill, O. P., "St. Thomas on the Membership of the Church," *Thomist* 27 (1963), especially 94–108. I will return to this article in my chapter on the Mystical Body.

27. Ibid., 98. The "state of the New Law" is the Catholic Church, with her sacraments.

28. 3, q.8, a.3, ad 3; emphasis added. I am using Colman O'Neill's translation of this text (O'Neill, "St. Thomas on the Membership of the Church," 94). The Latin reads, "*Et ideo antiqui Patres, servando legalia sacramenta, ferebantur in Christum per fidem et dilectionem eandem qua et nos in ipsum ferimur.*"

29. Aquinas frequently refers to this image of pedagogy. In 1–2, q.98, a.5, he argues that this pedagogy was given specially to the Jewish nation as a "prerogative of holiness" given Israel as part of the unique dignity of being chosen (gratuitously, not by merit) to be the nation from which Christ would be born. See 1–2, q.98, a.2, ad 2, and q.99, a.6.

30. In 1–2, q.98, a.6, Aquinas depicts this gradual improving of the human race as something that befits the right order that belongs to God as Wisdom: "With regard to good men, the Law was given to them as a help; which was most needed by the people, at the time when the natural law began to be obscured on account of the exuberance of sin: for it was fitting that this help should be bestowed on men in an orderly manner, so that they might be led from imperfection to perfection; wherefore it was becoming that the Old Law should be given between the law of nature and the law of grace."

31. Aquinas discusses this point (repeating much of what he has said earlier) in 1–2, q.106, a.3. See also 1–2, q.107, a.1, ad 2.

32. See 1–2, q.98, a.6, where Aquinas describes the two kinds of men; and 1–2, q.98, a.5, *sed contra*, where Aquinas notes that many (how many is not clear) of the Gentiles were saved. See also 2–2, q.2, a.7, ad 3. For the important place of the *sed contra* in Aquinas's theological argumentation, see Leo J. Elders, "Structure et fonction de l'argument 'sed contra' dans la Somme Théologique de Saint Thomas," *Divus Thomas* 80 (1977): 245–260.

33. Aquinas makes this clear in many places. One is 1–2, q.98, a.1, ad 3, where he interprets Psalm 119:32 (part of the great psalm, so often cited by Aquinas, composed entirely of praise of the Torah) to mean that the Psalmist is aware that he has received an inner principle of grace that enables him to follow the way of God's commandments. In 1–2, q.98, a.2, ad 4, he states, "Although the Old Law did not suffice to save man, yet another help from God besides the Law was available for man, viz., faith in the Mediator, by which the fathers of old were justified even as we are. Accordingly God did not fail man by giving him insufficient aids to salvation." I should also cite 1–2, q.106, a.1, ad 3, where Aquinas notes that

"whoever had the law of grace instilled into them belonged to the New Testament," even if they lived during the period prior to Christ. As Ulrich Kühn has shown, the view that the "New Law" *is* the grace of the Holy Spirit is an original contribution of Aquinas, moving beyond the Augustinian model (Kühn, *Via caritatis*, 192–197).

34. Aquinas describes "implicit" faith in 2–2, q.1, a.7. See also 1–2, q.107, a.1, ad 1.

35. See 1–2, q.98, a.2, ad 3.

36. See O'Neill, "St. Thomas on the Membership of the Church," 98–99.

37. See 2–2, q.2, a.7.

38. See O'Neill, "St. Thomas on the Membership of the Church," especially 96–97.

39. 3, q.49, a.5, ad 1. This explains the "hell of the just" to which Christ's soul descends after his death.

40. 1–2, q.106, a.3.

41. Wyschogrod, "A Jewish Reading," 138.

42. 1–2, q.99, a.1, ad 2 and ad 3.

43. 1–2, q.99, a.2.

44. See 1–2, q.99, a.1, ad 2.

45. 1–2, q.99, a.3.

46. We should bear in mind that the ceremonial precepts are not only those precepts that command direct acts of worship. Rather, Aquinas also counts as ceremonial those precepts that regard the preparation of the worshippers or the consecration of the instruments of worship. Thus precepts directing the construction of the tabernacle (an instrument of worship) or dictating what foods are unclean (an example of the preparation of the worshipper) belong to the ceremonial precepts. See 1–2, q.101, a.4.

47. Aquinas treats the Mosaic Law's precept about divorce (1–2, q.105, a.4, obj.8) in this way. Earlier (1–2, q.102, a.5, ad 3), in discussing the ceremonial precepts, he had noted that God could tolerate divorce under the Old Law since matrimony was not yet a sacrament. Another example of God's tolerating something not absolutely just is the precept that allows Jews to accept usury from foreigners, though not from fellow Jews (1–2, q.105, a.3, ad 3). Aquinas's discussion of slavery could be read in the same way, although in this case I am developing Aquinas's ideas. Concerning the precept that forbids Jews to enslave other Jews for more than seven years, Aquinas writes, "As the children of Israel had been delivered by the Lord from slavery, and for this reason were bound to the service of God, He did not wish them to be slaves in perpetuity" (1–2, q.105, a.4, ad 1). After Christ has redeemed human beings from slavery to sin and has bound all

human beings (potentially) to the service of God, slavery is recognized as unacceptable. This conclusion was reached by the great sixteenth-century Dominican theologian Bartolomé de Las Casas, who considered his theology of the status of Indians and of African slaves to be derived from Aquinas's principles. (See Gustavo Gutiérrez, *Las Casas: In Search of the Poor of Jesus Christ*, trans. Robert R. Barr [Maryknoll, NY: Orbis Books, 1993], 126–127, 319–330.)

48. See 1–2, q.105, a.2, ad 10.

49. The classification of the precepts precedes Aquinas, as we have noted above. Aquinas makes use of this threefold classification simply to identify the objects engaged by the various laws. His theology of fulfillment does not depend, therefore, upon retaining the threefold classification; rather, it depends upon the recognition of the various objects of the laws contained in the Torah.

50. See 1–2, q.99, a.3, *sed contra*. For the role of the Ten Commandments within the Old Testament, see the intriguing work of David Noel Freedman, *The Nine Commandments: Uncovering the Hidden Pattern of Crime and Punishment in the Hebrew Bible* (New York: Doubleday, 2000).

51. Aquinas is willing to admit that the ceremonies commanded by the precepts were "weak and imperfect" in their prefiguration of Christ, if only because of the "surpassing excellence" of the mystery of Christ (1–2, q.101, a.3, ad 1).

52. 1–2, q.104, a.2, ad 2.

53. Aquinas's use of the literal sense has been the subject of a number of valuable essays. See especially Mark F. Johnson, "Another Look at the Plurality of the Literal Sense," in *Medieval Philosophy and Theology*, vol. 2, ed. Mark D. Jordan et al. (Notre Dame, IN: University of Notre Dame Press, 1992), 117–141; Smalley, "William of Auvergne, John of La Rochelle, and St. Thomas Aquinas on the Old Law," in *St. Thomas Aquinas: Commemorative Studies*, vol. 2, ed. Maurer.

54. See 3, qq.46–49.

55. Aquinas describes this threefold fulfillment of the Mosaic Law in 3, q.47, a.2, ad 1. He makes the same point, though more briefly, in his discussion of the ceremonial precepts of the Mosaic Law (1–2, q.103, a.3, ad 2). Using as a hinge for his argument a text that serves the same purpose in the *tertia pars* (Jn 19:30, where Jesus says from the cross, "It is consummated"), Aquinas explains that "the mystery of the redemption of the human race [the end of divine law] was fulfilled in Christ's Passion. . . . Consequently the [ceremonial] prescriptions of the Law must have ceased then altogether through their reality being fulfilled." The cessation is a consummation, so the figure attains and participates in its end rather than merely being revoked.

56. 3, q.40, a.4.

57. 3, q.40, a.4, ad 1–3.

58. 3, q.40, a.4.

59. For Aquinas, of course, even the New Law is in a certain sense primarily figurative, since the life of grace (on earth) merely prefigures the life of glory that God's chosen people will enjoy in heavenly beatitude. Aquinas explains this point in 1–2, q.103, a.3. Any "triumphalism" on the part of the Roman Catholic Church is thereby preempted. It should be emphasized, however, that the claims advanced in this paragraph belong to Christian faith. I am not suggesting that Wyschogrod would find this view of Jesus' work persuasive.

60. The fullness of this identity is, for Aquinas, the life of glory, or perfect communion with God. The precepts of the Mosaic Law were intended to lead Israel into this perfect communion. However, only in Christ's passion does Israel achieve the *perfect fulfillment* of the law that merits perfect communion. The prophets and psalmists of Israel often bemoan their inability to fulfill the law perfectly and continually. In this sense, Aquinas holds that Christ conformed his conduct to the law in order to "deliver" the saints of Israel from "subjection" to the law. Aquinas here cites Gal 4:4–5: "God sent His Son . . . made under the Law, that He might redeem them who were under the Law" (3, q.40, a.4).

61. See Wyschogrod, "A Jewish Reading," 134–135.

62. 1–2, q.103, a.3, ad 1.

63. 1–2, q.103, a.4, ad 1 (see also ad 3).

64. 1–2, q.103, a.4; cf. *Summa contra Gentiles*, IV, ch. 57, where Aquinas compares the case of the Jews with that of the Nazarenes and Ebionites (early Christian heretics). The latter are in mortal sin because "while they observe the evangelical sacraments, they are professing that the Incarnation and the other mysteries of Christ have already been perfected; but, when they also observe the sacraments of the Law, they are professing that those mysteries are in the future." Although he fits it into his own framework, Aquinas derives this argument (as is so frequently the case) from St. Augustine. Otto Pesch provides a more negative construal of 1–2, q.103, a.4. According to Pesch, for Aquinas, the Jew who before Christ observes the Torah, but does so without any reference to a coming Messiah, commits sin; after Christ, moreover, observance of the ceremonial laws constitutes "*the* sin of the unbelieving Jew" (Otto Hermann Pesch, *Thomas von Aquin: Grenze und Grösse mittelalterlicher Theologie* [Mainz: Matthias-Grünewald-Verlag, 1988], 311–312). However, Aquinas distinguishes between the people and the priests of the Old Law: the priests, conversant with the prophesies about the Messiah, are expected by Aquinas to have had "more

explicit" faith, as would befit those who knew the prophesies, while the people were not held to this standard (1–2, q.102, a.4, ad 4). Second, in 1–2, q.103, a.4, Aquinas is interpreting St. Paul's warning to converts to Christianity that "if you receive circumcision, Christ will be of no advantage to you" (Gal 5:2). Like St. Paul, Aquinas specifically has in mind the "Jewish converts to Christianity," and he makes clear that he is referring to those who have made "a profession of faith." In this crucial discussion, Aquinas does not state that Jews, who have not accepted Christ, sin by continuing to observe the Torah's ceremonial precepts. In short, Pesch, by leaving out the context of Aquinas's response, exaggerates Aquinas's hostility toward Jews. Aquinas does not condemn the observance of Torah by Jews who do not believe in Jesus Christ, but *neither* does he condone not believing in Jesus Christ. Only by faith in Christ (implicit or explicit) are human beings healed of mortal sin, for reasons that will be explored more fully in the following chapters.

65. Scholars who find fulfillment models to be supersessionist will not be satisfied by my account, but it seems to me that the confession that the Messiah has come requires a fulfillment model. For contrasting views, from whom I have learned a good deal, see Mary C. Boys, *Has God Only One Blessing? Judaism as a Source of Christian Self-Understanding* (New York: Paulist Press, 2000), and R. Kendall Soulen, *The God of Israel and Christian Theology* (Minneapolis, MN: Fortress Press, 1996).

2 Incarnate Wisdom in Israel

1. Ben Witherington III, *John's Wisdom: A Commentary on the Fourth Gospel* (Louisville, KY: Westminster John Knox Press, 1995): 54. Similarly, Francis J. Moloney has affirmed the central claim of C. K. Barrett's well-known commentary: "What Barrett said of v.1 can be applied to vv.1–2: 'John intends that the whole of his gospel shall be read in light of this verse. The deeds and words of Jesus are the deeds and words of God; if this be not true the book is blasphemous'" (Francis J. Moloney, S. D. B., *The Gospel of John* [Collegeville, MN: Liturgical Press, 1998], 35).

2. Craig A. Evans, "Jesus' Self-Designation 'The Son of Man' and the Recognition of His Divinity," in *The Trinity: An Interdisciplinary Symposium on the Trinity*, ed. Stephen T. Davis, Daniel Kendall, and Gerald O'Collins, S. J. (Oxford: Oxford University Press, 1999), 29–47. See also Gordon D. Fee's contribution on Pauline theology to the same volume: "Paul and the Trinity: The Experience of Christ and the Spirit for Paul's Understanding of God," 49–72. For further argument that Jesus' deeds reveal his

belief in his authority to act in the place of Yahweh, see N. T. Wright, *Jesus and the Victory of God* (Minneapolis, MN: Fortress Press, 1996), 477ff.

3. To give this topic the full treatment it demands would require another book, but because of its importance for the theology of salvation it must be discussed here. For more thorough discussion, see the works cited in the footnotes below.

4. See Jean-Pierre Torrell, "S. Thomas d'Aquin et la science du Christ: Une relecture des Questions 9–12 de la *Tertia Pars* de la 'Somme de théologie,'" *Recherches thomasiennes* (Paris: Vrin, 2000), 198–213; also *Le Christ en ses mystères*, 135–149.

5. Torrell, *Le Christ en ses mystères*, 332–339. On this point, see Jacques Maritain, *On the Grace and Humanity of Jesus*, trans. J. W. Evans (New York: Herder & Herder, 1969). Aquinas gives the analogy of demonstrative knowledge not displacing the knowledge gained by the dialectical syllogism (3, q.9, a.3, ad 2).

6. Ibid., 338–339.

7. Ibid., 138–140. For Congar's position, see Yves Congar, O. P., *I Believe in the Holy Spirit*, trans. David Smith (New York: Crossroad, 1997), and *The Word and the Spirit*, trans. David Smith (San Francisco: Harper & Row, 1986). Similar views are expressed by Heribert Mühlen in *Der Heilige Geist als Person*, 5th ed. (Münster: Aschendorff, 1988).

8. For Raymond Brown's summary of these texts, see his helpful short book, *An Introduction to New Testament Christology* (New York: Paulist Press, 1994), 23–59, as well as his earlier *Jesus: God and Man* (New York: Macmillan, 1972).

9. For the patristic context, see Raymond Moloney, S. J., "Patristic Approaches to Christ's Knowledge, Part 1," *Milltown Studies* 37 (1996): 65–81. Moloney concludes that his survey "illustrates how a high Christology of Christ's knowledge flowed from Augustine into the middle ages" (78). Aquinas himself uses various expressions, such as *scientia beatorum*, *visio seu scientia beata*, and *fruitio beata*, but the meaning is the same. For recent systematic explanations in support of Aquinas's view, see Guy Mansini, O. S. B., "Understanding St. Thomas on Christ's Immediate Knowledge of God," *Thomist* 59 (1995): 91–124; Romanus Cessario, O. P., "Incarnate Wisdom and the Immediacy of Christ's Salvific Knowledge," in *Problemi teologici alla luce dell' Aquinate*, Studi Tomistici 44:5 (Vatican City: Libreria Editrice Vaticana, 1991), 334–340; Claude Sarrasin, *Plein de grâce et de vérité: Théologie de l'âme du Christ selon Thomas d'Aquin* (Vénasque: Éditions de Carmel, 1992); Albert Patfoort, O. P., "Vision béatifique et théologie de l'âme du Christ: À propos d'un ouvrage récent," *Revue Thomiste* 93 (1993): 635–639.

10. See Bernard Lonergan, S. J., *De Verbo Incarnato* (Rome: Gregorian University Press, 1964), and Karl Rahner, S. J., "Dogmatic Reflections on the Knowledge and Self-Consciousness of Christ," in *Theological Investigations*, vol.5, trans. K.-H. Kruger (Baltimore: Helicon Press, 1966), 193–215. See also Raymond Moloney, S. J., "The Mind of Christ in Transcendental Theology: Rahner, Lonergan, and Crowe," *Heythrop Journal* 25 (1984): 288–300. For recent systematic arguments based upon Lonergan's analysis and holding that Christ possessed "beatific vision" (once this term is properly understood), see Mansini, "Understanding St. Thomas"; Terry J. Tekippe, "Towards a Systematic Understanding of the Vision in Christ," *Method* 11 (1993): 77–101; Frederick E. Crowe, S. J., "The Mind of Jesus," *Communio* 1 (1974): 365–384, and "Eschaton and Worldly Mission in the Mind and Heart of Jesus," in Frederick E. Crowe, *Appropriating the Lonergan Idea*, ed. Michael Vertin (Washington, DC: Catholic University of America Press, 1989), 193–234.

11. Cessario, "Incarnate Wisdom," 338.

12. *Catechism of the Catholic Church* (Vatican City: Libreria Editrice Vaticana, 1994), #473, 478.

13. *Summa Theologiae* 1, q.45, a.6, *sed contra*.

14. 1, q.45, a.6. In ad 1, Aquinas remarks, "The processions of the divine Persons are the cause of creation." Ad 2 makes the same point. For a superb treatment of this issue, see Gilles Emery, O. P., *La Trinité créatrice* (Paris: Vrin, 1995).

15. Nonetheless, Aquinas holds that we can have an understanding of the attributes that pertain to God's "essence" (such as God's omnipotence and transcendence) apart from knowledge of the three divine Persons. If this were not so, then the ancient Israelites, for example, could not have known anything true about God as one without knowing the full mystery of the Trinity. On this point, see 3, q.3, a.3.

16. 3, q.3, a.2 (cf. a.4).

17. Ibid. In a.4, Aquinas provides a summary of his position: "Hence what has to do with action in the assumption is common to the three Persons; but what pertains to the nature of term [*ad rationem termini*] belongs to one Person in such a manner as not to belong to another; for the three Persons caused the human nature to be united to the one Person of the Son."

18. In 3, q.3, a.5, Aquinas defends the claim that each of the divine Persons could have assumed human nature. He notes, "Whatever the Son can do, so can the Father and the Holy Ghost, otherwise the power of the three Persons would not be one." To the objection that the Father cannot be sent and therefore cannot become incarnate, Aquinas replies that the

Incarnation of the Father would not be a sending but that it would none-theless be an Incarnation (ad 3).

19. 3, q.3, a.6. Joseph P. Wawrykow has pointed out (in response to theologians such as Karl Rahner and Ghislain Lafont) that Aquinas's "hypothetical questioning is warranted, ultimately, by the light it can shed on the actual Christian dispensation" (Wawrykow, "Wisdom in the Christology of Thomas Aquinas," in *Christ among the Medieval Dominicans*, ed. Kent Emery, Jr., and Joseph P. Wawrykow [Notre Dame, IN: University of Notre Dame Press, 1999], 181).

20. 3, q.3, a.6, ad 2.

21. These reasons, of course, are not proofs. Aquinas always begins from the principle that whatever God does is most fitting (and thus most beautiful). On this topic, see Gilbert Narcisse, O. P., "Les enjeux épistemologiques de l'argument de convenance selon saint Thomas d'Aquin," in *Ordo Sapientiae et Amoris*, ed. C.-J. Pinto de Oliveira (Fribourg: Éditions Universitaires, 1993): 143–167, and *Les raisons de Dieu: Argument de convenance et esthétique théologique selon saint Thomas d'Aquin et Hans Urs von Balthasar* (Fribourg: Éditions Universitaires, 1997). On the importance of arguments of fittingness for Aquinas's Christology, see also Wawrykow, "Wisdom in the Christology of Thomas Aquinas," 188.

22. 3, q.3, a.8. For development of this position, see 1, q.34, a.3 ("Whether the Name 'Word' Imports Relation to Creatures?"), and 1, q.44, a.3.

23. 3, q.3, a.8.

24. 3, q.3, a.8, ad 3. For explanation of this personal "name" of the Holy Spirit, see 1, q.38.

25. 1, q.29, especially a.4. See also 1, q.30 and q.39. On Aquinas's analogous use of the concept of person and related metaphysical issues pertaining to the Incarnation, see, among numerous studies, Horst Seidl, "The Concept of Person in St. Thomas Aquinas: A Contribution to Recent Discussion," *Thomist* 51 (1987): 435–460; Torrell, *Le Christ en ses mystères*, 153–165; E.-H. Weber, *Le Christ selon saint Thomas d'Aquin* (Paris: Desclée, 1988); Francis Ruello, *La Christologie de Thomas d'Aquin* (Paris: Beauchesne, 1987); Jean-Hervé Nicolas, *Synthèse dogmatique: De la Trinité à la Trinité* (Paris: Beauchesne, 1985), 301–358; Marie-Vincent Leroy, "L'union selon l'hypostase d'après S. Thomas d'Aquin," *Revue Thomiste* 74 (1974): 205–243; James A. Weisheipl, O. P., "The Concepts of 'Nature' and 'Person'," "The Mystery of the Incarnation," and "The Hypostatic Union," Appendices 3, 5, and 6 to St. Thomas Aquinas's *Commentary on Gospel of John* (Albany, NY: Magi Books, 1980), 458–468, 478–487, and 488–490; Alan Bäck, "Aquinas on the Incarnation," *New Scholasticism* 56 (1982): 127–145; and Ceslaus

Velecky, O. P., "Divine Relations" and "Divine Persons," Appendices 6 and 7 to *Summa Theologiae*, vol. 6, *The Trinity* (New York: McGraw-Hill, 1965), 141–148. The best succinct account of Aquinas's trinitarian doctrine is Gilles Emery, O. P., "Essentialisme ou personnalisme dans le traité de Dieu chez saint Thomas d'Aquin?" *Revue Thomiste* 98 (1998): 5–38.

26. See 3, q.2, a.4.

27. See 3, q. 2, a.11; 3, q.6, a.5; and elsewhere.

28. This means that Christ's human nature should not be described as a separate subject or "person" (in Aquinas's sense of "person"), as if it subsisted on its own "before" subsisting in the Word. On this point, see 1, q.29, a.1, ad 2; 3, q.2, a.2 and a.5; 3, q.4, a.2; 3, q.17; and 3, q.33, a.3. Were Christ to subsist on his own before subsisting in the Word, the Incarnation would have "to be looked upon as an ascent, as it were, of a man already existing and mounting up to the dignity of the Union" (3, q.33, a.3, ad 3).

29. 3, q.6, a.6. See also 3, q.2, aa.10–11. In a.11, Aquinas makes clear that "every operation of this man [Christ] followed the union" and therefore that the union of the Incarnation could not have been merited. In a.10, Aquinas explains that the grace of union is not a habit but belongs "by personal being" (i.e., subsistence) to Christ's human nature.

30. 3, q.6, a.6.

31. In Aristotelian terminology, the grace of union is "substantial," whereas habitual grace (the grace of the Holy Spirit) is "accidental." This point is clarified in 3, q.2, a.6 (see also 3, q.6, a.6, *sed contra* and ad 2).

32. Thus, when Gary D. Badcock faults Aquinas for refusing to see "the work of the Spirit in the humanity of Christ" as "the ground of the divine Sonship of Christ" (Badcock, *Light of Truth and Fire of Love: A Theology of the Holy Spirit* [Grand Rapids, MI: Eerdmans, 1997], 149), Aquinas would reply that Badcock misunderstands the nature of Christ's subsistence in the divine Person. This subsistence *is* the Word's subsistence and therefore cannot be "grounded" by the Spirit in the sense that Badcock seems to require.

33. 3, q.32, a.1.

34. In 3, q.32, a.1, obj.1, Aquinas quotes Augustine's *De Trinitate* to this effect. Similarly, in 3, q.32, a.1, ad 3, Aquinas approves Augustine's statement that "what is done by the Holy Ghost is done by the Son of God, because Theirs is one Nature and one Will." However, Aquinas also recognizes the significance of the relations of origin in shaping trinitarian act.

35. 3, q.32, a.1, ad 1 (cf. ad 2). Bruce Marshall eloquently explains appropriation theory *in Trinity and Truth* (Cambridge: Cambridge University Press, 2000), 251–256. He notes, "Every attribute and action common to the three persons belongs primarily to one of them. The primacy

here in question is that of likeness (*similitudo,* as the medievals put it) rather than of causality or existential dependence. . . . Every attribute and action common to the three persons belongs to each of them in a different way" (254). Marshall points out that this doctrine is found in Athanasius, Gregory of Nyssa, and others.

36. 3, q.32, a.1. In 3, q.32, a.2, Aquinas refers to the Holy Spirit as the "efficient cause" of the conception of Christ's human nature. On the other hand, Christ's human nature cannot be called (except in the analogous sense proper to the *imago dei* perfected by grace) the "son" of the Holy Spirit, since "sonship" properly refers to a perfect likeness, which a creature cannot have in relation to the Creator (see 3, q.32, a.3). When we name Christ the "Son of God," we are referring to his Person, which subsists in his human nature (see 3, q.16).

37. As Aquinas says in 3, q.2, a.12, ad 3, Christ "was conceived by the Holy Ghost, so that He might be the natural Son of God and of man."

38. 3, q.34, a.1, ad 1.

39. 3, q.7, a.9.

40. Christ, as man, does not "naturally" have access to the divine intellect that he has as God, since the infinite divine intellect cannot be fathomed by the human intellect in its natural state (see 3, q.7, a.1, ad 1 and 2). Aquinas emphasizes that even Christ's habitual grace does not mean that he "comprehends" the divine Word. As Aquinas points out, "the infinite is not comprehended by the finite" (3, q.10, a.1). Aquinas explains that "the soul of Christ sees the whole Essence of God, yet does not comprehend It; since it does not see It totally, i.e. not as perfectly as It is knowable" (3, q.10, a.1, ad 2). He makes the same point in describing beatific knowledge in 1, q.12, a.7.

41. 3, q.7, a.1.

42. 3, q.7, a.13. Aquinas suggests that this "order" fittingly corresponds to the immanent procession of the Spirit from the Son (and the Father).

43. Ibid. Regarding Christ's union with the Word taking place through the "medium" of his soul, see 3, q.6.

44. 3, q.7, a.12.

45. 3, q.7, a.1.

46. See 3, q.7, a.10.

47. 3, q.9, a.2.

48. See Matthew L. Lamb, "Nature, History, and Redemption," in *Jesus Crucified and Risen: Essays in Honor of Dom Sebastian Moore,* ed. William P. Loewe and Vernon J. Gregson (Collegeville, MN: Liturgical Press, 1998), 117–132; also Pope John Paul II, *Novo Millennio Ineunte* (Apostolic Letter), Vatican translation (Boston: Pauline Books and Media,

2001), #25–27. The Pope writes, "Jesus' cry on the cross, dear brothers and sisters, is not the cry of anguish of a man without hope, but the prayer of the Son who offers his life to the Father in love, for the salvation of all. At the very moment when he identifies with our sin, 'abandoned' by the Father, he 'abandons' himself into the hands of the Father. His eyes remain fixed on the Father. Precisely because of the knowledge and experience of the Father which he alone has, even at this moment of darkness he sees clearly the gravity of sin and suffers because of it. He alone, who sees the Father and rejoices fully in him, can understand completely what it means to resist the Father's love by sin. More than an experience of physical pain, his passion is an agonizing suffering of the soul. Theological tradition has not failed to ask how Jesus could possibly experience at one and the same time his profound unity with the Father, by its very nature a source of joy and happiness, and an agony that goes all the way to his final cry of abandonment. The simultaneous presence of these two seemingly irreconcilable aspects is rooted in the fathomless depths of the hypostatic union" (#26).

49. 3, q.9, a.2.

50. 3, q.7, a.5. The gifts, like the virtues, are "effects" of habitual grace (see 3, q.7, a.9). On the debate regarding the meaning of the gifts between those who consider them to be receptive habitus that dispose the person to obey the promptings of the Holy Spirit and those who consider them to infuse a supernatural mode of action, see Cruz Gonzalez Ayesta, *El don de sabiduria según santo Tomas: Divinizacion, filiacion y connaturalidad* (Pamplona: Eunsa, 1999).

51. Ibid.

52. 3, q.7, a.7.

53. Aquinas understands "tongues" to mean recognizable foreign languages, not gibberish.

54. 3, q.7, a.7. On this point, see Robert Barron, "Thomas Aquinas' Theological Method and the Icon of Jesus Christ," *Doctor Communis* 49 (1996): 103–125.

55. 3, q.8.

56. 3, q.8, a.5.

57. 3, q.8, a.1, emphasis added.

58. 3, q.8, a.6.

59. Aquinas explains Christ's causality in 3, q.8, a.1, ad 1: "To give grace or the Holy Ghost belongs to Christ as He is God, authoritatively; but instrumentally it belongs also to Him as man, inasmuch as His manhood is the instrument of His Godhead." For the efficient causality of Christ's saving work, see also 3, q.48, aa.1 and 6. For further discussion of the range of issues involved here, see most recently Paul G. Crowley, S.J.,

"Instrumentum Divinitatis in Thomas Aquinas: Recovering the Divinity of Christ," *Theological Studies* 52 (1991): 451–475.

60. Richard Schenk, O. P., *"Omnis Christi Actio Nostra Est Instructio:* The Deeds and Sayings of Jesus as Revelation in the View of Thomas Aquinas," in *La doctrine de la révélation divine de saint Thomas d'Aquin,* ed. Leo J. Elders (Vatican City: Libreria Editrice Vaticana, 1990), 104–131.

61. As suggested by Karl Rahner's Christology and taken to an extreme by Roger Haight, S. J.

62. Wright, *Jesus and the Victory,* 130. While the same point has been made by other New Testament exegetes, none has done so as forcefully and profoundly as Wright.

63. 3, q.40, a.1.

64. Ulrich Horst, O. P., "Christ, *Exemplar Ordinis Fratrum Praedicantium,* According to Saint Thomas Aquinas," in Emery and Wawrykow, *Christ among the Medieval Dominicans,* 263. Horst goes on to suggest that in this section of the *tertia pars,* Aquinas is seeking to respond to contemporary criticism of the mendicant orders and therefore depicts Christ's ministry as much like the practices of Dominicans. While Aquinas was seeking to defend the practices of his order, I would argue that his emphasis on the three purposes has a more profound significance, which becomes fully apparent only in light of his reading of the Old Law.

65. 3, q.36.

66. Gerald O'Collins, S. J., *The Tripersonal God* (New York: Paulist Press, 1999), 37, 38. Without citing Aquinas, O'Collins shows why Aquinas's approach to this issue, *pace* critics such as Yves Congar, remains valid.

67. 3, q.36, a.3.

68. Ibid.

69. 3, q.36, a.5.

70. 3, q.39, a.1.

71. 3, q.39, aa.1–3.

72. 3, q.39, a.5 (cf. ad 3) and a.6.

73. 3, q.40, a.1.

74. See 2–2, q.174, a.4, where Aquinas notes, "Although in some respect one or other of the prophets was greater than Moses, yet Moses was simply the greatest of all." Aquinas remarks that Moses is greatest, first, because, as Nm 12:8 says, he saw God "plainly and not by riddles." A prophet's greatness lies in the extent of his vision of the divine (salvific) realities, which God calls the prophet to reveal to the people. Like all medieval theologians, Aquinas takes literally the testimony of Dt 34:10, "There arose no more a prophet in Israel like unto Moses" (a.4, *sed contra*).

75. 3, q.40, a.1.

76. As Aquinas states, "Christ wished to make His Godhead known through His human nature" (3, q.40, a.1, ad 1). Earlier he had pointed out with regard to the fittingness (*convenientia*) of the Son of God's Incarnation: "It would seem most fitting that by visible things the invisible things of God should be made known; for to this end was the whole world made, as is clear from the word of the Apostle (Rom 1:20)" (3, q.1, a.1, *sed contra*).

77. See 3, q.40, a.1, ad 2 and 3. Aquinas suggests that Christ is thereby a pattern for a proper balance between action and contemplation.

78. 3, q.40, a.2.

79. 3, q.40, a.2, ad 2.

80. 3, q.40, a.2, ad 3.

81. Aquinas cites Mt 8:20 in a.3, *sed contra*.

82. 3, q.40, a.3, obj. and ad 2.

83. 3, q.40, a.3, ad 2.

84. This issue was forcefully debated in Aquinas's day (as, prompted by the Catholic Worker movement, it still is). For further elucidation, see Kevin Madigan, "Aquinas and Olivi on Evangelical Poverty: A Medieval Debate and Its Modern Significance," *Thomist* 61 (1997): 567–586.

85. 3, q.40, a.3. Aquinas cites Mk 1:38, where Jesus describes his task as one of preaching.

86. Ibid.

87. Ibid.

88. Ibid.

89. Ibid.

90. 3, q.40, a.4. The *sed contra* cites Mt 5:17, "Do not think that I am come to destroy the Law or the Prophets."

91. Ibid.

92. 3, q.41, a.1.

93. 3, q.41, a.3. Aquinas recognizes the fast of forty days as a parallel with Moses and Elijah.

94. 3, q.41, a.1.

95. 3, q.41, a.1, ad 3.

96. Ibid. In 3, q.41, a.4, Aquinas compares the temptation of Christ with the temptation of Adam, who was also without sin. He shows that in both cases the devil tempted in three steps: tempting first through food, then through vainglory, then through pride that extends to holding God in contempt.

97. 3, q.41, a.1, ad 2.

98. In 3, q.41, a.2, Aquinas remarks that "Christ of His own free-will exposed Himself to be tempted by the devil, just as by His own free-will He submitted to be killed by His members." This point emphasizes the reality

that Christ dies for all. Although the Roman soldiers (on the request of the Jewish leaders, abetted by Christ's own disciple) kill him, they are still Christ's "members."

99. 3, 1.41, a.4.

100. This connection between Christ's temptation and Christ's passion is not, of course, original to Aquinas. In 3, q.41, a.3, ad 3, Aquinas notes, "As Ambrose says on Luke 4:13, the devil departed from Christ *for a time* [after the temptation], *because, later on, he returned, not to tempt Him, but to assail Him openly*—namely, at the time of His Passion."

101. On this topic, see also Jean-Pierre Torrell, "Le semeur est sorti pour semer: L'image du Christ prêcheur chez frère Thomas d'Aquin," *La Vie spirituelle* 147 (1993): 657–670. Torrell argues that Aquinas interprets Christ's teaching/preaching role in light of the task of Christian preachers (especially Dominican friars). Since Christ's threefold office is participated in by Christians, this approach both reveals Aquinas's enthusiasm for his own vocation and has a profound theological rationale.

102. 3, q.42, a.1.

103. Ibid.

104. 3, q.42, a.2.

105. 3, q.42, a.2, ad 3.

106. 3, q.42, a.3, ad 2.

107. 3, q.42, a.3 (cf. ad 3).

108. 3, q.42, a.4 (cf. ad 2).

109. Ibid.

110. Ibid.

111. Ibid.

112. 3, q.42, a.4, ad 1. In our day, theologians such as Henri de Lubac, S. J., and Hans Urs von Balthasar have made an effort to recover this hermeneutical principle.

113. 3, q.43, a.1.

114. Ibid.

115. 3, q.43, a.2. Fallen angels do not have the power to work true miracles.

116. 3, q.43, a.1.

117. Ibid. In this regard, Aquinas cites Jn 10:36, 38.

118. 3, q.43, a.4. For further discussion of Christ's human action, see J. Montero, "La operación teándrica de Cristo, según la doctrina de Santo Tomás," *Studium* 7 (1967): 281–315; Kevin F. O'Shea, "The Human Activity of the Word," *Thomist* 22 (1959): 143–232; and Bernard Catão, *Salut et rédemption chez S. Thomas d'Aquin* (Paris: Aubier, 1965).

119. 3, q.43, a.3. Following Chrysostom and other Fathers, Aquinas rejects stories of Christ's childhood miracles as apocryphal and false (ad 1).

120. 3, q.43, a.2.

121. 3, q.43, a.4 and a.4, ad 3.

122. 3, q.43, a.3, ad 2. Aquinas here enunciates a crucial principle: "What the Divine power achieved in Christ was in proportion to the needs of the salvation of mankind, the achievement of which was the purpose of His taking flesh." Christ's miracles are never random but rather are ordered to furthering human salvation.

123. See 3, q.44, aa.1–4.

3 The Cross of Jesus Christ

1. Part of this chapter has appeared, in an earlier version, as Matthew Levering, "Israel and the Shape of Thomas Aquinas's Soteriology," *Thomist* 63 (1999): 65–82. No scholar has analyzed Aquinas's theology of salvation from the perspective of Christ's fulfillment of the Old Law, although this aspect has not been totally overlooked. Ulrich Kühn discusses Christ's fulfillment of the Old Law in his seminal work *Via caritatis: Theologie des Gesetzes bei Thomas von Aquin* (Göttingen: Vandenhoeck & Ruprecht, 1965), 203–206. Ghislain Lafont, O. S. B., in *Structures et méthode dans la Somme théologique de Saint Thomas d'Aquin* (Paris: Desclée, 1961), 417–418, emphasizes the significance of Christ's perfect obedience as the fulfillment of the Old Law, in that God wills to receive the "sacrifice of obedience" from his people. Jean-Pierre Torrell treats q.47, a.2, ad 1, in *Le Christ en ses mystères*, 355–356. While Torrell cautions that a focus on precepts can lead commentators to downplay Aquinas's emphasis on Christ's freedom and Christ's charity (356), Torrell is aware that Aquinas's account of the precepts of the Mosaic Law does not itself fall into this trap. On a related front, theologians such as Kühn, Max Seckler, Lafont, Yves Congar, Otto Pesch, and Torrell have sought to highlight the ways in which Aquinas's theology, while not organized according to the salvation-historical model of Hugh of St. Victor and his followers among the medieval Franciscans, nonetheless attends to the economy of salvation.

2. Torrell, *Le Christ en ses mystères*, 356.

3. Ibid.

4. Valkenberg, in *Words of the Living God*, has shown that Aquinas's discussion of the mysteries of Christ's life, in the *Summa Theologiae*, draws most heavily upon the Gospel of Matthew.

5. Donald Senior, C. P., *Matthew* (Nashville, TN: Abingdon Press, 1998): 55. The references are to John P. Meier, *The Vision of Matthew: Christ, Church and Morality in the First Gospel* (New York: Paulist Press, 1979), and Benno Przybylski, *Righteousness in Matthew and His World of Thought* (Cambridge: Cambridge University Press, 1980).

6. See Hans Urs von Balthasar, *The Glory of the Lord: A Theological Aesthetics*, Vol. 6, *The Old Covenant*, trans. Brian McNeil and Erasmo Leiva-Merikakis (San Francisco: Ignatius Press, 1991), especially 215–298, 402–414.

7. Hans Urs von Balthasar, *Theo-Drama*, vol. 4, *The Action*, trans. Graham Harrison (San Francisco: Ignatius Press, 1994): 263. For Balthasar's own substitutionary account of Christ's saving work, see *Theo-Drama*, vol. 4, 338–349, 357. Balthasar grounds Christ's substitution in the immanent relations of the Trinity (cf. *Theo-Drama*, vol. 5, *The Last Act*, trans. Graham Harrison [San Francisco: Ignatius Press, 1998], 85–98, 242ff.). See also Gérard Remy, "La déréliction du Christ: Terme d'une contradiction ou mystère de communion?" *Revue Thomiste* 98 (1998): 39–94, and "La substitution: Pertinence ou non-pertinence d'un concept théologique," *Revue Thomiste* 94 (1994): 559–600; Michele M. Schumacher, "The Concept of Representation in the Theology of Hans Urs von Balthasar," *Theological Studies* 60 (1999): 53–71.

8. 3, q.46, a.6, *sed contra*. Christ's passion, in this sense, is the prophesied "Day of Yahweh." Aquinas ties the passion to the Second Coming, which also constitutes the Day of Yahweh.

9. The significant differences between Aquinas's and Balthasar's theology of salvation should not obscure their shared divergence from Rahner's solution. As Balthasar writes, interpreting Aquinas with an eye toward Rahner, Christ's passion, for Aquinas, "is more than a sign of God's constant and antecedent desire to be reconciled with the world; it is more than a sacramental sign that God *is* reconciled to the world and is applying the fruits of this reconciliation to the world: it is in very truth the event *whereby* God's anger is turned away from the sinner, even if it remains the case that, from before all time, God has already specified Christ's Passion and satisfaction as the means whereby this is to be brought about" (Balthasar, *Theo-Drama*, vol. 4, 265). For further discussion, see Guy Mansini, O. S. B., "Rahner and Balthasar on the Efficacy of the Cross," *Irish Theological Quarterly* 63 (1998): 232–249.

10. Christ's suffering, therefore, is salvific *in itself*. Although he does not examine Christ's fulfillment of the Old Law's three kinds of precepts, Romanus Cessario, O. P., notes that Aquinas's theology of satisfaction affirms that Christ's suffering has positive value as a sin offering to God (restoring

the order of justice), not simply as an *exemplar* for the sinners joined to Christ by faith and charity (Cessario, *The Godly Image, Christ* 146).

11. In his recent commentary *The Gospel of John* (Collegeville, MN: Liturgical Press, 1998), Francis J. Moloney, S. D. B., similarly describes Jn 19:30: "Climaxing these indications of fulfillment, Jesus cries out '*tetelestai*' (v. 30a), an exclamation of achievement, almost of triumph. The task given to him by the Father (cf. 4:34; 5:36; 17:4) has now been consummately brought to a conclusion" (504).

12. The context established in the *Summa Theologiae*, as we have seen, by his extraordinary treatise on the Old Law in 1–2, qq.98–105.

13. Kenneth Hagen, *A Theology of Testament in the Young Luther: The Lectures on Hebrews* (Leiden: E. J. Brill, 1974), 48.

14. Ibid., 47–48.

15. See Cessario, *The Godly Image*, 148.

16. Aquinas conceives of cultic sacrifice as belonging to the "natural" virtue of religion, as well as to the Old Law. See 2–2, q.85, "Of Sacrifice," where he discusses sacrifice as part of the virtue of religion, which is in turn part of the virtue of justice. In this question, Aquinas conceives of sacrifice as part of holiness, rather than as a penance for sin. In q.85, a.1, he holds that offering sacrifice belongs to the natural law. It should be clear that Aquinas's reading of the Old Testament allows for a broader conception of sacrifice than does René Girard's influential theory of sacrificial scapegoating. On Girard's work, see especially the exchange between Roch Kereszty and Gil Bailie in *Communio* 26 (1999): 212–224. For further discussion of Aquinas's theory of sacrifice, see Serge-Thomas Bonino, O. P., "Le sacerdoce comme institution naturelle selon saint Thomas d'Aquin," *Revue Thomiste* 99 (1999): 33–57.

17. See my discussion of this relationship in chapter 1. The relationship of (proleptic) participation is described by Aquinas in 3, q.8, a.3, ad 3, and elsewhere.

18. Cf. Walter H. Principe, C. S. B., "Some Examples of Augustine's Influence on Medieval Christology," in *Collectanea Augustiniana: Mélanges T. J. Van Bavel*, vol. 2, ed. B. Bruning et al. (Leuven: Leuven University Press, 1990), 955–974.

19. Aquinas draws an analogy to "natural" love. The well-being of the state, he notes, requires a political love by which citizens "love the good of the state so that it might be preserved and defended. . . . So much is this so, that men would expose themselves to dangers of death or neglect of their own private good, in order to preserve or increase the good of the state" (Thomas Aquinas, *On Charity*, trans. Lottie H. Kendzierski [Milwaukee, WI: Marquette University Press, 1984], 43). Supernatural (infused) charity,

which transforms and elevates natural charity, must therefore require at least a willingness to sacrifice the life of the body. Christ's bloody self-sacrifice manifests this supernatural charity.

20. See Carlos-Josaphat Pinto de Oliveira, O. P., "Ordo rationis, ordo amoris: La notion d'ordre au centre de l'univers éthique de S. Thomas," in *Ordo Sapientiae et Amoris*, ed. C.-J. Pinto de Oliveira (Fribourg: Éditions Universitaires, 1993), 285–302. The order of the universe represents God's just distribution of goods to each creature according to its degree of being. Aquinas raises an important problem: God's distributive justice is grounded, on his side, in his wisdom; but distributive justice also regards what is "due" on the side of the one who receives. How can anything be "due," or owed by God, to a creature? Aquinas replies that God, in a sense, owes it to himself (as an expression of his goodness) that what he, in his wisdom, freely deems fitting for creatures should be fulfilled in creatures. It follows that justice is never something extrinsic to the relationship of creatures and God. The debt of punishment expresses the fact that if we sin, the order of justice by which God has connected us to himself does not simply disappear. Aquinas puts it succinctly: "whatever rises up against an order, is put down by that order or by the principle thereof" (1–2, q.27, a.1). This order and its principle—God's eternal law and God himself—cannot be understood outside the context of God's wisdom and love in freely creating and redeeming.

21. 1–2, q.87, a.3.

22. I have altered the translation by substituting *satisfies* for *atones*. The Latin is *satisfacit*.

23. See 1, q.97, a.1; 3, q.14, aa.1–3.

24. 1–2, q.87, a.6, ad 3. On the other hand, Aquinas emphasizes that if God "had willed to free man from sin without any satisfaction, He would not have acted against justice. . . . God has no one higher than Himself, for He is the sovereign and common good of the whole universe. Consequently, if He forgive sin, which has the formality of fault in that it is committed against Himself, He wrongs no one: just as anyone else, overlooking a personal trespass, without satisfaction, acts mercifully and not unjustly" (3, q.46, a.2, ad 3).

25. On Aquinas's development in the *Summa Theologiae* of Anselm's satisfaction theory, see especially Cessario, *The Godly Image*, 153. Similar conclusions are reached by Albert Patfoort, O. P., "Le vrai visage de la satisfaction du Christ selon S. Thomas," in Pinto de Oliveira, *Ordo Sapientiae et Amoris*, 247–266; W. Jerome Bracken, "Thomas Aquinas and Anselm's Satisfaction Theory," *Angelicum* 62 (1985): 503–530.

26. 3, q.49, a.4.

27. For a full overview of Aquinas's treatment of Christ as mediator (3, q.26), see two articles by Gérard Remy: "Le Christ médiateur dans l'oeuvre de saint Thomas," *Revue Thomiste* 93 (1993): 182–233, and "Sacerdoce et médiation chez saint Thomas," *Revue Thomiste* 99 (1999): 101–118. Aquinas connects Christ's mediation (which is a property of his humanity) with his satisfaction because Christ reconciles humankind to God by satisfying for sin: "it belongs to Him, as man, to satisfy for the sin of the human race. And in this sense He is called the Mediator of God and men" (3, q.26, a.2, ad 3).

28. See, for example, Dt 6:5, Lev 19:18, Is 1:11f., Ps 50:8–13, Sir 34:19–21, Mi 6:7. Aquinas makes clear that although the moral precepts of the Old Law concern "natural" virtues, it is impossible to fulfill the Old Law without the supernatural virtue of charity (see 1–2, q. 100, a.1; q.100, a.10, ad 3).

29. See q.47, a.4, ad 2; q.48, aa.2 and 3; q.49, a.4.

30. 2–2, q.24, a.1.

31. Merit thus is the "reward" due to the good acts that *grace* enables us to perform. For a comprehensive treatment of Aquinas's account of merit, see Wawrykow, *God's Grace and Human Action.*

32. See also Peter A. Kwasniewski's superb article, "St. Thomas, *Extasis,* and Union with the Beloved," *Thomist* 61 (1997): 587–603.

33. *Catechism of the Catholic Church,* trans. U.S. Catholic Conference (Vatican City: Libreria Editrice Vaticana, 1994), #478, emphasis added.

34. 3, q.46, a.3.

35. 3, q.49, a.1, ad 5.

36. 3, q.47, a.4, ad 1.

37. 3, q.47, a.1.

38. 3, q.48, a.2, ad 2.

39. Drawing upon the work of Bernard Lonergan, Matthew L. Lamb has remarked, "The more we love someone, the more our hearts are broken when they offend us. When Thomas Aquinas states that Jesus Christ in his human consciousness had not the light of faith, as we do, but the light of glory, that in no way dulled his pain or suffering. It did the opposite. The higher the created consciousness, the greater the suffering. Knowing and loving the Triune God both divinely and humanly, only such a human nature united hypostatically to the Word could take up into his human mind and heart each and every human being with all his and her sins and sufferings" (Matthew L. Lamb, "Apokalyptische Unterbrechung und Politische Theologie," in *Befristete Zeit,* ed. Jüergen Manemann [Münster: LIT Verlag, 1999], 239–240).

40. 3, q.46, a.1, ad 3.

41. Thus, Christ's suffering, not *simply* the charity with which he suffers, is salvific.

42. 1–2, q.105, a.2, ad 9.

43. 3, q.46, a.6, obj.6, cf. ad 6.

44. 3, q.46, a.7.

45. 3, q.46, a.8. In defending his own view that Christ was utterly hopeless on the cross, Hans Urs von Balthasar criticizes Aquinas's account as intelligible, in the modern context, only to "incorrigible school Thomists" (Hans Urs von Balthasar, *Theologik*, Vol. 2, *Wahrheit Gottes* [Einsiedeln: Johannes Verlag, 1985], 261, fn.9). Yet the testimony of some victims of torture indicates that it is possible for the most profound experience of suffering, of truly horrific torture, to be *joined* with profound inner peace. It seems to me that this is what Aquinas wishes to express. As Torrell remarks, not only have the mystics of every period spoken of various levels or regions of the soul, but also Sigmund Freud's theory of the unconscious or (in Maritain's terms) the supraconscious lends credibility to Aquinas's "topography of the soul" (Torrell, *Le Christ en ses mystères*, 338). On the normally devastating experience of torture, see William T. Cavanaugh, *Torture and Eucharist* (Oxford: Blackwell, 1998), 21–71.

46. 1, q.79, a.9. This distinction, as we will see in chapter 6, allows Aquinas to move away from an entirely "intellectualist" depiction of the state of glory.

47. 3, q.46, a.7.

48. 3, q.46, a.6.

49. Eleonore Stump overlooks this aspect of Aquinas's position. Stump remarks, "There is, however, one idea found in other, more familiar theories of the Atonement which is not mentioned in this paper because it is not in Aquinas; the fact that it is not seems to me a serious flaw in his account. Luther, for example, in his theory of the Atonement, emphasizes the idea that Christ somehow actually bears all human sin; that is, in some way all the sins ever committed in human history are transferred to Christ's soul in his suffering on the cross. (I will refer to this claim as 'Luther's idea,' for the sake of convenience only.) There is no similar or analogous claim in Aquinas's account. The problem for Aquinas, then, is to square his account with the New Testament story of the passion" (E. Stump, "Atonement According to Aquinas," in *Philosophy and the Christian Faith*, ed. Thomas V. Morris [Notre Dame, IN: University of Notre Dame Press, 1988], 84). Aquinas does not hold Luther's substitutionary view, but Aquinas *does* make a "similar or analogous claim" with regard to Christ's suffering for *all* sin.

50. 3, q.46, a.5.

51. 3, q.46, a.6, ad 2.

52. Guilt does not add any intensity to grief. Thomas points out that although a guilty man "grieves not merely on account of the penalty, but

also because of the crime," nonetheless the grief of an innocent man is more intense "by reason of his innocence, insofar as he deems the hurt to be the more undeserved" (q.46, a.6, ad 5).

53. 3, q.46, a.6, ad 4.

54. 3, q.46, a.6, ad 3.

55. 3, q.47, a.4. Donald Senior, who has written valuable commentaries on each of the four passion narratives, remarks (discussing the passion narrative of the Gospel of Matthew): "By making this prayer the death prayer of Jesus the evangelist catches up the motif of trust and vindication already raised in the mockery scene (cf. 27:32–44). Even though shredded by anguish Jesus, the Just One, prays a prayer of raw, unadorned faith in God. As he had from the very beginning of the Gospel, Matthew presents Jesus as the embodiment of Israel's faith, as the one who suffers with God's people and yet remains faithful. Only the first line [of Psalm 22] is quoted but the spirit of the entire psalm is at work here" (Donald Senior, *The Passion of Jesus in the Gospel of Matthew* [1985; reprint, Collegeville, MN: Liturgical Press, 1990], 136–137). This interpretation stands in sharp contrast to Balthasar's (and Moltmann's) view that Jesus' prayer indicates his utter hopelessness.

56. Here one may remark that by attending to the salvific significance of Christ's fulfillment of the Old Law, Aquinas draws together the themes of liberation and reconciliation that George A. Lindbeck, among others, has identified in the New Testament's descriptions of Christ's saving work (Lindbeck, "Atonement and the Hermeneutics of Social Embodiment," *Pro Ecclesia* 5 [1996]: 158). I might add that Lindbeck's "hermeneutics of social embodiment," which in his article refers to Christian ecclesial contexts, should be extended to consider Jesus' embodiment in Israel.

57. Geoffrey Wainwright, *For Our Salvation: Two Approaches to the Work of Christ* (Grand Rapids, MI: Eerdmans, 1997), 98–186.

58. Ibid., 100–115.

59. Ibid., 105, 118–119.

60. Ibid., 111.

61. Yves Congar, O.P., "Sur la trilogie: Prophète-roi-prêtre," *Revue des sciences philosophiques et théologiques* 67 (1983): 101.

62. Ibid., 101–102.

63. Ibid., 102.

64. Jean-Pierre Torrell, *Saint Thomas d'Aquin, maître spirituel* (Paris: Cerf, 1996), 198–200; Benoit-Dominique de La Soujeole, "Les *tria munera Christi*: Contribution de saint Thomas à la recherche contemporaine," *Revue Thomiste* 99 (1999): 59–74.

65. See Michael M. Waldstein, "On Scripture in the Summa Theologiae," *Aquinas Review* 1 (1994): 84–85.

66. 3, q.22.

67. 3, q.22, a.1, ad 3. La Soujeole states, "The doctrine of the threefold anointing of Christ specifies the content of the personal grace of Christ. And as this personal perfection only exists in order to communicate itself, it specifies also the content of the grace of Christians" ("Les *tria munera Christi*," 63).

68. 3, q.31, a.2.

69. Ibid.

70. Prologue to the *tertia pars*.

71. Aquinas makes this clear in, for example, 3, q.35, a.7, ad 1. Discussing why Christ selected Jerusalem as the place of his passion and death, Aquinas notes that "Jerusalem was at the same time a royal and a priestly city," since it contained both the Davidic monarchy and the Temple. Aquinas then makes the point that establishes the connection between Christ's threefold office and Christ's fulfillment of the Old Law: "Christ's priesthood and kingdom were *consummated* principally in His Passion." Discussing Christ's words from the cross, "*It is consummated*," Aquinas argues that these words refer to Christ's fulfillment of the Old Law (3, q.47, a.2, ad 1).

72. 2–2, q.174, a.4.

73. In 3, q.31, a.2 Aquinas describes Christ as "*rex, propheta, et sacerdos*"; in 3, q.22, a.1, ad 3, he describes Christ as *legislator, sacerdos, rex*.

74. See 1–2, q.99, a.4, and elsewhere.

75. Ibid.

76. See 3, q.46, a.5. Here one grasps why the "Day of Yahweh," prophesied so vividly by so many of the prophets, is fulfilled both by Christ's passion and eschatologically, at the Final Judgment.

77. See 3, q.59, a.4, and elsewhere.

78. In 3, q.2, Aquinas describes the union of the two natures in the Person of the Word. See especially a.2.

79. See my brief analysis of the metaphysics of the incarnation in chapter 2, with the accompanying footnote references. On this topic, Aquinas's discussion in 3, q.17, is particularly important. Aquinas insists in this question that Christ must be understood as *one* subject, with all that this entails. See also 3, q.4, a.2.

80. Aquinas treats this issue of predication in 3, q.16, a.4.

81. See the profound treatment of this point in two books by Thomas Weinandy, *Does God Change?* (Still River, MA: St. Bede's Publications, 1985), 67–100, and *Does God Suffer?* (Notre Dame, IN: University of Notre Dame Press, 2000), 1–146.

82. See 3, q.16, a.4. For a thorough discussion of how Aquinas attributes to Christ the characteristics of divinity and humanity (the "communication of idioms"), see Henk J.M. Schoot, *Christ the "Name" of God* (Leuven: Peeters, 1993).

83. This sense of extrinsicism will not, of course, be completely removed until one fully grasps the metaphysics of the hypostatic union. Such a project is beyond the scope of this study. It is worth pointing out, however, that Aquinas's metaphysical account avoids the need to imagine Christ's human nature, in itself, as a self-subsistent "I."

84. 3, q.18, a.1, ad 2. See also 3, q.19, a.1.

85. For discussions of how the faithful participate in Christ's offices, see, e.g., Gilles Emery, O.P., "Le sacerdoce spirituel des fidèles chez saint Thomas d'Aquin," *Revue Thomiste* 99 (1999): 211–243; Thomas R. Potvin, "Authority in the Church as Participation in the Authority of Christ According to Saint Thomas," *Église et Théologie* 5 (1974): 227–251; Albert Gauthier, O.P., "Comments on Father Potvin's Paper," *Église et Théologie* 5 (1974): 253–255.

86. 3, q.45, a.2.

87. Cf. 3, q.45, a.1 and 3, q.45, a.2, *sed contra*.

88. La Soujeole similarly points out that Christ's kingship is manifested by his entrance into the glory of Heaven ("Les *tres munera Christi*," 63). He then shows that Christ's office as prophet can be correlated with Christians' virtue of faith, Christ's office of priest with Christians' virtue of charity, and Christ's office of king with Christians' virtue of hope. Although I have suggested a different typology, La Soujeole's approach, I think, nicely complements my own.

89. This should not be taken to mean that external acts have nothing to do with the kingdom of God. Aquinas explains, "The kingdom of God consists chiefly in internal acts: but as a consequence all things that are essential to internal acts belong also to the kingdom of God. Thus if the kingdom of God is internal righteousness, peace, and spiritual joy, all external acts that are incompatible with righteousness, peace, and spiritual joy, are in opposition to the kingdom of God; and consequently should be forbidden in the Gospel of the kingdom" (1–2, q.108, a.1, ad 1).

90. 3, q.57, a.2.

91. 3, q.58, a.3. Aquinas notes that the grace of the hypostatic union raises Christ, as man, to the Father's right hand not as if Christ's humanity thereby became equal to his Godhead but in the sense that Christ's humanity comes to share in the Father's judiciary power. We should also note that, in Aquinas's view, this exaltation of Christ's humanity is caused

by the grace of the hypostatic union *and* by the merit of his passion. Aquinas argues in this regard, "There is nothing to hinder one and the same thing from being due to some one from various causes" (3, q.59, a.3).

92. 3, q.57, a.1. Aquinas recognizes that the Creed is using metaphors from human affairs. In human affairs, *to sit* may mean "to dwell," and the king's chancellor often sits at the king's right hand.

93. 3, q.36, a.8. Matthew's Gospel relates that the Magi inquire, "Where is he born king of the Jews?" (Mt 2:2), thereby causing Herod to fear for his throne.

94. 3, q.58, a.4, ad 2.

95. 3, q.59.

96. 3, q.59, a.1.

97. 3, q.59, a.2.

98. 3, q.59, a.2, ad 3. See also 3, q.9, a.3.

99. The judgment is primarily the victory of Christ, who brings his elect the ultimate end toward which all human affairs are ordered, namely beatitude (see 3, q.59, a.2, ad 2; 3, q.59, a.4). But insofar as some human beings refuse Christ's gift of justification, they are ordered by the "punishment of loss" to the justice established by Christ. It follows that the judgment can be described in terms of rewards and punishments (see 3, q.59, a.2).

100. In this regard, Aquinas repeatedly cites St. Paul's remark in 1 Cor 2:15, "The spiritual man judges all things" (3, q.59, a.2, ad 1, and many other places). The "spiritual man" shares in Christ's Spirit through the gifts of faith, hope, and love. Aquinas emphasizes, therefore, that "the saints judge only by Christ's authority" (3, q.59, a.6, *sed contra*).

101. 2–2, q.174, a.5.

102. 2–2, q.174, a.5, *sed contra.*

103. 2–2, q.174, a.5, ad 3. Aquinas says the same thing in 3, q.7, a.8 (including ad 1), which asks "Whether in Christ there was the gift of prophecy?"

104. 3, q.9, a.2.

105. 3, q.10, a.1. Aquinas here makes the point that Christ, in his human intellect, does not "comprehend" God in this sense.

106. 3, q.9, a.2 (cf. obj. 1, ad 1 and ad 3).

107. See 3, q.9, a.3, obj. and ad 1.

108. 3, q.9, a.3, ad 3.

109. 3, q.9, a.3.

110. 2–2, q.172, a.1. This article asks "Whether prophecy can be natural?" See also 2–2, q.173, a.2, where Aquinas differentiates various kinds of infused knowledge. He states that "prophetic revelation is conveyed sometimes by the mere infusion of light, sometimes by imprinting species anew,

or by a new co-ordination of species." The species may be first received by the senses or the imagination before being judged by the intellect or may be directly imprinted upon the intellect. In both ways, the prophecy is to be described as infused knowledge.

111. 2–2, q.172, a.1.

112. 2–2, q.171, a.2. See also 2–2, q.172, a.2, ad 3, where Aquinas notes that God uses the angels to reveal prophetic knowledge to human beings.

113. 3, q.9, a.3, obj.1 (cf. obj. 2 and 3).

114. 3, q.9, a.3.

115. See 3, q.7, a.8, ad 1.

116. See 2–2, q.174, a.6.

117. 3, q.11, a.1; 3, q.11, a.5. Aquinas also notes that Christ's infused knowledge pertained to several different intellectual *habitus* (3, q.11, a.6).

118. 1–2, q.107, a.2. See also 1–2, q.108.

119. 3, q.43, a.1. See also 2–2, q.171, a.1, where Aquinas argues that although prophecy consists primarily in infused knowledge, the prophetic office also involves proclamation and the performing of miracles.

120. See 3, q.42, a.4. Aquinas's point is that the Holy Spirit must be present in the hearer to enable the hearer to grasp the true significance of the spoken or written proclamation of the New Law.

121. 1–2, q.106, a.1.

122. 3, q.42, a.4, ad 2.

123. 3, q.7, a.9. In this regard, Aquinas likes to cite Jn 1:16, "And of His fullness we have all received, and grace for grace" (cf. 3, q.7, a.1). See also 3, q.8, a.6, where Aquinas explains, "Now the interior influx of grace is from no one save Christ, Whose manhood, through its union with the Godhead, has the power of justifying."

124. For a detailed exegetical analysis of the six articles of 3, q.22, see Jean-Pierre Torrell, O. P., "Le sacerdoce du Christ dans la *Somme de théologie*," *Revue Thomiste* 99 (1999): 75–100. Torrell points out that "Thomas appears to be the only one among his contemporaries to have treated this question. The reason is simple enough: Peter Lombard not having made it the object of any distinction in his *Sentences*, his commentators have not discussed it more than Thomas himself did in his own commentary on the *Sentences*" (ibid., 76). To grasp the influence of Aquinas's commentary on Hebrews upon his treatment of Christ's priesthood in the *Summa Theologiae*, see most recently Gilles Berceville, "Le sacerdoce du Christ dans le *Commentaire de l'Épître aux Hébreux* de saint Thomas d'Aquin," *Revue Thomiste* 99 (1999): 143–158.

125. 3, q.22, a.1.

126. 3, q.22, a.1, obj. 2 and 3.

127. 3, q.22, a.1, ad 2 and 3. In 3, q.22, a.6, Aquinas argues that Christ's priesthood is prefigured not only by the Levitical priesthood but also (and more fully) by the priesthood of Melchisedech, who offered bread and wine in the presence of Abraham.

128. 3, q.22, a.1 (keeping in mind that God does not change).

129. 3, q.22, a.3. In this regard, it is important to recall Aquinas's view that Christ's humanity is the living "instrument" of his divinity. Christ is a priest in his humanity, but since Christ's Personhood is divine, everything that Christ does in his humanity can be attributed to the divine Person. Aquinas concludes, "Hence insofar as His human nature operated by virtue of the Divine, that sacrifice [Christ's passion] was most efficacious for the blotting out of sins" (3, q.22, a.3, ad 1).

130. 3, q.22, a.2, obj. 1 and 2.

131. See also Augustine, *Confessions*, Book 10, Chapter 43.

132. 3, q.22, a.2. Christ's self-sacrifice was *for us*, not for himself.

133. 3, q.22, a.2, ad 1 and 2.

134. 3, q.22, a.5. Torrell discusses this point at length in "Le sacerdoce du Christ," 93–95.

135. 3, q.54, a.4, ad 1.

136. The main section of La Soujeole's article "Les *tria munera Christi*" focuses on showing how Christians share in Christ's threefold office. Although we have devoted less attention to this aspect, it should be clear that sharing, in this life, in Christ's threefold fulfillment of the law entails evangelizing (moral precepts, prophet), worshipping (ceremonial precepts, priest), and suffering (judicial precepts, king). In each area, the vocation of the laity is differentiated from that of the ministerial priest, without thereby compromising the priesthood of all believers. In eternal life, sharing in Christ's fulfillment of the law entails perfect charity, perfect worship, and perfect glory. It follows that sharing in Christ's fulfillment of the law is equivalent to sharing in Christ's fulfillment of the Temple.

4 To the Image of the Firstborn Son

1. Valkenberg, *Words of the Living God*, 2.

2. Levenson, *Sinai and Zion*, 12.

3. Levenson remarks, "What really happened on Mount Sinai? The honest historian must answer that we can say almost nothing in reply to this question" (17). He goes on to argue that the historical question is not of central importance for his project: "The experience of Sinai, whatever its historical basis, was perceived as so overwhelming, so charged with

meaning, that Israel could not imagine that any truth or commandment from God could have been absent from Sinai" (19).

4. Ibid., 39.

5. Ibid., 41. Levenson states, "This preference for historical terms over cosmic-primordial symbols sets the Sinai traditions off markedly from those of Zion."

6. Ibid., 44.

7. Ibid., 45.

8. Ibid., 50.

9. Ibid.

10. Ibid., 42f. (the section entitled "Mitsvot as the End of History").

11. Ibid., 22.

12. Ibid., 97.

13. For Levenson's historical analysis of the authorship, dating, and context of 1 Kgs 8, see Levenson, "From Temple to Synagogue: 1 Kgs 8," in *Traditions in Transformation*, ed. Baruch Halpern and Jon D. Levenson (Winona Lake, IN: Eisenbrauns, 1981), 143–166; and Levenson, "The Last Four Verses in Kings," *Journal of Biblical Literature* 103 (1984): 353–361.

14. Levenson, *Sinai and Zion*, 114. Levenson cites Eliade's *Patterns in Comparative Religion* (New York: Meridan, 1958), 367–387. A number of other works by Eliade could be cited.

15. Levenson, *Sinai and Zion*, 111ff. (the section entitled "Zion as the Cosmic Mountain"). In making this argument, Levenson frequently refers to Richard Clifford's *The Cosmic Mountain in Canaan and the Old Testament* (Cambridge: Harvard University Press, 1972). Like Levenson, Clifford is indebted to Eliade for the category of "cosmic mountain."

16. Levenson, *Sinai and Zion*, 125.

17. Ibid.

18. Ibid.

19. Ibid., 138.

20. Ibid., 142. Levenson cites Tillich's *Dynamics of Faith* (New York: Harper & Row, 1958), 42. This account of symbol as grounded in a theory of participation has affinities with medieval neo-Platonic thought, which influenced Aquinas through Pseudo-Dionysius and Albert the Great. It is well known that participation theory is central to Aquinas's theology.

21. Levenson, *Sinai and Zion*, 172.

22. Ibid., cf. 182.

23. In referring to "ancient Israel's history," I am aware that the authors who wrote the biblical texts were continually interpreting new events in light of the earlier narratives and were often reinterpreting earlier events in light of developing theological claims. On this point, see espe-

cially Michael Fishbane, *Biblical Interpretation in Ancient Israel* (Oxford: Oxford University Press, 1985); Richard B. Hays, *Echoes of the Scripture in the Letters of Paul* (New Haven, CT: Yale University Press, 1989); and N. T. Wright, *The New Testament and the People of God* (Minneapolis, MN: Fortress Press, 1992).

24. Levenson, *Sinai and Zion*, 44.

25. *Commentary on the Epistle to the Hebrews*, in *S. Thomae Aquinatis Opera Omnia*, ed. Robert Busa, S.J. (Stuttgart: Frommann-Holzboorg, 1980), Chapter 1, Lecture 1; cf. Chapter 7, Lecture 3, where Aquinas, following Hebrews, explains why Christians do not retain the Levitical priesthood or the ceremonial laws associated with it.

26. See 1–2, q.98, a.1; 1–2, q.103, a.4; 1–2, q.104, a.3. Aquinas holds that observing the ceremonial and the judicial precepts constitutes, *for those who recognize Christ*, a "mortal sin" (i.e., a sin against divine charity) if the precepts are observed with the idea that such observance is necessary for salvation.

27. *Commentary on the Epistle to the Hebrews*, Chapter 9, Lecture 4. The difference between Aquinas's position and linear supersessionism is contained in his use of the verbs *consummare* and *terminare*. As the one who brings to completion or consummates the Old Law, Christ is the "term" of the Old Law, which has its end in Christ. As Aquinas uses it, *terminare* has the teleological sense of fruition or resting in the end.

28. Jewish theologians, since the destruction of the Temple, have interpreted the people of Israel as the present embodiment of the Temple, in a way somewhat analogous to the Christian claim that the Mystical Body of Christ fulfills the Temple. See, e.g., Jacob Neusner and Bruce D. Chilton, *The Body of Faith: Israel and the Church* (Valley Forge, PA: Trinity Press International, 1996). Neusner writes, "The doctrine of Israel implicit throughout the Mishnah, which was compiled around 200 C.E., and explicit in many of its details may be stated very simply: the community now stands in the place of the Temple of Jerusalem, destroyed in 70 C.E. . . . The holiness of the life of Israel, the people, a holiness that had formerly centered on the Temple, now endured and transcended the physical destruction of the building and the cessation of sacrifices. The Mishnah's theology stated in countless details that Israel the people was holy, was the medium and the instrument of God's sanctification" (31–32). See also Michael Wyschogrod, *The Body of Faith: God and the People Israel*, 2nd ed. (Northvale, NJ: Jacob Aronson, 1996). Wyschogrod specifies that God is not "incarnated" in Israel but rather dwells "among or alongside" Israel in a unique way (11–12).

29. Baruch Halpern, *The First Historians: The Hebrew Bible and History* (University Park: Pennsylvania State University Press, 1996), 3–4.

I should note that Halpern's criticism is leveled against all "confessional" readings (including Jewish ones), not simply against the "christological" reading.

30. It is impossible here to describe fully Aquinas's understanding of God's providence. Suffice it to say that Aquinas holds that human (and angelic) free will *never* operates outside of God's providence, even when free will (through no fault of God, though permitted by God) falls short of the perfect good that God wills for creatures. This is so because God's providence entails knowing *and* willing, from eternity (i.e., in God's eternal presence), both free will and, in a real sense, all the contingent events that involve the exercise of this free will.

31. 1, q.1, a.10. When Aquinas notes that God has the power to signify his meaning not merely by words but also by *res ipsas*, his point is that God, in his providence, can use a certain historical reality to signify future historical realities (the allegorical sense), ethical realities (the moral sense), and/or eschatological realities (the anagogical sense).

32. In this sense, Aquinas does approach other texts critically. See, for example, his *Commentary on the Book of Causes*, trans. Vincent A. Guagliardo, O.P., et al. (Washington, DC: Catholic University of America Press, 1996).

33. 1, q.1, a.10 and ad 3.

34. Given the appreciation of Aquinas and other Christian theologians for the details of ancient Israel's religion, it seems rather unfair for Levenson to assert regarding the modern project of "biblical theology": "One would have expected biblical theologians of Christian persuasion to have asked whether Jewish tradition sheds any light upon the religion of most ancient Israel *which their own religious orientation has prevented them from glimpsing for nearly two thousand years*" (Levenson, *Sinai and Zion*, 1, emphasis added).

35. See, e.g., Smalley, "William of Auvergne, John of La Rochelle and St. Thomas Aquinas on the Old Law," in *St. Thomas Aquinas: Commemorative Studies*, vol. 2, ed. Maurer; Hood, *Aquinas and the Jews*; Wyschogrod, "A Jewish Reading of St. Thomas Aquinas on the Old Law," in *Understanding Scripture*, ed. Thoma and Wyschogrod.

36. 1–2, q.102, a.4, ad 1.

37. Aquinas does not, as some modern exegetes do, interpret the building of the Temple as an act of arrogance on the part of Solomon. Rather, he assumes (on the basis of biblical texts) that God commissions and approves the Temple. He states in 1, q.27, a.1, that "to have a temple is God's prerogative."

38. Cited in 1–2, q.102, a.4, obj.1.

39. In 1–2, q.102, a.4, ad 2, Aquinas connects the building of the Temple with the emergence of a powerful and stable monarchy. In ad 3, he argues that centralized worship aided the development of monotheism, which serves as an explanation for why God willed to have Israel replace the movable tabernacle with a Temple. In this case, as almost always when he seeks to explain the "historical" reason for why Israel did certain things, Aquinas draws his reasoning from Moses Maimonides. Following Maimonides, Aquinas also suggests that the Temple was built on the place where Abraham had been instructed to sacrifice Isaac (ad 2).

40. 2–2, q.2, a.7, ad 3.

41. See DiNoia, *The Diversity of Religions: A Christian Perspective.*

42. 1–2, q.102, a.4, ad 4.

43. 1–2, q.102, a.4, ad 6. I should emphasize, however, that Aquinas is not trying to make an exact determination of the ways in which the various things connected with the Temple prefigure Christ. For example, he suggests that the candlestick might prefigure Christ as the light of the world or might signify the Church's teaching and faith as enlightening. Aquinas's point is only that every aspect of the Temple's liturgy draws the participant, in God's plan, into the saving work of the Messiah.

44. 1–2, q.102, a.4, ad 9. The Church, as the "Body of Christ," is the visible manifestation of the Mystical Body. On the other hand, the Mystical Body is certainly not limited to members of the Church.

45. 1–2, q.106, a.1.

46. *Commentary on the Gospel of John*, Part I, Chapter 3, Lecture 1.

47. Aquinas makes this point, citing the text from Romans, in 3, q.30, a.1, ad 3, and elsewhere.

48. Although Levenson criticizes the Christian tendency to exclude law from soteriology and notes that the Jewish idea of "deliverance" is not the same as what he considers to be the individualistic Christian understanding of "salvation" (*Sinai and Zion*, 44), he recognizes that the Old Testament is a history of God's redemptive work (184). Levenson should not, therefore, be seen as attacking the whole notion of soteriology.

49. See 3, qq.27–33. Scholarly attention to Aquinas's discussion of the Virgin Mary has tended to focus instead upon the fact that Aquinas, while recognizing the Virgin Mary's sanctification in the womb and her avoidance of sin, does not think that the Virgin Mary was sanctified at the instant of her conception. In my view, this focus upon Aquinas's opposition to the details of the later dogma of the Immaculate Conception has obscured the important contribution of his treatise on the Virgin Mary to theological understanding of Christ's saving work.

50. 3, q.27, a.2, *sed contra.*
51. 3, q.28, a.3 *sed contra.*
52. Aquinas's argument may be worth quoting in full. He states, "God so prepares and endows those, whom He chooses for some particular office, that they are rendered capable of fulfilling it. . . . Now the Blessed Virgin was chosen by God to be His Mother. Therefore there can be no doubt that God, by His grace, made her worthy of that office" (3, q.27, a.4).
53. 3, q.27, a.4.
54. In 3, q.28, a.3, Aquinas remarks that the Holy Spirit's *"shrine [sacrarium]* was the virginal womb, wherein He had formed the flesh of Christ."
55. Levenson, *Sinai and Zion*, 170, 139, 125 respectively.
56. 3, q.30, a.1.
57. Ibid.
58. *Commentary on the Gospel of John*, Part I, Chapter 2, Lecture 1.
59. Ibid., p.161.
60. Cf. 1–2, q.102, a.4, ad 8 and 9.
61. *Commentary on the Gospel of John*, Part I, Chapter 2, Lecture 1 (p. 155).
62. The hypostatic union far surpasses, of course, the indwelling of the Trinity in the soul of a mere human being. In this sense, it would be misleading to describe Christ as the perfect Temple of God because Christ *is* God. On the other hand, Christ's human nature is indwelt by the Holy Spirit. In this sense Aquinas describes him as the perfect tabernacle or Temple, according to the description of the mission of the Holy Spirit that Aquinas gives in 1, q.43, a.3: "God is in all things by His essence, power, and presence, according to His one common mode, as the cause existing in the effects which participate in His goodness. Above and beyond this common mode, however, there is one special mode [sanctifying grace] belonging to the rational nature wherein God is said to be present as the object known is in the knower, and the beloved in the lover. And since the rational creature by its operation of knowledge and love attains to God Himself, according to this special mode God is said not only to exist in the rational creature, but also to dwell therein as in His own *temple*" (emphasis added).
63. For further discussion of trinitarian indwelling, see, among numerous studies, Gilles Emery, *La Trinité créatrice* (Paris: Vrin, 1995), 384–413; Luc-Thomas Somme, *Fils adoptifs de Dieu par Jésus Christ* (Paris: Vrin, 1997); Emile Bailleux, "A l'image du Fils premier-né," *Revue Thomiste* 76 (1976): 181–207; Francis L. B. Cunningham, O.P., *The Indwelling of the Trinity* (Dubuque, IA: Priory Press, 1955), 178–211; William J. Hill, O.P., *The Three-Personed God* (Washington, DC: Catholic University of America

Press, 1982), 284–296; and Albert Patfoort, O. P., "Missions divines et expérience des Personnes divines selon S. Thomas," *Angelicum* 63 (1986): 545–559. Rahner's theory that trinitarian indwelling occurs by divine quasi-formal causality has been succinctly critiqued by Hill, *The Three-Personed God*, 293–294.

64. Bonaventure, *Disputed Questions on the Mystery of the Trinity*, trans. Zachary Hayes, O. F. M. (St. Bonaventure, NY: Franciscan Institute of St. Bonaventure University, 1979), Question 1, Article 2, Respondeo (p. 132), emphasis added.

65. See, e.g., Balthasar, *Theo-Drama*, vol. 4, *The Action*, and vol. 5, *The Last Word*. See also Guy Mansini, O. S. B., "Balthasar and the Theo-dramatic Enrichment of the Trinity," *Thomist* 64 (2000): 499–519; Brian J. Spence, "The Hegelian Element in Von Balthasar's and Moltmann's Understanding of the Suffering of God," *Toronto Journal of Theology* 14 (1998): 45–60; and Steffen Lösel, "Murder in the Cathedral: Hans Urs von Balthasar's New Dramatization of the Doctrine of the Trinity," *Pro Ecclesia* 5 (1996): 427–439.

66. *Summa Theologiae* 3, q.2, a.6, ad 1. (The reference is to Augustine's *Octoginta trium Quaestionum*.) See also 3, q.16, a.6, ad 2.

67. The unity of soul and body according to Aquinas is analyzed by Kevin White, "Aquinas on the Immediacy of the Union of the Soul and Body," in *Studies in Thomistic Theology*, ed. Paul Lockey (Houston: Center for Thomistic Studies, 1995), 209–280.

68. 3, q.45, a.1.

69. Ibid.

70. The structure here is that of *imitatio Christi*. See Thomas S. Hibbs, "*Imitatio Christi* and the Foundation of Aquinas's Ethics," *Communio* 18 (1991): 556–573; P. de Cointet, "'Attache-toi au Christ!' L'imitation du Christ dans la vie spirituelle selon S. Thomas d'Aquin," *Sources* 124 (1989): 64–74; Torrell, *Saint Thomas d'Aquin, maître spirituel*, especially 489–493; Torrell, "Imiter Dieu comme des enfants bien-aimés: La conformité à Dieu et au Christ dans l'oeuvre de saint Thomas," in *Novitas et Veritas Vitae*, ed. C.-J. Pinto de Oliveira (Fribourg, Éditions Universitaires, 1991), 53–65; Torrell, "Le Christ dans la 'spiritualité' de saint Thomas," in *Christ among the Medieval Dominicans*, ed. Kent Emery, Jr., and Joseph P. Wawrykow (Notre Dame, IN: University of Notre Dame Press, 1999), 197–219. Torrell's work is the definitive treatment of the subject. For a wide-ranging study of the theme of imitation of Christ in the patristic and medieval periods, see Giles Constable, *Three Studies in Medieval Religious and Social Thought* (Cambridge: Cambridge University Press, 1995), 143–248.

71. 3, q.45, a.1.

72. 3, q.45, a.1, obj.3.

73. Ibid., ad 3.

74. Ibid.

75. Aquinas repeatedly affirms that in creatures, being is distinct from doing. He thus rejects any functionalist notion of the person. See 1, q.77, a.1, where Aquinas distinguishes the essence of the human soul from its power.

76. 3, q.45, a.2.

77. Ibid.

78. Ibid., ad 1.

79. Ibid., ad 3.

80. Ibid. The reference is to Gregory the Great's *Moralia in Job*, xxxii.

81. 3, q.45, a.3.

82. Ibid., ad 3.

83. Cf. Paul McPartlan, *Sacrament of Salvation: An Introduction to Eucharistic Ecclesiology* (Edinburgh: T.&T. Clark, 1995).

84. 3, q.45, a.4. For a comprehensive discussion of this topic, see Somme, *Fils adoptifs*.

85. Ibid., ad 2.

86. Ibid.

87. Ibid., ad 4.

88. Ibid.

89. For further discussion, see Jean-Pierre Torrell, "La causalité salvifique de la résurrection du Christ selon saint Thomas," *Revue Thomiste* 96 (1996): 179–208; Montague Brown, "Aquinas on the Resurrection of the Body," *Thomist* 56 (1992): 165–207.

90. 3, q.53, a.1. Agreeing with Augustine, Aquinas later states specifically that Christ "merited" his resurrection by virtue of the perfect humility and charity of his passion (3, q.53, a.4, ad 2). Of course, Christ's perfect humility and charity were gifts of grace, resulting from the Holy Spirit conforming his human nature to his divine nature. As is especially evident in the case of the God-man, by rewarding merit, God rewards his own gifts.

91. 3, q.52. Descent should not be interpreted as spatial motion, since the soul is a spiritual entity. Aquinas states, "Christ's soul descended into hell not by the same kind of motion as that whereby bodies are moved, but by that kind whereby the angels are moved" (3, q.52, a.1, ad 3).

92. See 3, q.52, aa. 1–2, 5, 8.

93. 3, q.52, a.1, ad 1. It is worth noting that in a.2, ad 2–4, Aquinas addresses texts, such as Acts 2:24, 1 Pt 3:19, and Christ's parable about the rich man and Lazarus, that appear to refer to hell.

94. 3, q.52, a.1.

95. 3, q.52, a.2.

96. Ibid. Aquinas notes that "while remaining in one part of hell, He wrought this effect in a measure in every part of hell, just as while suffering in one part of the earth He delivered the whole world by His Passion." In a.6, Aquinas emphasizes that "when Christ descended into hell He worked by the power of His Passion. Consequently, His descent into hell brought the fruits of deliverance to them only who were united to His Passion through faith quickened by charity, whereby sins are taken away." Aquinas thus "demythologizes" the descent of Christ's soul into hell. Christ's soul works through the power of his passion, so the drama fundamentally takes place on earth, not in hell.

97. 3, q.52, a.1, ad 2.

98. 3, q.52, a.7.

99. 3, q.52, a.5. Of course, this interpretation is not original to Aquinas. Augustine held a similar view, as did most of the Fathers and medieval theologians.

100. Ibid., ad 3.

101. 3, q.53, a.1.

102. Ibid. Aquinas puts this another way in ad 3: "Christ's Passion wrought our salvation, properly speaking, by removing evils; but the Resurrection did so as the beginning and exemplar of all good things."

103. 3, q.53, a.2, ad 1; cf. q.53, a.3, where Aquinas distinguishes between rising to immortality (as Christ did) and the "imperfect resurrection" to further (mortal) life, as in the case of Lazarus and others.

104. 3, q.54, a.4.

105. Ibid.

106. Ibid.

107. Ibid., ad 1.

108. 3, q.55, a.1.

109. Aquinas points out that maleness is not a requirement for being a "higher person": "if women burn with greater charity, they shall also attain greater glory from the Divine vision: because the women whose love for our Lord was more persistent—so much so that *when even the disciples withdrew* from the sepulchre *they did not depart,*—were the first to see Him rising in glory" (3, q.55, a.1, ad 3). The italicized section indicates a quotation from Gregory the Great, *Hom.* 25.

110. 3, q.55, a.3. In aa.5–6, Aquinas affirms that Christ's postresurrection appearances to the disciples constitute "most evident signs" or "proofs [*argumenta*]" that he has truly risen. Still, Aquinas distinguishes such signs or proofs from "proof" in the sense of an argument used to demonstrate something syllogistically. Faith in the resurrection, Aquinas notes, "is

beyond human reason" and therefore cannot be proved by a demonstration based upon rational principles (a.5).

111. 3, q.56, a.1.

112. Ibid., ad 3. For further discussion of the salvific causality of Christ's Resurrection, see Torrell, "La causalité salvifique."

113. 3, q.56, a.2, ad 3.

5 Israel, the Church, and the Mystical Body of Christ

1. Frederick Christian Bauerschmidt, "Theo-Drama and Political Theology," *Communio* 25 (1998): 533.

2. Aquinas holds that law (in the fallen world) has two purposes, one positive and one negative: to induce people to live virtuously and to prevent them from fully and unrestrainedly enacting their disordered desires. To the degree that positive law accomplishes either of these tasks, it is ordered to the Church's mission. For Aquinas's account of the relationship of human ("positive") law to the mission and "divine law" of the Church, see 1–2, q.96, especially aa.4–5. Aquinas is well aware that positive laws may contradict divine law and must in such cases be disobeyed. William Cavanaugh's remark contrasting Pope Pius XII's and Dorothy Day's responses to World War II—"In the theology of the Catholic Worker, the mystical body of Christ does not hover above national boundaries but dissolves them, making possible Christian resistance to the nation-state's designs" (*Torture and Eucharist* [Oxford: Blackwell, 1998], 221)—indicates the complexity of the distinctions that more Thomistic theologies of Christ's Mystical Body must draw. For Aquinas, the Mystical Body is not an otherworldly reality; rather, the Mystical Body describes the suffering of Christ's eucharistic people here and now, in light of their vocation to eternal glory. However, the Mystical Body, as conceived by Aquinas, does not displace systems of positive law or mandate pacifism as the only Christian response to Nazi Germany's genocidal activities.

3. Scott Bader-Saye, *Church and Israel after Christendom: The Politics of Election* (Boulder, CO: Westview Press, 1999), 26. He is drawing upon George Lindbeck's "The Church," in *Keeping the Faith*, ed. Geoffrey Wainwright (Philadelphia: Fortress Press, 1988), 190.

4. Ibid., 55.

5. Ibid., 57, 59.

6. See Torrell, "*Ecclesia Iudaeorum:* Quelques jugements positifs de saint Thomas d'Aquin à l'égard des Juifs et du judaïsme," 1732–1741.

7. See *Lumen Gentium*, #7–13.

8. 3, q.61, a.4, ad 1. Aquinas cites Dionysius's work *The Ecclesiastical Hierarchy*, which conceives of the "states" in terms of liturgy or worship.

9. 3, q.83, a.1.

10. This approach has been anticipated, with a somewhat different purpose in mind (that of clarifying Aquinas's thought in relationship to Pius XII's encyclical *Mystici Corporis*), by Colman E. O'Neill, O.P., in his article "St. Thomas on the Membership of the Church," *The Thomist* 27 (1963): 88–140. O'Neill identifies four "states"—before the law, under the law, the time of grace, and glory—that correspond to "four diverse liturgies" (95–96). Only the heavenly worship is without figurative ceremonies. O'Neill remarks, "Old and New Law are not wholly diverse, since it is the same God who gives both of them and both are directed towards the same end, namely, the submission of man to God. They are distinct in the manner that two parts of the same motion are distinct, according as one part is nearer to the term than the other, which is to say that the relation of the New Law to the old is that of what is perfect to what is imperfect in the same genus" (97).

11. Aquinas's emphasis on liturgy in his account of salvation can hardly be overemphasized. Until recently, Thomists had not followed the suggestions provided briefly by O'Neill or later (indirectly) by Liam Walsh, O.P., in his article "Liturgy in the Theology of St. Thomas," *Thomist* 38 (1974): 557–583. Recent exceptions include Torrell's *Saint Thomas d'Aquin, maître spirituel*, and A.N. Williams, *The Ground of Union: Deification in Aquinas and Palamas* (Oxford: Oxford University Press, 1999).

12. I use the word *communio* to suggest, if only in passing, the important links between Aquinas's conception of the Mystical Body and the best examples of contemporary "communion ecclesiology." These links have been drawn out more fully in Pedro Rodríguez, "La Iglesia como 'communio' en la perspectiva de la gracia capital de Cristo," in *Problemi teologici alla luce d ell' Aquinate*, Studi Tomistici 44:5 (Vatican City: Libreria Editrice Vaticana, 1991), 296–303, and Janez Vodopivec, "La 'gratia capitis' in San Tommaso in relazione all'ecclesiologia di comunione," in *Prospettive teologiche moderne*, Studi Tomistici 13:4 (Vatican City: Libreria Editrice Vaticana, 1981), 327–338. On the diversity of approaches that presently lay claim to being "communion ecclesiologies," see Dennis M. Doyle, "Journet, Congar, and the Roots of Communion Ecclesiology," *Theological Studies* 58 (1997): 462.

13. See 1–2, q.106, a.3, ad 2; 1–2, q.102, a.5, ad 4; 1–2, q.107, a.1, ad 2; 3, q.8, a.3, ad 3; 3, q.45, a.3; 3, q.49, a.5, ad 1; 3, q.62, a.6; and elsewhere.

14. 2–2, q.2, a.7, ad 3.

15. Aquinas notes that every nation "contains two kinds of men" (1–2, q.101, a.3; cf. 1–2, q.98, a.6).

16. In discussing the "sacraments" of the natural law and of the Old Law, Aquinas succinctly expresses his view of history as composed of both continuity and change. He writes, "The state of the human race after sin and before Christ can be considered from two points of view. First, from that of faith: and thus it was always one and the same: since men were made righteous, through faith in the future coming of Christ. Secondly, according as sin was more or less intense, and knowledge concerning Christ more or less explicit. For as time went on sin gained a greater hold on man, so much so that it clouded man's reason, the consequence being that the precepts of the natural law were insufficient to make man live aright, and it became necessary to have a written code of fixed laws, and together with these certain sacraments of faith. For it was necessary, as time went on, that the knowledge of faith should be more and more unfolded" (3, q.61, a.3, ad 2).

17. See 1, q.95.

18. 1–2, q.91, a.6. Aquinas is following St. Paul's account of history in Rom 2.

19. In Aquinas's words, by "the time of Abraham" it was clear that "man had fallen headlong into idolatry and the most shameful vices" (1–2, q.98, a.6). He is not arguing that human beings lost the *ability* to perceive, as rational creatures, the "natural law." He does say, however, that over time "the dictate of the natural law" was "darkened by habitual sinning" (1–2, q.98, a.6).

20. 1–2, q.98, a.4. Following Gal 3:16, Aquinas argues that the promises given to Abraham signified, at least implicitly, the future birth of the Savior from among the descendants of Abraham.

21. See 1–2, q.92, a.1.

22. 1–2, q.99, a.1, ad 2.

23. 1–2, q.99, a.2. The purpose of divine law is to lead man into a deeper communion with God than would have been possible naturally, but divine law does so by restoring man to justice in *all* his relationships. The Old Law stands between the natural law and the New Law in that it is neither the law of grace nor merely the law of nature (since it prepares for and foreshadows Christ).

24. Following Gal 3:24, Aquinas frequently describes the Old Law as a "pedagogue" (see 1–2, q.91, a.5).

25. Aquinas cites Jer 31:31, 33: "Behold the days shall come, saith the Lord; and I will perfect unto the house of Israel, and unto the house of Juda, a new testament. . . . For this is the testament which I will make to

the house of Israel. . . . I will give my laws into their mind, and in their heart will I write them" (1–2, q.106, a.1, *sed contra*).

26. Aquinas cites Rom 8:3–4: "what the Law could not do in that it was weak through the flesh, God sent His own Son, . . .that the justification of the Law might be fulfilled in us" (1–2, q.98, a.6). Since the Old Law outlines the way in which people may act justly but does not itself embody the inner principle of grace necessary for people to act justly, the Old Law directs people toward recognizing their need for the New Law (see 1–2, q.98, a.2, ad 3). The Old Law also, by setting forth precepts that both declare what should be done and establish punishment for those who fail to do what should be done (an example given by Aquinas is the punishment of stoning for idolatry [see 1–2, q.105, a.2, ad 9]), helped make people just by means of the force of law. In this sense, Aquinas notes that because in the divine pedagogical plan the Old Law was "given to men who were imperfect," the Old Law "was called the *law of fear*, inasmuch as it induced men to observe its commandments by threatening them with penalties, and is spoken of as containing temporal promises" (1–2, q.107, a.1, ad 2).

27. Adoptive sonship in the Son does not mean that human beings, in the state of glory, are placed in the Son's unique relationship to the Father. Rather, adoptive sonship is to the whole Trinity. On the other hand, the *incarnate* Son mediates this relationship of glorified human beings to the whole Trinity, so in this sense human beings are said to enjoy beatitude "in the Son." For elaboration of this point, see H. P. C. Lyons, S. J., "The Grace of Sonship," *Ephemerides theologicae Lovanienses* 27 (1951): 438–466.

28. 1–2, q.98, a.5, ad 3.

29. 1–2, q.99, a.6.

30. 1–2, q.98, a.5, ad 2.

31. 1–2, q.106, a.3.

32. 1–2, q.105, a.1, *sed contra*.

33. 1–2, q.100, a.5.

34. 1–2, q.105, a.2, obj.1 and 4. In his response to obj.1, Aquinas notes that Dt 23:24 ends with the injunction (not cited in the objection) that the person eating the fruit of the vineyard may *not* also bring a basket to fill up. The point of the objection remains valid, however.

35. The commandments to love God and to love neighbor are found in Dt 6:5 and Lv 19:18, respectively (see 1–2, q.107, obj.2).

36. Aquinas uses this phrase to describe the end of human law (1–2, q.98, a.1).

37. 1–2, q.105, a.2, ad 1.

38. 1–2, q.105, a.2, ad 4.

39. See 1–2, q.98, a.1.

40. Aquinas uses this phrase in 1–2, q.98, a.4; similarly, in 1–2, q.98, a.5, he refers to Israel's "prerogative of holiness."

41. Aquinas generally explains the fact that Israel is not itself the "end" but is striving toward the "end" in terms of the relationship of the imperfect to the perfect. He states, "In things ordained to an end, there is perfect goodness when a thing is such that it is sufficient in itself to conduce to the end: while there is imperfect goodness when a thing is of some assistance in attaining the end, but is not sufficient for the realization thereof" (1–2, q.98, a.1). Israel's community is to be understood in the latter way.

42. 1–2, q.98, a.4.

43. 1–2, q.92, a.1.

44. 1–2, q.90, a.3, ad 1.

45. Aquinas believes that Christ is the redeemer of all humankind, so he does not try to imagine an Israel abstracted from its ordering to Christ. This does not rule out dialogue with Jewish theologians, since the prophets also point to a coming Messiah, even if Jewish theologians do not consider this promise to have been fulfilled as yet. The claim that the Messiah has come does not mean that God has "abandoned" the Jewish people, or his covenant with the Jewish people, since the time of Christ. Neither does it mean that the practices of Jewish faith have no value. But it does mean that the Messiah, as Jewish theologians would expect, is (having come) the center of salvation history and the source of ultimate salvation for all people.

46. As we have seen, Aquinas argues in 3, q.47, a.2, ad 1, that Christ fulfills the Old Law by his passion. It is significant, therefore, that 3, q.47, a.2, asks "Whether Christ Died Out of *Obedience?*" (emphasis added).

47. The Mystical Body shows how Christ's fulfillment of the law is also the fulfillment of the Temple. Employing the neoscholastic language of "objective" and "subjective" redemption, Emilio Sauras, O. P., makes somewhat the same point. See his "Thomist Soteriology and the Mystical Body," *Thomist* 15 (1952): 543–571.

48. Aquinas holds that Christ does, in fact, fulfill the letter of the law as well (see 1–2, q.107, a.2).

49. This is not to say, of course, that Christ's fulfillment of the judicial precepts is not prefigured in the Old Testament. On the contrary, Aquinas cites a number of texts that he thinks prefigure Christ in this way, such as Is 53:4: "Surely he hath carried our sorrows"; Lam 1:12: "O all ye that pass by the way attend, and see if there be any sorrow like unto my sorrow"; and Jer 12:7: "I have given my dear soul into the hands of her enemies" (3, q.46, a.6).

50. We should emphasize again that Aquinas holds that divine law, although twofold (Old and New), has one "end": "The unity of faith under both Testaments witnesses to the unity of end" (1–2, q.107, a.1, ad 2).

51. 1–2, q.108, a.4, *sed contra*.

52. St. Augustine, *De Trinitate*, Book 4: cited by Aquinas in 3, q.48, a.3.

53. 1–2, q.104, a.3, ad 3.

54. 3, q.7, aa. 1, 9, 10. Aquinas cites Jn 1:16: "And of his fulness we have all received, and grace for grace" (3, q.7, a.1). When he states that Christ (as God or, instrumentally, as man) gives grace, he always means that Christ's merits and satisfaction enable the Holy Spirit to initiate the *reditus* of the believer to the Trinity (see 3, q.8, a.1, ad 1).

55. 3, q.7, a.2. See also 2–2, q.24, aa.3 and 4, where Aquinas describes the infusion of charity. In a.4 he notes that the quantity of charity "depends, not on any natural virtue, but on the sole grace of the Holy Ghost Who infuses charity."

56. Aquinas holds that Christ merits his bodily resurrection because "Divine Justice" will "exalt them who humble themselves for God's sake" (3, q.53, a.1; cf. 3, q.19, a.4; 3, q.53, a.4, ad 2).

57. That is, Christ's fulfillment of the Torah.

58. Christ's grace of headship, and the corresponding reality of his Mystical Body, are discussed in 3, q.8. See also Fernando Ocáriz, "La elevación sobrenatural como re-creación en Cristo," in *Prospettive teologiche moderne*, Studi Tomistici 13:4 (Vatican City: Libreria Editrice Vaticana, 1981), 281–292, and José Antonio Riestra, "El influjo de Cristo en la gloria de los santos," in *Prospettive teologiche moderne*, Studi Tomistici 13:4 (Vatican City: Libreria Editrice Vaticana, 1981), 232–240.

59. 3, q.8, a.3.

60. 1–2, q.106, a.1.

61. Aquinas explains the nature of a "sacrament" in 3, q.60. He argues that a sacrament is a sensible sign that always signifies three things: "the very cause of our sanctification, which is Christ's passion; the form of our sanctification, which is grace and the virtues; and the ultimate end of our sanctification, which is eternal life" (3, q.60, a.3). In 1–2, q.101, a.4, he argues that the ceremonies of the Old Law should be divided into four categories: sacrifices, sacred things, sacraments, and observances. The "sacraments" of the Old Law, in this technical sense, refer only to "a sort of consecration either of the people or of the ministers." On the other hand, when treating of the sacraments of the New Law, Aquinas applies a less technical sense of "sacrament" to the Old Law. In 3, q.61, a.3, therefore, he includes such things as the sacrifice of the Paschal Lamb among the "sacraments" of the Old Law.

62. 3, q.61, a.1. See also 3, q.60, a.4; 3, q.61, a.4, ad 1, and elsewhere. By emphasizing this principle, Aquinas is able to show that sacraments belong to the divine *pedagogy*, which takes account of the order of creation. He notes that because "Divine wisdom provides for each thing according to its mode," it was most fitting that sacraments be given to human beings, whose intellects "acquire knowledge of the intelligible from the sensible" (3, q.60, a.4).

63. 3, q.61, a.4.

64. 3, q.61, a.1, *sed contra*. The text comes from *Contra Faustum*, Book 19.

65. 3, q.61, a.4.

66. The importance of sacramental grace—the power of the sacraments to cause and to deepen the "new creation" that enables the human being to enjoy *friendship* with God—is emphasized by Charles B. Crowley, O.P., "The Role of Sacramental Grace in Christian Life," *Thomist* 3 (1940): 519–545. Crowley draws especially upon the thought of John of St. Thomas.

67. 3, q.62, a.6.

68. 3, q.61, a.3.

69. 1–2, q.101, a.2, ad 1. Aquinas holds that among the people of Israel, as among the members of the Church, the degree of explicit faith varied among individuals. In both Israel and the Church, the learned are expected to have more explicit faith (see 2–2, qq.6–8).

70. 2–2, q.3.

71. 3, q.62, a.4 (see also a.3).

72. 3, q.62, a.5.

73. 3, q.62, a.5; see also 3, q.64, a.3. As an analogy, Aquinas suggests the relationship of the hand (a "united instrument") to a stick (a "separate instrument"). In emphasizing the importance of Christ's passion, Aquinas is not ignoring Christ's resurrection. Rather, as he explains in 3, q.62, a.5, ad 3, "Justification is ascribed to the Resurrection by reason of the term *whither*, which is newness of life through grace. But it is ascribed to the Passion by reason of the term *whence*, i.e. in regard to the forgiveness of sin."

74. 3, q.62, a.1. The causality of the sacraments is instrumental, since only God can be the "principal" cause of grace. However, an instrumental cause can be an efficient cause. Thus the sacraments can be said to cause grace directly or efficiently.

75. 3, q.62, a.2.

76. Aquinas describes this action succinctly in 3, q.62, a.1, ad 2, where he states that "the corporeal sacraments by their operation, which they exercise on the body that they touch, accomplish through the Divine

institution an instrumental operation on the soul; for example, the water of baptism, in respect of its proper power, cleanses the body, and thereby, inasmuch as it is the instrument of the Divine power, cleanses the soul: since from soul and body one thing is made." The spiritual action of the Word through the corporeal element is signified, Aquinas notes, by the fact that certain words are required to be used in performing each sacrament (3, q.60, aa.6–8).

77. 3, q.63. The word "character" is the same in Latin and English.

78. For insight into Aquinas's conception of the distinction between baptism and confirmation, see B.-M. Perrin, "Le caractère de la confirmation chez saint Thomas," *Revue Thomiste* 98 (1998): 225–265.

79. 3, q.63, aa.3, 5. Using a definition developed by St. Albert, Aquinas states, "Some define character thus: A character is a distinctive mark printed in a man's rational soul by the eternal Character, whereby the created trinity [i.e. the *imago dei*] is sealed with the likeness of the creating and re-creating Trinity, and distinguishing him from those who are not so enlikened, according to the state of faith" (3, q.63, a.3, *sed contra*). It is worth emphasizing that for Aquinas, the primary aspect of being conformed to the "figure" or "character" of Christ is sharing in the worship that the slain and victorious Lamb offers to the Father: the eternal liturgy lies at the heart of Aquinas's vision, in the same way as it does for many of the Eastern Fathers.

80. 3, q.63, aa.2, 6. Thus although the sacrament of ordination provides a special character, baptism also provides a character, so one can speak of the "universal priesthood of believers." The universal priesthood of believers, however, represents a passive or receptive power. For further elucidation of this point, see Gilles Emery, O.P., "Le sacerdoce spirituel des fidèles chez saint Thomas d'Aquin." Emery places the priesthood of all believers in the context of the participation of believers, through the grace of the Holy Spirit, in Christ's threefold office.

81. Aquinas points out that since "the power of the sacrament is from God alone, it follows that God alone can institute the sacraments" (3, q.64, a.2). From this he concludes that "those things that are essential to the sacrament, are instituted by Christ Himself, Who is God and man" (3, q.64, a.2, ad 1).

82. This is true even though baptism is the most necessary sacrament, as the means of entrance into the Christian life, since baptism restores the *imago dei* by taking away every sin through initiating the person into sacramental participation in the power of Christ's passion. Incorporated by baptism into the life of grace, the newly baptized person no longer suffers

from the impediments of sin that previously obstructed the full interior working of the Holy Spirit (3, q.65, a.3; q.69, a.1; cf. q.69, a.7).

83. 3, q.73, a.3; see also q.68, a.2. In the latter article, Aquinas states that in certain cases "God, Whose power is not tied to visible sacraments, sanctifies man inwardly."

84. 3, q.65, a.3.

85. On this topic, see especially Martin Morard, "L'Eucharistie, clé de voûte de l'organisme sacramental chez saint Thomas d'Aquin," *Revue Thomiste* 95 (1995): 217–250.

86. 3, q.73, a.5, ad 1. For analysis of the connection between Christ's passion and the Eucharist, see Thierry-Dominique Humbrecht, O.P., "L'Eucharistie, 'représentation' du sacrifice du Christ, selon saint Thomas," *Revue Thomiste* 98 (1998): 355–386.

87. On charity as friendship with God, see Guy Mansini, O.S.B., "*Similitudo, Communicatio*, and the Friendship of Charity in Aquinas," in *Thomistica*, ed. E. Manning (Leuven: Peeters, 1995): 1–26; Anthony W. Keaty, "Thomas's Authority for Identifying Charity as Friendship: Aristotle or John 15?" *Thomist* 62 (1998): 581–601; and Fergus Kerr, O.P., "Charity as Friendship," in *Language, Meaning and God*, ed. Brian Davies, O.P. (London: Geoffrey Chapman, 1987), 1–23.

88. 3, q.73, a.5.

89. For further reflection on this theme, see Gilles Emery, O.P., "Le fruit ecclésial de l'Eucharistie chez saint Thomas d'Aquin," *Nova et Vetera* 72 (1997): 25–40.

90. Bader-Saye, *Church and Israel after Christendom*, 140.

91. 3, q.83, a.1.

92. This point indicates once again the unity between Aquinas's conception of the fulfillment of Torah and his conception of the fulfillment of the Temple.

93. 3, q.61, a.1, *sed contra*.

94. 3, q.64, a.2, ad 2.

95. In 2–2, q.1, aa.1 and 2, Aquinas emphasizes that the object of faith is God, not propositions about God. Nonetheless, propositions about God play an important role in elucidating the "material object" of faith, since a "thing known is in the knower according to the mode of the knower" (2–2, q.1, a.2).

96. See 2–2, q.1, a.9, *sed contra* and ad 5; and elsewhere.

97. 2–2, q.1, a.10. On Aquinas's view of the papacy, see Serge-Thomas Bonino, O.P., "La place du pape dans l'Église selon saint Thomas d'Aquin," *Revue Thomiste* 86 (1986): 392–422. The unity of the Church extends to

the glorified Mystical Body, although in heaven no ecclesial hierarchy will be needed. Human companionship does not add anything to the vision of God, but nonetheless beatitude should not be conceived apart from this unity. This point has been excellently made by R. C. Petry in "The Social Character of Heavenly Beatitude According to the Thought of St. Thomas Aquinas," *Thomist* 7 (1944): 65–79.

6 The Heavenly Jerusalem

1. *Sacrosanctum Concilium*, #8. Cited in the *Catechism of the Catholic Church*, #1090.

2. On the anagogical sense, see 1, q.1, a.10; for an example of the method, see 1–2, q.102, a.2.

3. Cited in 1, q.1, a.10. The quote is from the *Celestial Hierarchy*, although Pseudo-Dionysius makes the same point in *Ecclesiastical Hierarchy*, from which Aquinas quotes in 1–2, q.106, a.4, ad 1.

4. 1–2, q. 103, a.3. Aquinas makes the same point in 1–2, q.106, a.4, ad 1, where he is addressing the issue of whether the New Law will last until the end of the world: "there is a threefold state of mankind; the first was under the Old Law; the second is that of the New Law; the third will take place not in this life, but in heaven. But as the first state is figurative and imperfect in comparison with the state of the Gospel; so is the present state figurative and imperfect in comparison with the heavenly state, with the advent of which the present state will be done away as expressed in that very passage (1 Cor. 13:12): *We see now through a glass in a dark manner; but then face to face.*" See also his threefold description of "spiritual regeneration" in his *Commentary on the Gospel of John*, Part 1, Chapter 3, Lecture 1. Spiritual regeneration exists imperfectly and symbolically in the Old Law, imperfectly and evidently in the New Law, and perfectly and evidently in the state of glory.

5. 1–2, q.103, a.3, ad 1.

6. The continuity between the state of the Old Law, the state of the New Law, and the state of glory is shown by the reality that Christ's priesthood is eternal. On this point, see Denis Chardonnens, O. C. D., "Éternité du sacerdoce du Christ et effet eschatologique de l'Eucharistie," *Revue Thomiste* 99 (1999): 159–180.

7. See Jean-Pierre Torrell, O. P., *Saint Thomas Aquinas*, vol. 1, *The Person and His Work*, trans. Robert Royal (Washington, DC: Catholic University of America Press, 1996), 289. Torrell notes that Aquinas had been experiencing contemplative ecstasies during this period (284–289).

8. Pesch, *Thomas von Aquin*, 189–190.

9. Ibid., 189; see also Torrell, *Saint Thomas Aquinas*, vol. 1, 333. We will cite the *Commentary on the Sentences* directly.

10. Otto Pesch notes that we can address the question of how Aquinas would have modified his treatise only on a case-by-case basis. In Pesch's view, the Supplement remains a valuable source for understanding Aquinas's thought and influence (Pesch, *Thomas von Aquin*, 189–190). For discussion of Aquinas's account of the state of glory, see William J. Hoye, *Actualitas Omnium Actuum: Man's Beatific Vision of God as Apprehended by Thomas Aquinas* (Meisenheim am Glan: Verlag Anton Hain, 1975); Jean-Pierre Torrell, "La vision de Dieu 'per essentiam' selon saint Thomas d'Aquin," *Micrologus* 5 (1997): 43–68; Montague Brown, "Aquinas on the Resurrection of the Body," *Thomist* 56 (1992): 165–207; and Carlo Leget, *Living with God: Thomas Aquinas on the Relation between Life on Earth and "Life" after Death* (Leuven: Peeters, 1997). On the *imago dei*, see Torrell, *Saint Thomas d'Aquin, maître spirituel*, 105ff.

11. See Simon Tugwell, O. P., *Human Immortality and the Redemption of Death* (Springfield, IL: Templegate, 1990), 145–155. Tugwell notes that in Aquinas's "*Compendium [of Theology]*, as in the commentary on the Sentences, Thomas still feels obliged to say that beatitude is incomplete until the soul is reunited with the body" (150). In the *Compendium*, Aquinas offers arguments for this position that further develop those in the *Commentary on the Sentences:* "final perfection presupposes the 'first perfection' of being complete according to the nature of what you are, and, in the case of human beings, that means being bodily, since a disembodied human soul is not a complete human being. So man's final beatitude requires that the soul should be reunited with the body" (150). In the *Summa Theologiae* (1–2, q.4, a.5, and 3, q.59, a.5), in contrast, Aquinas argues that the beatified separated soul already enjoys perfect beatitude, since beatitude is a spiritual perfection proper to the soul. Even here, however, Aquinas finds a place for the body: "Thomas makes a distinction between what is necessary for something to exist and what is necessary for its bene esse. A soul is necessary for a human being to exist at all; it is necessary in the first sense. Good looks and quick wits are not necessary in this sense, but they do contribute to human *bene esse*. It is only in this weaker sense that the body is necessary for beatitude" (152). The issues that Tugwell raises are important, but they are not the ones that I wish to pursue in this chapter. This chapter will explore Aquinas's account of eternal life in terms of the liturgical fulfillment of the Temple.

12. Richard Bauckham and Trevor Hart, *Hope against Hope: Christian Eschatology at the Turn of the Millennium* (Grand Rapids, MI: Eerdmans, 1999), 178.

13. Ibid., 179.

14. Cf. the title of Catherine Pickstock, *After Writing: On the Liturgical Consummation of Philosophy* (Oxford: Blackwell, 1998).

15. Pesch, *Thomas von Aquin*, 192–195.

16. *Commentary on the Sentences*, in Robert Busa, S. J., ed., *S. Thomae Aquinatis Opera Omnia*, vol. 1 (Stuttgart: Frommann-Holzboog, 1980), IV, dist.43, q.1, a.3, q.la 1; cf. Suppl., q.77, a.1.

17. On this topic, he cites Augustine's *De Trinitate*, Book III, ch.4.

18. *Commentary on the Sentences*, IV, dist.43, q.1, a.3, q.la 1; cf. Suppl., q.77, a.1.

19. Aquinas makes two exceptions to this rule about higher and lower bodies rising together at the end of time: Christ and the Virgin Mary. Although he never discusses it at length, he accepts the tradition of the Virgin Mary's bodily assumption into heaven. In treating the Virgin Mary's sanctification, for example, he takes as evidence for her sanctification in the womb the fact that she was assumed bodily into heaven. He attributes this argument to Augustine, although modern scholarship has concluded that the tractate in fact belongs to a later author. See 3, q.27, a.1; cf. 3, q.25, a.5, obj.1, *Commentary on the Sentences*, IV, dist.43, q.1, a.3, q.la 1, and 3, q.27, a.5. Her bodily assumption is a "special privilege of grace" and flows (like the resurrection of all human beings) from the efficacy of Christ's resurrection. Aquinas handles Mt 27:52, which implies that certain saints of the Old Testament rose from their graves before Christ's resurrection, with caution. While suggesting that these saints may have been truly resurrected (rather than simply resuscitated), he notes: "It must, however, be observed that, although the Gospel mentions their resurrection before Christ's, we must take this statement as made in anticipation, as is often the case with writers of history. For none rose again with a true resurrection before Christ, since He is the *firstfruits of them that sleep* (1 Cor. 15:20)" (*Commentary on the Sentences*, IV, dist.43, q.1, a.3, q.la 1; cf. Suppl., q.77, a.1, ad 3). Aquinas's comment about the methods of writers of history should not be overlooked.

20. *Commentary on the Sentences*, IV, dist.43, q.1, a.2, q.la 2; cf. Suppl., q.76, a.2. Aquinas notes that this interpretation derives from Gregory the Great's *Moralia*; it is also the position taken by Albert in his *Commentary on the Sentences*.

21. Ibid.

22. *Commentary on the Sentences*, IV, dist.43, q.1, a.1, q.la 1; cf. Suppl., q.75, a.1; on the nature of happiness or beatitude, see 1–2, qq.1–5, especially q.4, aa.5–6, where Aquinas shows that perfection of the body, while not necessary for happiness in a strict sense (since the separated soul may

enjoy the beatific vision, which suffices for happiness), is necessary for human happiness to be in all ways perfect. See also the discussion in Tugwell, *Human Immortality.*

23. *Commentary on the Sentences,* IV, dist.43, q.1, a.1, q.la 2; cf. Suppl., q.75, a.2, ad 3.

24. See *Commentary on the Sentences,* IV, dist.43, q.1, a.1, q.la 3 (Suppl., q.75, a.3), where Aquinas explains that resurrection is not a natural occurrence, even though it fulfills a natural dynamism of the rational creature.

25. 3, q.8, a.3.

26. Ibid.

27. Ibid.; see also *Commentary on the Sentences,* IV, dist.46, q.1, a.3 (Suppl., q.99, a.1), where Aquinas (following Augustine) explains that "sin renders a person worthy to be altogether cut off from the fellowship of God's city, and this is the effect of every sin committed against charity, which is the bond uniting this same city together."

28. *Commentary on the Sentences,* IV, dist.48, q.1, a.3; cf. Suppl., q.90, a.3.

29. 3, q.59, aa.2, 4.

30. *Commentary on the Sentences,* IV, dist.47, q.1, a.2, q.la 1; cf. Suppl., q.89, a.1.

31. These saints will be those who, like Christ, lived humbly and chose voluntary poverty. Aquinas notes that "of all things that make man contemptible in this world poverty [*paupertas*] is the chief: and for this reason the excellence of judicial power is promised to the poor, so that he who humbles himself for Christ's sake shall be exalted." See *Commentary on the Sentences,* IV, dist.47, q.1, a.2, q.la 2; cf. Suppl., q.89, a.2.

32. *Commentary on the Sentences,* IV, dist.47, q.1, a.2, q.la 2; cf. Suppl., q.89, a.2, ad 4 and 3, q.59, a.3.

33. On this difficult subject, see *Commentary on the Sentences,* IV, dist.50, q.2, a.4; cf. Suppl., q.94. Many people naturally recoil at the idea that the blessed do not *pity* the damned. This reaction involves a misunderstanding of the nature of charity. Charity is not an emotion. Rather, charity is rational love of the good. Those who reject Christ's love and thereby choose freely to remain in original sin (i.e., in a state of disordered will, turned away from love), are lovable not for the disordered condition of their wills but for the goodness of their existence, which even the damned retain. The blessed continue to love this created good in the damned, but they do not love the *lack* of good that characterizes disordered wills.

34. *Commentary on the Sentences,* IV, dist.44, q.1, a.1, q.la 2; cf. Suppl., q.79, a.2.

35. *Commentary on the Sentences*, IV, dist.44, q.1, a.3, q.la 1; cf. Suppl., q.81, a.1.

36. *Commentary on the Sentences*, IV, dist.44, q.1, a.3, q.la 2; cf. Suppl., q.81, a.2. Aquinas also affirms that the distinction between male and female will remain in eternal life but that the hierarchical relationship between male and female, as Aquinas conceived of it, will no longer hold. He states, "Woman is subject to man on account of the frailty of nature, as regards both vigor of soul and strength of body. After the resurrection, however, the difference in those points will be not on account of the difference of sex, but by reason of the difference of merits" (*Commentary on the Sentences*, IV, dist.44, q.1, a.3, q.la 3; cf. Suppl., q.81, a.3, ad 2).

37. *Commentary on the Sentences*, IV, dist.44, q.2, a.1, q.la 3; cf. Suppl., q.82, a.3.

38. *Commentary on the Sentences*, IV, dist.44, q.2, a.1, q.la 4; cf. Suppl., q.82, a.4.

39. *Commentary on the Sentences*, IV, dist.44, q.2, a.1, q.la 1; cf. Suppl., q.82, a.1, especially ad 2.

40. Ibid.; cf. Suppl., q.82, a.1, ad 5.

41. *Commentary on the Sentences*, IV, dist.44, q.2, a.2, q.la 1, *sed contra*; cf. Suppl., q.83, a.1, *sed contra*.

42. *Commentary on the Sentences*, IV, dist.44, q.2, a.2; cf. Suppl., q.83, aa.1–5. Aquinas notes that by divine power (i.e. a miracle), two bodies can be in the same place. As examples, he gives the miracle of the risen Christ's entering through closed doors and the miracle of the Virgin Mary's perpetual virginity (q.la 3).

43. *Commentary on the Sentences*, IV, dist.44, q.2, a.3, q.la 1; cf. Suppl., q.84, a.1.

44. *Commentary on the Sentences*, IV, dist.44, q.2, a.3, q.la 2; cf. Suppl., q.84, a.2.

45. *Commentary on the Sentences*, IV, dist.44, q.2, a.4, q.la 1, *sed contra* (Suppl., q.85, a.1, *sed contra*); see also *Commentary on the Sentences*, IV, dist.44, q.2, a.3, q.la 2, *sed contra* (Suppl., q.84, a.2, *sed contra*).

46. *Commentary on the Sentences*, IV, dist.44, q.2, a.4, q.la 1; cf. Suppl., q.85, a.1.

47. Ibid., cf. Suppl., q.85, a.1, ad 2.

48. *Commentary on the Sentences*, IV, dist.44, q.2, a.4, q.la 2; cf. Suppl., q.85, a.2, ad 2.

49. *Commentary on the Sentences*, IV, dist.48, q.2, a.1, *sed contra*; cf. Suppl., q.91, a.1, *sed contra*.

50. *Commentary on the Sentences*, IV, dist.48, q.2, a.1; cf. Suppl., q.91, a.1.

51. Ibid.

52. Alasdair MacIntyre, *Dependent Rational Animals: Why Human Beings Need the Virtues* (Chicago: Open Court, 1999).

53. *Commentary on the Sentences*, IV, dist.48, q.2, a.1; cf. Suppl., q.91, a.1, ad 5.

54. *Commentary on the Sentences*, IV, dist.48, q.2, aa.3–4; cf. Suppl., q.91, aa.3–4.

55. *Commentary on the Sentences*, IV, dist.48, q.2, a.2; cf. Suppl., q.91, a.2.

56. *Commentary on the Sentences*, IV, dist.48, q.2, a.5; cf. Suppl., q.91, a.5.

57. Ibid.

58. On this topic, see Torrell, "La vision de Dieu." Aquinas discusses the Persons in relation to the essence at various points. He devotes 1, q.39 to this issue. As he notes in 1, q.39, a.1, "in creatures relations are accidental, whereas in God they are the divine essence itself. Thence it follows that in God essence is not really distinct from person; and yet that the persons are really distinguished from each other. For person, as above stated (q.29, a.4), signifies relation as subsisting in the divine nature. But relation as referred to the essence does not differ therefrom really, but only in our way of thinking; while as referred to an opposite relation, it has a real distinction by virtue of that opposition." The vision of the divine essence is not different from the vision of the divine processions, although the divine processions are really distinct from each other.

59. See 1, q.12, aa.1, 2, 4–6. A. N. Williams has argued persuasively that Aquinas's account of the beatific vision corresponds to the meaning of deification or theosis among Eastern Orthodox theologians (Williams, *The Ground of Union*, 159–160).

60. 1, q.12, a.2.

61. Ibid.

62. 1, q.12, a.2, ad 3; see also a.4.

63. 1, q.12, a.7, ad 2.

64. 1, q.12, a.4.

65. Ibid.

66. 1, q.12, a.5; see also 1–2, q.110.

67. 1, q.12, a.5, ad 2.

68. For further discussion of this point, see Williams, *The Ground of Union*.

69. 1, q.12, a.6.

70. This point is emphasized by Williams, *The Ground of Union*, 39.

71. 3, q.23, a.1.

72. 3, q.22, a.5, ad 1.
73. Ibid.
74. See 3, q.26.

Conclusion

1. Pope Pius XII, *Mystici Corporis*, #80; translation cited from *The Papal Encyclicals*, vol. 4: 1939–1958, ed. Claudia Carlin Ihm (Raleigh, NC: McGrath Publishing, 1981), 53.

2. A. N. Williams, *The Ground of Union*.

3. N. T. Wright, *The Climax of the Covenant: Christ and the Law in Pauline Theology* (Minneapolis, MN: Fortress Press, 1992), 262, 266. Wright argues against "two-covenant" models of salvation, which hold that God institutes one covenant for the salvation of Jews and another covenant for the salvation of Gentiles. Two-covenant models fail to account for the claim, made by the entire New Testament, that Jesus is the Messiah of Israel who fulfills God's covenants with Israel and extends them to the nations. On the other hand, it cannot be emphasized too strongly that "fulfillment" theories, such as that of Aquinas, require *neither* the revoking of the earlier covenants *nor* the view that those who continue to follow the Mosaic Law, as most Jews have done, are now outside of God's plan for salvation. As we have seen, while affirming that God saves humankind through Christ Jesus, Aquinas does not limit "through Christ Jesus" only to those who explicitly confess faith in Christ. The scandal of particularity cannot be avoided either by Judaism, which affirms that Israel is God's elect people, or by Christianity.

4. Valkenberg, *Words of the Living God*, 208.

5. See the *pars secunda secundae* of the *Summa Theologiae*.

Bibliography

Primary

Abelard, Peter. *Ethical Writings: Ethics and Dialogue between a Philosopher, a Jew, and a Christian* (c.1136). Trans. Paul Vincent Spade. Indianapolis, IN: Hackett, 1995.

———. *Opera Theologica.* Ed. Eligius M. Buytaert. Corpus Christianorum 11. Vol. 1: *Commentaria in Epistolam Pauli ad Romanos; Apologia contra Bernardum.* Turnholt: Typographi Brepols Editores Pontificii, 1969.

Albert the Great. *Opera Omnia.* Vol. 21, Part 1: *Super Matthaeum.* Ed. Bernhard Schmidt. Münster: Aschendorff, 1987.

———. *Opera Omnia.* Vol. 24: *Ennarationes in Joannem.* Ed. A. Borgnet and E. Borgnet. Paris: 1899.

———. *Opera Omnia.* Vol. 28: *Commentarium in III Sententiarum.* Ed. A. Borgnet. Paris: 1894.

Alexander of Hales. *Summa Theologica seu "Summa Fratris Alexandri."* 4 vols. Florence: Collegii S. Bonaventurae, 1924–1948.

Anselm of Canterbury. *Why God Became Man.* Trans. Joseph M. Colleran. New York: Magi Books, 1969.

Aquinas, Thomas. *Commentary on the Book of Causes.* Trans. Vincent A. Guagliardo et al. Washington, DC: Catholic University of America Press, 1996.

———. *Commentary on the Gospel of John.* Part I. Trans. James A. Weisheipl and Fabian R. Larcher. Albany, NY: Magi Books, 1980.

———. *Commentary on the Gospel of John.* Part II. Trans. James A. Weisheipl and Fabian R. Larcher. Petersham, MA: St. Bede's Publications, 1999.

———. *S. Thomae Aquinatis Opera Omnia.* Ed. Robert Busa, S. J. 6 vols. Stuttgart: Frommann-Holzboog, 1980.

————. *Summa Theologica.* 5 vols. Trans. Fathers of the English Dominican Province. Westminster, MD: Christian Classics, 1981 [reprint of 1920 edition].

————. *Summa Theologiae.* 3 vols. Ed. Petrus Caramello. Turin: Marietti, 1952.

Bernard of Clairvaux. *Life and Works of St. Bernard.* 2 vols. Trans. and ed. Dom John Mabillon, O. S. B., and Samuel J. Eales. London: Burns & Oates, 1889–1896.

Bonaventure. *Disputed Questions on the Mystery of the Trinity.* Trans. Zachary Hayes, O. F. M. St. Bonaventure, NY: Franciscan Institute of St. Bonaventure University, 1979.

————. *Opera Omnia.* Vol. 3: *Commentarium in III Sententiarum.* Rome: Quaracchi, 1882.

————. *Opera Omnia.* Vol. 6: *Commentarii in Sacram Scripturam.* Rome: Quaracchi, 1893.

Fairweather, Eugene R., ed. *A Scholastic Miscellany: Anselm to Ockham.* Philadelphia: Westminster, 1956.

Gratian. *The Treatise on Laws (Decretum dd.1–20) with the Ordinary Gloss.* Trans. Augustine Thompson, O. P., and James Gordley. Washington, DC: Catholic University of America Press, 1993.

Grosseteste, Robert. *De Cessatione Legalium* (1231). Ed. Richard C. Dales and Edward B. King. London: Oxford University Press, 1986.

Lombard, Peter. *Opera Omnia.* Patrologiae Latinae. Vols. 191–192: *Collectanea in Omnes D. Pauli Apostoli Epistolas* (1140). Ed. J.-P. Migne. Paris: 1854–1855.

————. *Sententiae in IV libris distinctae.* Vol. 2, books 3–4. Ed. Ignatius Brady, O. F. M. Rome: Editiones Collegii S. Bonaventurae ad Claras Aquas, 1981.

Maimonides, Moses. *The Guide for the Perplexed.* Trans. (from the original Arabic text) M. Friedlander. 2nd ed. New York: Dover, 1956.

Secondary

Aertsen, J. A. "Aquinas and the Classical Heritage: A Response to Arvin Vos." In *Christianity and the Classics.* Ed. Wendy E. Helleman. New York: University Press of America, 1990: 83–89.

————. "Beauty in the Middle Ages: A Forgotten Transcendental?" In *Medieval Philosophy and Theology.* Vol. 1. Ed. Mark D. Jordan et al. Notre Dame, IN: University of Notre Dame Press, 1991: 68–97.

———. "Natural Law in the Light of the Doctrine of Transcendentals." In *Lex et Libertas*. Studi Tomistici 30. Ed. Leo Elders and K. Hedwig. Vatican City: Libreria Editrice Vaticana, 1987: 99–112.

———. *Nature and Creature: St. Thomas Aquinas's Way of Thought*. Trans. H. D. Morton. Leiden: E. J. Brill, 1988.

Aillet, Marc. *Lire la Bible avec S. Thomas: Le passage de la littera à la res dans la Somme Theologique*. Fribourg: Éditions Universitaires, 1993.

Akinwale, Anthony, O.P. *The Theology of the Passion of Christ in St. Thomas Aquinas and Its Possible Relevance to Liberation Theology*. Dissertation, Boston College, 1996.

Arias Reyero, Maximino. *Thomas von Aquin als Exeget: Die Prinzipien seiner Schriftdeutung und seine Lehre von den Schriftsinnen*. Einsiedeln: Johannes Verlag, 1971.

Aubert, Jean-Marie. *Loi de Dieu, loi des hommes*. Paris: Desclée, 1964.

———. "Nature de la relation entre 'Lex Nova' et 'Lex Naturalis' chez Saint Thomas d'Aquin." In *Morale e diritto nella prospettiva tomistica*. Studi Tomistici 15:6. Vatican City: Libreria Editrice Vaticana, 1982: 34–38.

Aulén, Gustav. *Christus Victor*. Trans. A. G. Hebert. New York: Macmillan, 1979.

Ayesta, Cruz Gonzalez. *El don de sabiduria según santo Tomas: Divinización, filiación y connaturalidad*. Pamplona: Eunsa, 1999.

Bäck, Allan. "Aquinas on the Incarnation." *New Scholasticism* 56 (1982): 127–145.

Backes, Ignaz. *Die Christologie des hl. Thomas von Aquin und die griechischen Kirchenväter*. Paderborn: Ferdinand Schöningh Verlag, 1931.

Badcock, Gary D. *Light of Truth and Fire of Love: A Theology of the Holy Spirit*. Grand Rapids, MI: Eerdmans, 1997.

Bader-Saye, Scott. *Church and Israel after Christendom: The Politics of Election*. Boulder, CO: Westview Press, 1999.

Bailleux, Emile. "A l'image du Fils premier-né." *Revue Thomiste* 76 (1976): 181–207.

Balthasar, Hans Urs von. *Explorations in Theology*. Vol. 1: *The Word Made Flesh*. Trans. A. V. Littledale and Alexander Dru. San Francisco: Ignatius Press, 1989.

———. "*Fides Christi*: An Essay on the Consciousness of Christ." Trans. Edward T. Oakes, S.J. In *Explorations in Theology*. Vol. 2: *Spouse of the Word*. San Francisco: Ignatius Press, 1991: 43–79.

———. *The Glory of the Lord: A Theological Aesthetics*. Vol. 6: *Theology: The Old Covenant*. Trans. Erasmo Leiva-Merikakis and Brian McNeil, C.R.V. San Francisco: Ignatius Press, 1991.

————. *The Glory of the Lord: A Theological Aesthetics*. Vol. 7: *Theology: The New Covenant*. Trans. Brian McNeil, C.R.V. San Francisco: Ignatius Press, 1989.

————. *Mysterium Paschale*. Trans. Aidan Nichols, O.P. Grand Rapids, MI: Eerdmans, 1990.

————. *Theo-Drama*. Vol. 3: *Dramatis Personae: Persons in Christ*. Trans. Graham Harrison. San Francisco: Ignatius Press, 1992.

————. *Theo-Drama*. Vol. 4: *The Action*. Trans. Graham Harrison. San Francisco: Ignatius Press, 1994.

————. *Theo-Drama*. Vol. 5: *The Last Act*. Trans. Graham Harrison. San Francisco: Ignatius Press, 1998.

————. *Theologik*. Vol. 2: *Wahrheit Gottes*. Einsiedeln: Johannes Verlag, 1985.

Barron, Robert. "The Liturgy as Display of God's Justice." *Antiphon* 4 (1999): 19–24.

————. *Thomas Aquinas: Spiritual Master*. New York: Crossroad, 1996.

————. "Thomas Aquinas' Theological Method and the Icon of Jesus Christ." *Doctor Communis* 49 (1996): 103–125.

Barth, Karl. *Church Dogmatics*. Vol. 4, Part 1: *The Doctrine of Reconciliation*. Trans. G. W. Bromiley. Edinburgh: T. & T. Clark, 1956.

Basso, Domingo M. "La ley eterna en la teologia de Santo Tomás." *Teologia* 11 (1974): 33–63.

Bataillon, Louis J., O.P. "Saint Thomas et les Pères: De la *Catena* a la *tertia pars*." In *Ordo Sapientiae et Amoris*. Ed. C.-J. Pinto de Oliveira, O.P. Fribourg: Éditions Universitaires, 1993: 15–36.

Bauckham, Richard, and Trevor Hart. *Hope against Hope: Christian Eschatology at the Turn of the Millennium*. Grand Rapids, MI: Eerdmans, 1999.

Bauerschmidt, Frederick Christian. "Theo-Drama and Political Theology." *Communio* 25 (1998): 532–552.

Beckwith, Roger T., and Martin J. Selman, eds. *Sacrifice in the Bible*. Grand Rapids, MI: Baker, 1995.

Bellemare, Rosaire. "La Somme de Théologie et la lectura de la Bible." *Eglise et Théologie* 5 (1974): 257–270.

Bellomo, Manlio. *The Common Legal Past of Europe, 1000–1800*. 2nd ed. Trans. Lydia G. Cochrane. Washington, DC: Catholic University of America Press, 1995.

Berceville, Gilles, O.P. "Le sacerdoce du Christ dans le *Commentaire de l'Épître aux Hébreux* de saint Thomas d'Aquin." *Revue Thomiste* 99 (1999): 143–158.

Bermudez, Catalina. "Hijos de Dios por la Gracia en los comentarios de Santo Tomás a las cartas paulinas." In *Storia del tomismo*. Studi Tomistici 45:6. Vatican City: Libreria Editrice Vaticana, 1992: 78–89.

Biffi, Inos. "I misteri della vita di Cristo nei commentari biblici di S. Tommaso d'Aquino." *Divus Thomas* 79 (1976): 217–254.

Blazquez, Niceto. "Los tratados sobre la ley antigua y nueva en la *Summa Theologiae*." *Scripta Theologica* (Pamplona) 15 (1983): 421–468.

Bonino, Serge-Thomas, O. P. "La place du pape dans l'Église selon saint Thomas d'Aquin," *Revue Thomiste* 86 (1986): 392–422.

———. "Le sacerdoce comme institution naturelle selon saint Thomas d'Aquin." *Revue Thomiste* 99 (1999): 33–57.

Bordoni, D. Marcello. "Il significato ecclesiologico del concetto Tomista di incarnazione nella *Summa Teologica*." In *Prospettive teologiche moderne*. Studi Tomistici 13:4. Vatican City: Libreria Editrice Vaticana, 1981: 320–326.

Bouesse, Humbert, O. P. "La causalité efficiente instrumentale et la causalité méritoire de la sainte humanité du Christ." *Revue Thomiste* 44 (1938): 256–298.

Bougerol, Jacques Guy, O. F. M. "Le mystère pascal chez saint Bonaventure." In *Ordo Sapientiae et Amoris*. Ed. C.-J. Pinto de Oliveira, O. P. Fribourg: Éditions Universitaires, 1993: 387–398.

Bourke, David. Introduction to *Summa Theologiae*, vol. 29: *The Old Law*. New York: McGraw-Hill, 1969.

Bouthillier, Denise. "Le Christ en son mystère dans les *Collationes* du *Super Isaiam* de saint Thomas d'Aquin." In *Ordo Sapientiae et Amoris*. Ed. C.-J. Pinto de Oliveira, O. P. Fribourg: Éditions Universitaires, 1993: 37–64.

Boyle, John F. "St. Thomas Aquinas and Sacred Scripture." *Pro Ecclesia* 4 (1995): 92–104.

———. *The Structural Setting of Thomas Aquinas' Theology of the Grace of Christ as He Is Head of the Church in the* Summa Theologiae. Dissertation, University of Toronto, 1989.

———. "The Twofold Division of St. Thomas's Christology in the *Tertia pars*." *Thomist* 60 (1996): 439–447.

Boyle, Leonard. *The Setting of the* Summa Theologiae *of St. Thomas*. Toronto: Pontifical Institute of Medieval Studies, 1982.

Boys, Mary C. *Has God Only One Blessing? Judaism as a Source of Christian Self-Understanding*. New York: Paulist Press, 2000.

Bracken, W. Jerome, C. P. "Thomas Aquinas and Anselm's Satisfaction Theory." *Angelicum* 62 (1985): 503–530.

————. *Why Suffering in Redemption? A New Interpretation of the The-ology of the Passion in the* Summa Theologica, 3, 46–49, *by Thomas Aquinas.* Dissertation, Fordham University, 1978.

Brown, Montague. "Aquinas on the Resurrection of the Body." *Thomist* 56 (1992): 165–207.

Brown, Raymond E., S. S. *An Introduction to New Testament Christology.* New York: Paulist Press, 1994.

————. *Jesus: God and Man.* New York: Macmillan, 1967.

Buckley, James J. "Balthasar's Use of the Theology of Aquinas." *Thomist* 59 (1995): 517–545.

Burns, J. Patout, S. J. "The Concept of Satisfaction in Medieval Redemption Theory." *Theological Studies* 36 (1975): 285–304.

Caprioli, P. Mario, O. C. D. "Il sacerdozio di Christo nella *Somma Teologica* e nel commento *Super Epistolam ad Hebraeos.*" In *Storia del tomismo.* Studi Tomistici 45:6. Vatican City: Libreria Editrice Vaticana, 1992: 96–105.

Carl, Maria. "Law, Virtue, and Happiness in Aquinas's Moral Theory." *Thomist* 61 (1997): 425–447.

Catão, Bernard. *Salut et rédemption chez S. Thomas d'Aquin.* Paris: Aubier, 1965.

Catechism of the Catholic Church. Trans. U. S. Catholic Conference. Vatican City: Libreria Editrice Vaticana, 1994.

Cavanaugh, William T. *Torture and Eucharist.* Oxford: Blackwell, 1998.

Cessario, Romanus, O. P. *Christian Faith and the Theological Life.* Washington, DC: Catholic University of America Press, 1996.

————. *The Godly Image: Christ and Satisfaction in Catholic Thought from Anselm to Aquinas.* Petersham, MA: St. Bede's Publications, 1990.

————. "Incarnate Wisdom and the Immediacy of Christ's Salvific Knowledge." In *Problemi teologici alla luce dell' Aquinate.* Studi Tomistici 44:5. Vatican City: Libreria Editrice Vaticana, 1991: 334–340.

————. "Is Aquinas's *Summa* Only about Grace?" In *Ordo Sapientiae et Amoris.* Ed. C.-J. Pinto de Oliveira, O. P. Fribourg: Éditions Universitaires, 1993: 197–209.

————. "St. Thomas Aquinas on Satisfaction, Indulgences, and Crusades." *Medieval Philosophy and Theology* 2 (1992): 74–96.

————. "Toward Understanding Aquinas' Theological Method: The Early Twelfth-Century Experience." In *Studies in Thomistic Theology.* Ed. Paul Lockey. Houston: Center for Thomistic Studies, 1995: 17–89.

Chamorro, Juan Fernando, O. P. "Ley nueva y ley antigua en Santo Tomás." *Studium* 7 (1967): 317–380.

Chardonnens, Denis, O. C. D. "Éternité du sacerdoce du Christ et effet eschatologique de l'Eucharistie: La contribution de saint Thomas d'Aquin à un thème de théologie sacramentaire." *Revue Thomiste* 99 (1999): 159–180.

Châtillon, Jean. "La Bible dans les écoles du XIIe siècle." In *Le Moyen Âge et la Bible*. Ed. Pierre Riché and Guy Lobrichon. Paris: Beauchesne, 1984: 163–197.

Chenu, Marie-Dominique, O. P. *Nature, Man, and Society in the Twelfth Century: Essays on New Theological Perspectives in the Latin West.* Ed. and trans. Jerome Taylor and Lester K. Little. 1968. Reprint. Toronto: University of Toronto Press, 1997.

———. "The Renewal of Moral Theology: The New Law." *Thomist* 34 (1970): 1–12.

———. *La théologie comme science au XIII siècle.* 3rd ed. Paris: J. Vrin, 1957.

———. "La théologie de la loi ancienne selon S. Thomas." *Revue Thomiste* 61 (1961): 485–497.

———. *Toward Understanding St. Thomas.* Trans. A.-M. Landry, O. P., and D. Hughes, O. P. Chicago: Henry Regnery, 1964.

Chroust, A.-H. "The Philosophy of Law from St. Augustine to St. Thomas Aquinas." *New Scholasticism* 20 (1946): 26–71.

Clerk, D. M. de. "Droits du demon et necessité de la rédemption: Les Écoles d'Abelard et de Pierre Lombard." *Recherches de Théologie ancienne et médiévale* 14 (1947): 32–64.

———. "Questions de soteriologie medievale." *Recherches de Théologie ancienne et médiévale* 13 (1946): 150–184.

Cointet, P. de. "'Attache-toi au Christ!' L'imitation du Christ dans la vie spirituelle selon S. Thomas d'Aquin." *Sources* 124 (1989): 64–74.

Colish, Marcia L. *Medieval Foundations of the Western Intellectual Tradition, 400–1400.* New Haven, CT: Yale University Press, 1997.

———. *Peter Lombard.* Vol. 1. New York: E. J. Brill, 1994.

———. "Peter Lombard as an Exegete of St. Paul." In *Ad Litteram.* Ed. M. D. Jordan and K. Emery, Jr. Notre Dame, IN: University of Notre Dame Press, 1992: 71–92.

Collins, Joseph, O. P. "God's Eternal Law." *Thomist* 23 (1960): 497–532.

Congar, Yves, O. P. *I Believe in the Holy Spirit.* Trans. David Smith. New York: Crossroad, 1997.

———. "The Idea of the Church in St. Thomas Aquinas." In *The Mystery of the Church.* Baltimore: Helicon Press, 1965: 97–117.

———. "Saint Augustin et le traité scolastique 'De Gratia Capitis.'" *Augustinianum* 20 (1980): 79–93.

————. "Saint Thomas Aquinas and the Infallibility of the Papal Magisterium." *Thomist* 38 (1974): 81–105.

————. "Sur la trilogie: Prophète-roi-prêtre." *Revue des sciences philosophiques et théologiques* 67 (1983): 97–115.

————. *Thomas d'Aquin: Sa vision de théologie et de l'Église.* London: Variorum Reprints, 1984.

————. *The Word and the Spirit.* Trans. David Smith. San Francisco: Harper & Row, 1986.

Conley, Kieran, O. S. B. *A Theology of Wisdom: A Study in St. Thomas.* Dubuque, IA: Priory Press, 1963.

Constable, Giles. *Three Studies in Medieval Religious and Social Thought.* Cambridge: Cambridge University Press, 1995.

Corbin, Michel. *Le chemin de la théologie chez Thomas d'Aquin.* Paris: Beauchesne, 1972.

Cousar, Charles B. *A Theology of the Cross: The Death of Jesus in the Pauline Letters.* Minneapolis, MN: Fortress Press, 1990.

Crowe, Frederick E., S. J. "Eschaton and Worldly Mission in the Mind and Heart of Jesus." In Frederick E. Crowe, *Appropriating the Lonergan Idea.* Ed. Michael Vertin. Washington, DC: Catholic University of America Press, 1989: 193–234.

————. "The Mind of Jesus." *Communio* 1 (1974): 365–384.

Crowley, Charles B., O. P. "The Role of Sacramental Grace in Christian Life." *Thomist* 3 (1940): 519–545.

Crowley, Paul G., S. J. "*Instrumentum Divinitatis* in Thomas Aquinas: Recovering the Divinity of Christ." *Theological Studies* 52 (1991): 451–475.

Cunningham, Francis L. B., O. P. *The Indwelling of the Trinity.* Dubuque, IA: Priory Press, 1955.

Daly, R. J., S. J. *Christian Sacrifice: The Judeo-Christian Background before Origen.* Washington, DC: Catholic University of America Press, 1978.

DiNoia, J. A., O. P. *The Diversity of Religions: A Christian Perspective.* Washington, DC: Catholic University of America Press, 1992.

Dittoe, John T. "Sacramental Incorporation into the Mystical Body." *Thomist* 9 (1946): 469–514.

Dodds, Michael J., O. P. "Thomas Aquinas, Human Suffering, and the Unchanging God of Love." *Theological Studies* 52 (1991): 330–344.

————. "Ultimacy and Intimacy: Aquinas on the Relation between God and the World." In *Ordo Sapientiae et Amoris.* Ed. C.-J. Pinto de Oliveira, O. P. Fribourg: Éditions Universitaires, 1993: 211–227.

————. *The Unchanging God of Love: A Study of the Teaching of St. Thomas Aquinas on Divine Immutability in View of Certain Contemporary Criticisms of This Doctrine.* Fribourg: Éditions Universitaires, 1986.

Donneaud, Henry, O.P. "Hans Urs von Balthasar contre saint Thomas d'Aquin sur la foi du Christ." *Revue Thomiste* 97 (1997): 335–354.

———. "Insaisissable sacra doctrina? À propos d'une réédition récente." *Revue Thomiste* 98 (1998): 179–224.

Doyle, Dennis M. "Journet, Congar, and the Roots of Communion Ecclesiology." *Theological Studies* 58 (1997): 461–479.

Dulles, Avery, S.J. "The Church According to Thomas Aquinas." In Avery Dulles, S.J., *A Church to Believe In.* New York: Crossroad, 1985: 149–169.

———. "Criteria of Catholic Theology." *Communio* 22 (1995): 303–315.

Dwyer, John C. "The Implications of Tillich's Theology of the Cross for Catholic Theology." In *Paul Tillich: A New Catholic Assessment.* Ed. Raymond F. Bulman and Frederick J. Parrella. Collegeville, MN: Liturgical Press, 1994: 73–90.

Elders, Leo J. "Aquinas on Holy Scripture as the Medium of Divine Revelation." In *La doctrine de la révélation divine de saint Thomas d'Aquin.* Ed. Leo J. Elders. Vatican City: Libreria Editrice Vaticana, 1990: 132–152.

———. "La relation entre l'ancienne et la nouvelle Alliance, selon saint Thomas d'Aquin." *Revue Thomiste* 100 (2000): 580–602.

———. "Le Saint-Esprit et la 'Lex Nova' dans les commentaires bibliques de S. Thomas d'Aquin." In *Credo in Spiritum Sanctum: Atti del Congresso Teologico Internazionale di Pneumatologia.* Vol. 2. Vatican City, 1983: 1195–1205.

———. "St. Thomas Aquinas and Holy Scripture." Unpublished lecture delivered at the 2000 Summer Thomistic Institute at the University of Notre Dame.

———. "Structure et fonction de l'argument 'sed contra' dans la *Somme théologique* de Saint Thomas." *Divus Thomas* 80 (1977): 245–260.

———. "Thomas Aquinas and the Fathers of the Church." In *The Reception of the Church Fathers in the West: From the Carolingians to the Maurists.* Vol. 1. Ed. Irena Backus. New York: E. J. Brill, 1997: 337–366.

Emery, Gilles, O.P. "Essentialisme ou personnalisme dans le traité de Dieu chez saint Thomas d'Aquin?" *Revue Thomiste* 98 (1998): 5–38.

———. "Le fruit ecclésial de l'Eucharistie chez S. Thomas d'Aquin." *Nova et Vetera* 72, no. 4 (1997): 25–40.

———. "La procession du Saint-Esprit *a Filio* chez saint Thomas d'Aquin." *Revue Thomiste* 96 (1996): 531–574.

———. "Le sacerdoce spirituel des fidèles chez saint Thomas d'Aquin." *Revue Thomiste* 99 (1999): 211–243.

———. *La Trinité créatrice.* Paris: Vrin, 1995.

Etienne, J. "Loi et grâce: Le concept de loi nouvelle dans la *Somme théologique* de St. Thomas d'Aquin." *Revue théologique de Louvain* 16 (1985): 5–22.

Evans, Craig A. "Jesus' Self-Designation 'The Son of Man' and the Recognition of His Divinity." In *The Trinity: An Interdisciplinary Symposium on the Trinity*. Ed. Stephen T. Davis, Daniel Kendall, S. J., and Gerald O'Collins, S. J. Oxford: Oxford University Press, 1999: 29–47.

Evans, Gillian R. "*Cur Deus Homo*: St. Bernard's Theology of the Redemption. A Contribution to the Contemporary Debate." *Studia Theologica* 36 (1982): 27–36.

———. *The Language and Logic of the Bible: The Earlier Middle Ages*. Cambridge: Cambridge University Press, 1984.

———. *Old Arts and New Theology*. Oxford: Clarendon Press, 1980.

Fabro, Cornelio. *Participation et causalité selon S. Thomas d'Aquin*. Paris: Éditions Béatrice Nauwelaerts, 1961.

Faricy, Robert, S. J. "The Charism of Prophecy in the Church." In *Prospettive teologiche moderne*. Studi Tomistici 13:4. Vatican City: Libreria Editrice Vaticana, 1981: 371–380.

Fatula, Mary Ann, O. P. *Thomas Aquinas: Preacher and Friend*. Collegeville, MN: Liturgical Press, 1993.

Fee, Gordon D. "Paul and the Trinity: The Experience of Christ and the Spirit for Paul's Understanding of God." In *The Trinity: An Interdisciplinary Symposium on the Trinity*. Ed. Stephen T. Davis, Daniel Kendall, S. J., and Gerald O'Collins, S. J. Oxford: Oxford University Press, 1999: 49–72.

Finnis, John. *"Historical Consciousness" and Theological Foundations*. The Etienne Gilson Series 14. Toronto: Pontifical Institute of Medieval Studies, 1992.

Fiorenza, Francis Schüssler. "Critical Social Theory and Christology: Toward an Understanding of Atonement and Redemption as Emancipatory Solidarity." *CTSA Proceedings* 30 (1975): 63–110.

Fishbane, Michael. *Biblical Interpretation in Ancient Israel*. Oxford: Oxford University Press, 1985.

Forster, William J. *The Beatific Knowledge of Christ in the Theology of the 12th and 13th Centuries*. Dissertation, Angelicum, 1958.

Franks, Robert. *The Work of Christ: A Historical Study of Christian Doctrine*. London: Thomas Nelson & Sons, 1962.

Freedman, David Noel. *The Nine Commandments: Uncovering the Hidden Pattern of Crime and Punishment in the Hebrew Bible*. New York: Doubleday, 2000.

Frei, Hans W. *The Eclipse of Biblical Narrative*. New Haven, CT: Yale University Press, 1974.

Friedman, Lee M. *Robert Grosseteste and the Jews*. Cambridge, MA: Harvard University Press, 1934.

Funkenstein, Amos. "Gesetz und Geschichte: Zur historisierenden Hermeneutik bei Moses Maimonides und Thomas von Aquin." *Viator: Medieval and Renaissance Studies* 1 (1970): 147–178.

Gallarand, H. "La rédemption dans les écrits d'Anselme et d'Abelard." *Revue de l'Histoire des Religions* 92 (1925): 212–241.

Gauthier, Albert, O.P. "Comments on Father Potvin's Paper." *Église et Théologie* 5 (1974): 253–255.

Geenan, G. "The Place of Tradition in the Theology of St. Thomas." *Thomist* 15 (1952): 110–135.

Gherardini, Brunero. "La 'satisfactio vicaria' in San Tommaso." *Doctor Communis* 37 (1984): 103–122.

Gibson, M. T. "The Place of the *Glossa ordinaria* in Medieval Exegesis." In *Ad Litteram: Authoritative Texts and Their Medieval Readers*. Ed. M. D. Jordan and K. Emery, Jr. Notre Dame, IN: University of Notre Dame Press, 1992: 5–27.

Gillon, L.-B. *Christ and Moral Theology*. Staten Island, NY: Alba House, 1967.

———. "La notion de conséquence de l'union hypostatique, dans le cadre de IIIa, qq.2–26." *Angelicum* 15 (1938): 17–34.

Goergen, Donald, O.P. "Albert the Great and Thomas Aquinas on the Motive of the Incarnation." *Thomist* 44 (1980): 523–538.

Gorringe, Timothy. *God's Just Vengeance: Crime, Violence, and the Rhetoric of Salvation*. Cambridge: Cambridge University Press, 1996.

Grabmann, Martin. *Thomas Aquinas*. Trans. Virgil Michel, O.S.B. New York: Longmans, Green, 1928.

Gribomont, Jean, O.S.B. "Le lien des deux testaments selon la théologie de S. Thomas." *Ephemerides theologiae Lovanienses* 22 (1946): 70–89.

Guindon, André. La pédagogie de la crainte dans l'histoire du salut selon Thomas d'Aquin. Tournai: Desclée, 1975.

Guindon, Roger, O.M.I. Béatitude et théologie morale chez saint Thomas d'Aquin. Ottawa: Editions de l'Université d'Ottawa, 1956.

Gutiérrez, Gustavo. *Las Casas: In Search of the Poor of Jesus Christ*. Trans. Robert R. Barr. Maryknoll, NY: Orbis Books, 1993.

Gy, P.-M. "La relation au Christ dans l'Eucharistie selon S. Bonaventure et S. Thomas d'Aquin." In *Sacrements de Jésus-Christ*. Ed. J. Doré. Paris: Desclée, 1983: 69–106.

Hagen, Kenneth. *Hebrews Commenting from Erasmus to Bèze, 1516–1598.* Tübingen: Mohr, 1981.

——. "Luther on Atonement—Reconfigured." *Concordia Theological Quarterly* 61 (1997): 251–276.

——. *A Theology of Testament in the Young Luther: The Lectures on Hebrews.* Leiden: E. J. Brill, 1974.

Halpern, Baruch. *The First Historians: The Hebrew Bible and History.* University Park: Pennsylvania State University Press, 1996.

Hankey, Wayne. "Aquinas and the Passion of God." In *Being and Truth.* Ed. Alistair Kee and Eugene T. Long. London: SCM Press, 1986: 318–331.

Hardy, Louis. *La doctrine de la rédemption chez S. Thomas.* Paris: Desclée, 1936.

Harrington, Daniel J., S. J. "What and Why Did Jesus Suffer According to Mark?" *Chicago Studies* 34 (1995): 32–41.

Hart, D. Bentley. "A Gift Exceeding Every Debt: An Eastern Orthodox Appreciation of Anselm's *Cur Deus Homo.*" *Pro Ecclesia* 7 (1998): 333–349.

Haskins, Charles Homer. *The Renaissance of the Twelfth Century.* Cambridge: Harvard University Press, 1933.

Hays, Richard B. *Echoes of Scripture in the Letters of Paul.* New Haven, CT: Yale University Press, 1989.

——. "Response to Robert Wilken, 'In Dominico Eloquio.'" *Communio* 25 (1998): 520–528.

Hibbs, Thomas S. *Dialectic and Narrative in Aquinas.* Notre Dame, IN: University of Notre Dame Press, 1995.

——. "*Imitatio Christi* and the Foundation of Aquinas's Ethics." *Communio* 18 (1991): 556–573.

Hick, John. "Is the Doctrine of the Atonement a Mistake?" In *Reason and the Christian Religion: Essays in Honor of Richard Swinburne.* Ed. Alan G. Padgett. Oxford: Clarendon Press, 1994: 247–263.

Hill, William J., O. P. *The Three-Personed God.* Washington, DC: Catholic University of America Press, 1982.

——. "Uncreated Grace: A Critique of Karl Rahner." *Thomist* 27 (1963): 333–356.

Holtz, F. "La valeur sotériologique de la résurrection du Christ selon saint Thomas." *Ephemerides theologicae Lovanienses* 29 (1953): 609–645.

Hood, John Y. B. *Aquinas and the Jews.* Philadelphia: University of Pennsylvania Press, 1995.

Horst, Ulrich, O. P. "Christ, *Exemplar Ordinis Fratrum Praedicantium,* According to Saint Thomas Aquinas." In *Christ among the Medieval Dominicans.* Ed. Kent Emery, Jr., and Joseph P. Wawrykow. Notre Dame, IN: University of Notre Dame Press, 1999: 256–270.

Hoye, William J. *Actualitas Omnium Actuum: Man's Beatific Vision of God as Apprehended by Thomas Aquinas.* Meisenheim am Glan: Verlag Anton Hain, 1975.

Humbrecht, Thierry-Dominique, O. P. "L'Eucharistie, 'représentation' du sacrifice du Christ, selon saint Thomas." *Revue Thomiste* 98 (1998): 355–386.

Hunt, Anne. *The Trinity and the Paschal Mystery: A Development in Recent Catholic Theology.* Collegeville, MN: Liturgical Press, 1997.

Jamros, Daniel P., S. J. "Satisfaction for Sin: Aquinas on the Passion of Christ." *Irish Theological Quarterly* 56 (1990): 307–328.

Janz, Denis R. "Syllogism or Paradox: Aquinas and Luther on Theological Method." *Theological Studies* 59 (1998): 3–21.

Jenkins, John I. *Knowledge and Faith in Thomas Aquinas.* Cambridge: Cambridge University Press, 1997.

John Paul II. Apostolic Letter *Novo Millennio Ineunte.* Vatican Translation. Boston: Daughters of St. Paul, 2001.

Johnson, Luke Timothy. *Living Jesus: Learning the Heart of the Gospel.* New York: HarperCollins, 1999.

———. *The Writings of the New Testament.* Philadelphia: Fortress Press, 1986.

Johnson, Mark F. "Another Look at the Plurality of the Literal Sense." In *Medieval Philosophy and Theology.* Vol. 2. Ed. Mark D. Jordan et al. Notre Dame, IN: University of Notre Dame Press, 1992: 117–141.

———. "God's Knowledge in Our Frail Mind: The Thomistic Model of Theology." *Angelicum* 76 (1999): 25–45.

———. "The Sapiential Character of the First Article of the Summa Theologiae." In *Philosophy and the God of Abraham.* Ed. R. James Long. Toronto: Pontifical Institute of Mediaeval Studies, 1991: 85–98.

Jordan, Mark D. "The Modes of Thomistic Discourse: Questions for Corbin's *Le chemin de la théologie chez Thomas d'Aquin.*" *Thomist* (1981): 80–98.

Kaczynsky, Edward, O. P. "'Lex nova' in S. Tommaso." *Divinitas* 15 (1981): 22–33.

———. "'Lex spiritus' in S. Paolo e la sua interpretazione in S. Tommaso." In *Credo in Spiritum Sanctum: Atti del Congresso teologico internazionale di Pneumatologia.* Vol. 2. Vatican City: Libreria Editrice Vaticana, 1983: 1207–1222.

Katz, Steven T. *The Holocaust in Historical Context.* Vol. 1: *The Holocaust and Mass Death before the Modern Age.* Oxford: Oxford University Press, 1994.

Keaty, Anthony W. "Thomas's Authority for Identifying Charity as Friendship: Aristotle or John 15?" *Thomist* 62 (1998): 581–601.

Kereszty, Roch, O. Cist. "Historical Research, Theological Inquiry, and the Reality of Jesus: Reflections on the Method of J. P. Meier." *Communio* 19 (1992): 576–600.

———. *Jesus Christ: Fundamentals of Christology*. Ed. J. Stephen Maddux. New York: Alba House, 1991.

———. "A Response to Gil Bailie's, 'Girard's Contribution to the Church of the 21st Century." *Communio* 26 (1999): 212–216.

Kerr, Fergus, O. P. "Charity as Friendship." In *Language, Meaning and God*. Ed. Brian Davies, O. P. London: Geoffrey Chapman, 1987: 1–23.

Kries, Douglas Lee. *Friar Thomas and the Politics of Sinai: An Inquiry Concerning the Status of the Mosaic Law in the Christian Theology of Thomas Aquinas*. Dissertation, Boston College, 1988.

Kühn, Ulrich. *Via caritatis: Theologie des Gesetzes bei Thomas von Aquin*. Göttingen: Vandenhoeck & Ruprecht, 1965.

Kurz, William S., and Kevin E. Miller. "The Use of Scripture in the *Catechism of the Catholic Church*." *Communio* 23 (1996): 480–507.

Kwasniewski, Peter A. "St. Thomas, *Extasis* and Union with the Beloved." *Thomist* 61 (1997): 587–603.

Lachance, Louis, O. P. *Le concept de droit selon Aristote et S. Thomas*. 2nd ed. Montreal: Éditions du Levrier, 1948.

Lafont, Ghislain, O. S. B. *Peut-on connaître Dieu en Jésus-Christ?* Paris: Cerf, 1969.

———. *Structures et méthode dans la* Somme théologique *de Saint Thomas d'Aquin*. Paris: Desclée, 1961.

Laje, Enrique, S. J. "A proposito de una teologia de la redención en Santo Tomás de Aquino." *Stromata* 22 (1966): 79–81.

———. "La redención por la muerte de Christo en el pensamiento de Santo Tomás." *Ciencia y Fe* 20 (1964): 403–418.

———. "Satisfacción y pena en el pensamiento de Santo Tomás." *Ciencia y Fe* 21 (1965): 267–289.

Lamb, Matthew L. "Apokalyptische Unterbrechung und politische Theologie." In *Befristete Zeit*. Ed. Jürgen Manemann. Münster: LIT Verlag, 1999: 232–240.

———. Introduction to St. Thomas Aquinas's *Commentary on Saint Paul's Epistle to the Ephesians*. Albany, NY: Magi Books, 1966: 3–36.

———. "Nature, History, and Redemption." In *Jesus Crucified and Risen: Essays in Honor of Dom Sebastian Moore*. Ed. William P. Loewe and Vernon J. Gregson. Collegeville, MN: Liturgical Press, 1998: 117–132.

Landgraf, A. M. "Die Gnadenökonomie des Alten Bundes nach der Lehre der Frühscholastik." *Zeitschrift für katholische Theologie* 57 (1933): 215–253.

Langston, Douglas. "Scotus' Departure from Anselm's Theory of the Atonement." *Recherches de théologie ancienne et médiévale* 50 (1983): 227–241.

La Soujeole, Benoit-Dominique de, O. P. "Les tria munera Christi: Contribution de saint Thomas à la recherche contemporaine." *Revue Thomiste* 99 (1999): 59–74.

Leblanc, Marie, O. S. B. "Le péché originel dans la pensée de S. Thomas." *Revue Thomiste* 93 (1993): 567–600.

Le Bras, G. "Les Écritures dans le décret de Gratien." *Zeitschrift für Rechtsgeschichte* 27 (1938): 47–80.

Lécuyer, Joseph. "La causalité efficiente des mystères du Christ selon saint Thomas d'Aquin." *Doctor Communis* 6 (1953): 91–120.

———. "Les étapes de l'enseignement thomiste sur l'épiscopat." *Revue Thomiste* 57 (1957): 29–52.

———. "Note sur une définition thomiste de la satisfaction." *Doctor Communis* 8 (1955): 21–31.

Lee, Patrick. "Permanence of the Ten Commandments: St. Thomas and His Modern Commentators." *Theological Studies* 42 (1981): 422–443.

Leget, Carlo. *Living with God: Thomas Aquinas on the Relation between Life on Earth and "Life" after Death.* Leuven: Peeters, 1997.

Leithart, Peter J. "Marcionism, Postliberalism, and Social Christianity." *Pro Ecclesia* 8 (1999): 85–97.

Lemeer, Benedictus M., O. P. "De Relatione inter Regnum Dei et Ecclesiam in Doctrina S. Thomae." In *Prospettive teologiche moderne.* Studi Tomistici 13:4. Vatican City: Libreria Editrice Vaticana, 1981: 339–349.

Leroy, Marie-Vincent. "L'union selon l'hypostase d'après S. Thomas d'Aquin." *Revue Thomiste* 74 (1974): 205–243.

Levenson, Jon D. "From Temple to Synagogue: 1 Kings 8." In *Traditions in Transformation.* Ed. Baruch Halpern and Jon D. Levenson. Winona Lake, IN: Eisenbrauns, 1981: 143–166.

———. *The Hebrew Bible, the Old Testament, and Historical Criticism.* Louisville, KY: Westminster/John Knox Press, 1993.

———. "The Last Four Verses in Kings." *Journal of Biblical Literature* 103 (1984): 353–361.

———. *Sinai and Zion: An Entry into the Jewish Bible.* San Francisco: Harper & Row, 1985.

Lienhard, Joseph T., S. J. *The Bible, the Church, and Authority*. College-ville, MN: Liturgical Press, 1995.

Lindbeck, George A. "Atonement and the Hermeneutics of Social Embodiment." *Pro Ecclesia* 5 (1996): 144–160.

Lohaus, Gerd. *Die Geheimnisse des Lebens Jesu in der Summa theologiae des heiligen Thomas von Aquin*. Freiburg: Herder, 1985.

Lonergan, Bernard, S. J. *De Verbo Incarnato*. Rome: Gregorian University Press, 1964.

Long, Steven A. "Nicholas Lobkowicz and the Historicist Inversion of Thomistic Philosophy." *Thomist* 62 (1998): 41–74.

Lösel, Steffen. "Murder in the Cathedral: Hans Urs von Balthasar's New Dramatization of the Doctrine of the Trinity." *Pro Ecclesia* 5 (1996): 427–439.

Lottin, Odon, O. S. B. "Le concept de justice chez les théologiens du moyen âge avant l'introduction d'Aristote." *Revue Thomiste* 44 (1938): 511–521.

Lubac, Henri de. *Medieval Exegesis*. Vol. 1: *The Four Senses of Scripture*. Trans. Mark Sebanc. Grand Rapids, MI: Eerdmans, 1998.

Lyons, H. P. C., S. J. "The Grace of Sonship." *Ephemerides theologicae Lovanienses* 27 (1951): 438–466.

MacIntyre, Alasdair. *Dependent Rational Animals: Why Human Beings Need the Virtues*. Chicago: Open Court, 1999.

Madigan, Kevin. "Aquinas and Olivi on Evangelical Poverty: A Medieval Debate and Its Modern Significance." *Thomist* 61 (1997): 567–586.

Mahoney, John. "'The Church of the Holy Spirit' in Aquinas." *Heythrop Journal* 15 (1974): 18–36.

Mailhiot, M. D. "La pensée de S. Thomas sur le sens spirituel." *Revue Thomiste* 59 (1959): 613–663.

Mansini, Guy, O. S. B. "Balthasar and the Theodramatic Enrichment of the Trinity." *Thomist* 64 (2000): 499–519.

———. "Rahner and Balthasar on the Efficacy of the Cross." *Irish Theological Quarterly* 63 (1998): 232–249.

———. "St. Anselm, *Satisfactio*, and the Rule of St. Benedict." *Revue Bénédictine* 97 (1987): 101–121.

———. "*Similitudo, Communicatio*, and the Friendship of Charity in Aquinas." In *Thomistica. Recherches de théologie ancienne et médié-vale*, Supplement 1. Ed. E. Manning. Leuven: Peeters, 1995: 1–26.

———. "Understanding St. Thomas on Christ's Immediate Knowledge of God." *Thomist* 59 (1995): 91–124.

Maritain, Jacques. *On the Grace and Humanity of Jesus*. Trans. Joseph W. Evans. New York: Herder and Herder, 1969.

Marquardt, Friedrich-Wilhelm. *Das christliche Bekenntnis zu Jesus, dem Jude: Eine Christologie.* 2 vols. Munich: C. Kaiser, 1990.

Marshall, Bruce. "Christ and the cultures: The Jewish People and Christian Theology." In *The Cambridge Companion to Christian Doctrine.* Ed. Colin E. Gunton. Cambridge: Cambridge University Press, 1997: 81–100.

———. *Trinity and Truth.* Cambridge: Cambridge University Press, 2000.

Martínez, F. "La Eucaristía y la unidad de la Iglesia en Santo Tomás de Aquino." *Studium* 9 (1969): 377–404.

Maurer, Armand, C. S. B. "Reflections on Thomas Aquinas' Notion of Presence." In *Philosophy and the God of Abraham.* Ed. R. James Long. Toronto: Pontifical Institute of Mediaeval Studies, 1991: 113–127.

———. "St. Thomas on the Sacred Name 'Tetragrammaton.'" *Mediaeval Studies* 34 (197): 275–286.

Mbaki, Mayemba, O. P. *De saint Dominique à saint Thomas d'Aquin: Comment parler de la spiritualité de l'order les frères prêcheurs au XIIIe siècle?* Fribourg: Éditions Universitaires, 1988.

McCool, Gerald A., S. J. *From Unity to Pluralism: The Internal Evolution of Thomism.* New York: Fordham University Press, 1989.

McDermott, Brian O., S. J. *Word Become Flesh: Dimensions of Christology.* Collegeville, MN: Liturgical Press, 1993.

McGrath, Alister. "Homo Assumptus? A Study in the Christology of the Via Moderna, with Particular Reference to William of Ockham." *Ephemerides theologicae Lovanienses* 60 (1984): 283–297.

———. *Luther's Theology of the Cross: Martin Luther's Theological Breakthrough.* Oxford: Basil Blackwell, 1985.

———. "The Moral Theory of the Atonement: An Historical and Theological Critique." *Scottish Journal of Theology* 38 (1985): 205–220.

———. "Some Observations Concerning the Soteriology of the Schola Moderna." *Recherches de théologie ancienne et médiévale* 52 (1985): 182–193.

McGregor, Bede, O. P. "Revelation, Creeds and Salvific Mission." In *La doctrine de la révélation divine de saint Thomas d'Aquin.* Ed. Leo J. Elders. Vatican City: Libreria Editrice Vaticana, 1990: 196–211.

McGuckin, T. "Saint Thomas Aquinas and Theological Exegesis of Sacred Scripture." *Louvain Studies* 16 (1991): 99–120.

McPartlan, Paul. *Sacrament of Salvation: An Introduction to Eucharistic Ecclesiology.* Edinburgh: T. & T. Clark, 1995.

Meier, John P. *The Vision of Matthew: Christ, Church, and Morality in the First Gospel.* New York: Paulist Press, 1979.

Ménard, Etienne. *La tradition: Révélation, Écriture, Église selon saint Thomas d'Aquin*. Paris: Desclée, 1964.

Mersch, Emile, S. J. *The Whole Christ: The Historical Development of the Doctrine of the Mystical Body in Scripture and Tradition*. Trans. John R. Kelly, S. J. Milwaukee, WI: Bruce Publishing, 1938.

Milano, A. "Il sacerdozio nella ecclesiologia di san Tommaso d'Aquino." *Asprenas* 17 (1970): 59–107.

Milbank, John. "The Name of Jesus: Incarnation, Atonement, Ecclesiology." *Modern Theology* 7 (1991): 311–333.

Molloy, Noel. "Hierarchy and Holiness: Aquinas on the Holiness of the Episcopal State." *Thomist* 39 (1975): 198–252.

Moloney, Francis J., S. D. B. *The Gospel of John*. Collegeville, MN: Liturgical Press, 1998.

Moloney, Raymond, S. J. "The Mind of Christ in Transcendental Theology: Rahner, Lonergan, and Crowe." *Heythrop Journal* 25 (1984): 288–300.

———. "Patristic Approaches to Christ's Knowledge, Part 1." *Milltown Studies* 37 (1996): 65–81.

Montero, J. "La operación teándrica de Cristo, según la doctrina de Santo Tomás." *Studium* 7 (1967): 281–315.

Morard, Martin. "L'Eucharistie, clé de voûte de l'organisme sacramental chez saint Thomas d'Aquin." *Revue Thomiste* 95 (1995): 217–250.

———. "Les expressions 'corpus mysticum' et 'persona mystica' dans l'oeuvre de saint Thomas d'Aquin." *Revue Thomiste* 95 (1995): 653–664.

———. "Sacerdoce du Christ et sacerdoce des chrétiens dans le *Commentaire des Psaumes* de saint Thomas d'Aquin." *Revue Thomiste* 99 (1999): 119–142.

Moreno, A., O. P. "The Nature of St. Thomas' Knowledge 'Per Connaturalitatem.'" *Angelicum* 47 (1970): 44–62.

Mühlen, Heribert. *Der Heilige Geist als Person*. 5th ed. Münster: Aschendorff, 1988.

Muller, Earl, S. J. "Real Relations and the Divine: Issues in Thomas's Understanding of God's Relation to the World." *Theological Studies* 56 (1995): 673–695.

Murphy, Richard T. A. Introduction, notes, and appendices to *Summa Theologiae*, vol. 54: *The Passion of Christ*. New York: McGraw-Hill, 1965.

Narcisse, Gilbert, O. P. "Les enjeux épistemologiques de l'argument de convenance selon saint Thomas d'Aquin." In *Ordo Sapientiae et Amoris*. Ed. C.-J. Pinto de Oliveira. Fribourg: Éditions Universitaires, 1993: 143–167.

———. "Participer à la vie trinitaire." *Revue Thomiste* 96 (1996): 107–128.

———. *Les raisons de Dieu: Argument de convenance et esthétique théologique selon saint Thomas d'Aquin et Hans Urs von Balthasar.* Fribourg: Éditions Universitaires, 1997.

Neusner, Jacob, and Bruce D. Chilton. *The Body of Faith: Israel and the Church.* Valley Forge, PA: Trinity Press International, 1996.

Nichols, Aidan, O.P. "St. Thomas Aquinas on the Passion of Christ: A Reading of *Summa Theologiae* IIIa, q.46." *Scottish Journal of Theology* 43 (1990): 447–459.

Nicolas, Jean-Hervé. "Le Christ est mort pour nos péchés selon les Écritures." *Revue Thomiste* 96 (1996): 209–234.

———. "Réactualisation des mystères rédempteurs dans et par les sacrements." *Revue Thomiste* 58 (1958): 20–54.

———. *Synthèse dogmatique: De la Trinité à la Trinité.* Paris: Beauchesne, 1985.

Nicolas, M.-J. "L'idée de nature dans la pensée de saint Thomas d'Aquin." *Revue Thomiste* 74 (1974): 533–590.

———. "La théologie des mystères selon saint Thomas d'Aquin." In *Mens concordet voci.* Paris: Desclée, 1983: 489–496.

Noonan, John T. "Agency, Bribery and Redemption in Thomas Aquinas." *Recherches de théologie ancienne et médiévale* 49 (1982): 159–173.

Nuth, Joan. "Two Medieval Soteriologies: Anselm of Canterbury and Julian of Norwich." *Theological Studies* 53 (1992): 611–645.

O'Brien, T. C. "'Sacra Doctrina' Revisited: The Context of Medieval Education." *Thomist* 41 (1977): 475–509.

Ocáriz, Fernando. "La elevación sobrenatural como re-creación en Cristo." In *Prospettive teologiche moderne.* Studi Tomistici 13:4. Vatican City: Libreria Editrice Vaticana, 1981: 281–292.

Ocker, Christopher. "Medieval Exegesis and the Origin of Hermeneutics." *Scottish Journal of Theology* 52 (1999): 328–345.

O'Collins, Gerald, S.J. *Christology: A Biblical, Historical, and Systematic Study of Jesus Christ.* Oxford: Oxford University Press, 1995.

———. "Images of Jesus: Reappropriating Titular Christology." *Theology Digest* 44 (1997): 303–318.

———. "Thomas Aquinas and Christ's Resurrection." *Theological Studies* 31 (1970): 512–522.

———. *The Tripersonal God.* New York: Paulist Press, 1999.

O'Collins, Gerald, S.J., and Daniel Kendall, S.J. *The Bible for Theology: Ten Principles for the Theological Use of Scripture.* New York: Paulist Press, 1997.

O'Collins, Gerald, S.J., Stephan Kendall, S.J., and Stephen Davis. *The Trinity: An Interdisciplinary Symposium on the Trinity*. Oxford: Oxford University Press, 1999.

Ols, Daniel, O.P. *Le Christologie contemporànee e le lóro posizióni fondamentali al vàglio délla dottrina di S. Tommaso*. Studi Tomistici 39. Vatican City: Libreria Editrice Vaticana, 1991.

O'Meara, Thomas F., O.P. "Grace as a Theological Structure in the *Summa Theologiae* of Thomas Aquinas." *Recherches de Théologie ancienne et médiévale* 55 (1988): 130–153.

———. "Tarzan, Las Casas, and Rahner: Aquinas's Theology of Wider Grace." *Theology Digest* 45 (1998): 319–327.

———. *Thomas Aquinas Theologian*. Notre Dame, IN: University of Notre Dame Press, 1997.

———. "Virtues in the Theology of Thomas Aquinas." *Theological Studies* 58 (1997): 254–285.

O'Neill, Colman E., O.P. Appendices to *Summa Theologiae*, vol. 50: *The One Mediator*. New York: McGraw-Hill, 1963.

———. *Meeting Christ in the Sacraments*. Rev. ed. Ed. Romanus Cessario, O.P. New York: Alba House, 1991.

———. "The Rule Theory of Doctrine and Propositional Truth." *Thomist* 49 (1985): 417–442.

———. *Sacramental Realism*. Chicago: Midwest Theological Forum, 1998.

———. "St. Thomas on the Membership of the Church." *Thomist* 27 (1963): 88–140.

O'Shea, Kevin F. "The Human Activity of the Word." *Thomist* 22 (1959): 143–232.

Patfoort, Albert, O.P. "Missions divines et expérience des Personnes divines selon S. Thomas." *Angelicum* 63 (1986): 545–559.

———. "Théorie de la théologie ou reflexion sur le corpus des Écritures? Le vrai sense, ans l'oeuvre de S. Thomas, des prologues du *Super Libros Sententiarum* et de la *Somme Théologique*." *Angelicum* 54 (1977): 459–488.

———. "Vision béatifique et théologie de l'âme du Christ: À propos d'un ouvrage récent." *Revue Thomiste* 93 (1993): 635–639.

———. "Le vrai visage de la satisfaction du Christ selon S. Thomas." In *Ordo Sapientiae et Amoris*. Ed. C.-J. Pinto de Oliveira, O.P. Fribourg: Éditions Universitaires, 1993: 247–266.

Perrin, B.-M. "Le caractère de la confirmation chez saint Thomas." *Revue Thomiste* 98 (1998): 225–265.

Pesch, Otto Hermann. *Das Gesetz: Kommentar zu* Summa Theologiae I-II 90–105. Deutsche Thomas edition. Vol. 13. Heidelberg: Graz, 1977.

———. "Paul as Professor of Theology: The Image of the Apostle in St. Thomas's Theology." *Thomist* 38 (1974): 584–605.

———. "Sittengebote, Kultvorschriften, Rechtssatzungen: Zur Theologie-geschichte von *Summa Theologiae* I-II 99, 2–5." In *Thomas von Aquino: Interpretation und Rezeption*. Ed. Willehad Paul Eckert, O.P. Mainz: Matthias-Grünewald-Verlag, 1974: 488–518.

———. *Theologie der Rechtfertigung bei Martin Luther und Thomas von Aquin: Versuch eines systematisch-theologischen Dialogs.* 1967. Reprint. Mainz: Matthias-Grünewald-Verlag, 1985.

———. *Thomas von Aquin: Grenze und Grösse mittelalterlicher Theologie.* Mainz: Matthias-Grünewald-Verlag, 1988.

Petry, R. C. "The Social Character of Heavenly Beatitude According to the Thought of St. Thomas Aquinas." *Thomist* 7 (1944): 65–79.

Pickstock, Catherine. *After Writing: On the Liturgical Consummation of Philosophy.* Oxford: Blackwell, 1998.

Pinckaers, Servais, O.P. "La loi de l'Évangile ou loi nouvelle selon S. Thomas." In *Loi et évangile.* Ed. Jean-Marie Aubert and Servais Pinckaers. Geneva: Labor et Fidés, 1981: 57–79.

———. *The Sources of Christian Ethics.* 3rd ed. Trans. Sr. Mary Thomas Noble, O.P. Washington, DC: Catholic University of America Press, 1995.

Pinto de Oliveira, Carlos-Josaphat, O.P. "Ordo rationis, ordo amoris: La notion d'ordre au centre de l'univers éthique de S. Thomas." In *Ordo Sapientiae et Amoris.* Ed. C.-J. Pinto de Oliveira, O.P. Fribourg: Éditions Universitaires, 1993: 285–302.

Pius XII. *Mystici Corporis.* In The Papal Encyclicals. Vol. 4: 1939–1958. Ed. Claudia Carlin Ihm. Raleigh, NC: McGrath Publishing, 1981: 37–63.

Potvin, Thomas R. "Authority in the Church as Participation in the Authority of Christ According to Saint Thomas." *Église et Théologie* 5 (1974): 227–251.

———. *The Theology of the Primacy of Christ According to St. Thomas and Its Scriptural Foundations.* Fribourg: Éditions Universitaires, 1973.

Prades, J. *"Deus specialiter est in sanctis per gratiam": El misterio de la in-habitación de la Trinidad, en los escritos de Santo Tomás.* Rome: Gregorian University, 1993.

Preus, James Samuel. *From Shadow to Promise: Old Testament Interpreta-tion from Augustine to the Young Luther.* Cambridge, MA: Harvard University Press, 1969.

Principe, Walter H., C.S.B. "Some Examples of Augustine's Influence on Medieval Christology." In *Collectanea Augustiniana: Mélanges T.J.*

Van Bavel. Vol. 2. Ed. B. Bruning. Leuven: Leuven University Press, 1990: 955–974.

———. *Thomas Aquinas' Spirituality*. The Etienne Gilson Series 7. Toronto: Pontifical Institute of Medieval Studies, 1984.

———. "'The Truth of Human Nature' According to Thomas Aquinas: Theology and Science in Interaction." In *Philosophy and the God of Abraham*. Ed. R. James Long. Toronto: Pontifical Institute of Mediaeval Studies, 1991: 161–177.

Prouvost, G. *Thomas d'Aquin et les thomismes: Essai sur l'histoire des thomismes*. Paris: Cerf, 1996.

Przybylski, Benno. *Righteousness in Matthew and His World of Thought*. Cambridge: Cambridge University Press, 1980.

Qualizza, Marino. "La condizione spirituale di Israele nel Vecchio Tetamento secondo San Tommaso." In *Prospettive teologiche moderne*. Studi Tomistici 13:4. Vatican City: Libreria Editrice Vaticana, 1981: 407–413.

Quinn, Philip L. "Abelard on Atonement: 'Nothing Unintelligible, Arbitrary, Illogical, or Immoral about It.'" In *Reasoned Faith: Essays in Philosophical Theology in Honor of Normal Kretzmann*. Ed. Eleonore Stump. Ithaca, NY: Cornell University Press, 1993: 281–300.

———. "Aquinas on Atonement." In *Trinity, Incarnation, and Atonement*. Ed. Ronald J. Feenstra and Cornelius Plantinga, Jr. Notre Dame, IN: University of Notre Dame Press, 1989: 153–177.

Rahner, Karl, S.J. "Dogmatic Reflections on the Knowledge and Self-Consciousness of Christ." In *Theological Investigations*. Trans. Karl-H. Kruger. Vol. 5. Baltimore: Helicon Press, 1966: 193–215.

———. *The Trinity*. Trans. Joseph Donceel. New York: Crossroad, 1998.

Rashdall, Hastings. *The Idea of Atonement in Christian Theology*. London: Macmillan, 1919.

Ratzinger, Joseph. *Gospel, Catechesis, Catechism*. San Francisco: Ignatius Press, 1997.

———. "Interreligious Dialogue and Jewish-Christian Relations." *Communio* 25 (1998): 29–41.

Remy, Gérard. *Le Christ médiateur dans l'oeuvre de saint Augustin*. 2 vols. Paris: Champion, 1979.

———. "Le Christ médiateur dans l'oeuvre de saint Thomas." *Revue Thomiste* 93 (1993): 182–233.

———. "Le Christ médiateur et tête de l'Église selon le sermon Dolbeau 26 d'Augustin." *Revue des Sciences religieuses* 72 (1998): 3–19.

———. "La déréliction du Christ: Terme d'une contradiction ou mystère de communion?" *Revue Thomiste* 98 (1998): 39–94.

———. "Du Logos intermédiaire au Christ médiateur chez les Pères grecs." *Revue Thomiste* 96 (1996): 397–452.

———. "Sacerdoce et médiation chez saint Thomas." *Revue Thomiste* 99 (1999): 101–118.

———. "La substitution: Pertinence ou non-pertinence d'un concept théologique." *Revue Thomiste* 94 (1994): 559–600.

———. "La théologie de la médiation selon saint Augustin, son actualité." *Revue Thomiste* 91 (1991): 580–623.

Riestra, José Antonio. "Experiencia mística y visión beatífica en Cristo, según Santo Tomás." In *Problemi teologici alla luce dell' Aquinate*. Studi Tomistici 44:5. Vatican City: Libreria Editrice Vaticana, 1991: 318–325.

———. "El influjo de Cristo en la gloria de los santos." In *Prospettive teologiche moderne*. Studi Tomistici 13:4. Vatican City: Libreria Editrice Vaticana, 1981: 232–240.

Rivière, J. *The Doctrine of the Atonement: A Historical Essay*. Trans. Luigi Cappadelta. 2 vols. St. Louis, MO: B. Herder, 1909.

———. *Le dogme de la rédemption au début du moyen âge*. Paris: Vrin, 1934.

———. "Le dogme de la rédemption au XIIe siècle d'après les dernières publications." *Revue du moyen âge latin* 2 (1946): 101–112, 219–230.

———. "Sur les premières applications du terme 'satisfactio' à l'oeuvre du Christ." *Bulletin de Litterature Écclesiastique* 25 (1924): 285–297; 353–369.

———. "Sur l'origine des furmules 'de condigno,' 'de congruo.'" *Bulletin de litterature écclesiastique* 28 (1927): 75–88.

Rodríguez, Pedro. "La Iglesia como 'communio' en la perspectiva de la gracia capital de Cristo." In *Problemi teologici alla luce dell' Aquinate*. Studi Tomistici 44:5. Vatican City: Libreria Editrice Vaticana, 1991: 296–303.

———. "Spontanéité et caractère légal de la loi nouvelle." In *Lex et Libertas*. Studi Tomistici 30. Ed. Leo Elders and K. Hedwig. Vatican City: Libreria Editrice Vaticana, 1987: 254–264.

Rogers, Eugene F., Jr. "How the Virtues of an Interpreter Presuppose and Perfect Hermeneutics: The Case of Thomas Aquinas." *Journal of Religion* 76 (1996): 64–81.

———. *Thomas Aquinas and Karl Barth: Sacred Doctrine and the Natural Knowledge of God*. Notre Dame, IN: University of Notre Dame Press, 1995.

Rossi, Margherita Maria. "(L')Attenzione a Tommaso d'Aquino esegeta." *Angelicum* 76 (1999): 73–104.

Ruello, Francis. *La Christologie de Thomas d'Aquin.* Paris: Beauchesne, 1987.

Sabra, George. *Thomas Aquinas' Vision of the Church: Fundamentals of an Ecumenical Ecclesiology.* Mainz: Matthias-Grunewald-Verlag, 1987.

Santagada, Osvaldo D. "Ley antigua y culto: Los preceptos ceremoniales de la ley antigua en la *Suma Teologica* de Santo Tomás de Aquino." *Teologia* (Buenos Aires) 11 (1974): 64–117.

Sarrasin, Claude. *Plein de grâce et de vérité: Théologie de l'âme du Christ selon Thomas d'Aquin.* Vénasque: Éditions de Carmel, 1992.

Sauras, Emilio, O.P. "Esquema tomista de una teologia sobre la 'Iglesia del Espiritu.'" In *Prospettive teologiche moderne.* Studi Tomistici 13:4. Vatican City: Libreria Editrice Vaticana, 1981: 307–319.

———. "Thomist Soteriology and the Mystical Body." *Thomist* 15 (1952): 543–571.

Scheffczyk, Leo. "Die Bedeutung der Mysterien des Lebens Jesu für Glauben und Leben des Christen." In *Die Mysterien des Lebens Jesu und die christliche Existenz.* Ed. L. Scheffcyzk. Aschaffenburg: P. Pattloch, 1984: 17–34.

———. "Die Stellung des Thomas von Aquin in der Entwicklung der Lehre von den Mysteria Vitae Christi." In *Renovatio et Reformatio.* Ed. M. Gerwing and G. Ruppert. Münster: Aschendorff, 1985: 44–70.

Schenk, Richard, O.P. "Christ, Christianity, and Non-Christian Religions: Their Interrelation in the Theology of Robert Kilwardby." In *Christ among the Medieval Dominicans.* Ed. Kent Emery, Jr., and Joseph P. Wawrykow. Notre Dame, IN: University of Notre Dame Press, 1998: 344–363.

———. "*Omnis Christi Actio Nostra Est Instructio:* The Deeds and Sayings of Jesus as Revelation in the View of Thomas Aquinas." In *La doctrine de la révélation divine de saint Thomas d'Aquin.* Ed. Leo J. Elders. Vatican City: Libreria Editrice Vaticana, 1990: 104–131.

Schenker, Adrian, O.P. "Die Rolle der Religion bei Maimonides und Thomas von Aquin: Bedeutung der rituellen und liturgischen Teile der Tora nach dem *Führer der Unschlussigen* und der *Theologischen Summe.*" In *Ordo Sapientiae et Amoris.* Ed. C.-J. Pinto de Oliveira, O.P. Fribourg: Éditions Universitaires, 1993: 169–193.

Schleiermacher, Friedrich. *The Christian Faith.* Translation of the German 2nd ed. Edinburgh: T. & T. Clark, 1989.

Schönborn, Christoph, O.P. *From Death to Life: The Christian Journey.* Trans. Brian McNeil. San Francisco: Ignatius Press, 1995 [1988].

Schoot, Henk J. M. *Christ the "Name" of God: Thomas Aquinas on Naming God.* Leuven: Peeters, 1993.

Schumacher, Michele M. "The Concept of Representation in the Thought of Hans Urs von Balthasar." *Theological Studies* 60 (1999): 53–71.

Seckler, Max. *Das Heil in der Geschichte: Geschichtstheologisches Denken bei Thomas von Aquin.* Munich: Kösel Verlag, 1964.

Seidl, Horst. "The Concept of Person in St. Thomas Aquinas: A Contribution to Recent Discussion." *Thomist* 51 (1987): 435–460.

Seitz, Christopher R. "Of Mortal Appearance: The Earthly Jesus and Isaiah as a Type of Christian Scripture." *Ex Auditu* 14 (1998): 31–41.

———. *Word without End: The Old Testament as Abiding Theological Witness.* Grand Rapids, MI: Eerdmans, 1998.

Senior, Donald, C.P. *Matthew.* Abingdon New Testament Commentaries. Nashville, TN: Abingdon Press, 1998.

———. *The Passion of Jesus in the Gospel of John.* 1985; reprint, Collegeville, MN: Liturgical Press, 1990.

———. *The Passion of Jesus in the Gospel of Matthew.* Collegeville, MN: Liturgical Press, 1985.

Sentis, L. "La lumière dont nous faisons usage: La règle de la raison et la loi divine selon Thomas d'Aquin." *Revue des sciences philosophiques et théologiques* 79 (1995): 49–69.

Shanley, Brian J., O.P. "Aquinas on Pagan Virtue." *Thomist* 63 (1999): 553–577.

———. "*Sacra Doctrina* and the Theology of Disclosure." *Thomist* 61 (1997): 163–187.

Siegfried, E. "Thomas von Aquin als Ausleger des Alten Testaments." *Zeitschrift für wissenschaftliche Theologie* 37 (1894): 603–625.

Smalley, Beryl. "An Early Twelfth-Century Commentator on the Literal Sense of Leviticus." *Recherches de théologie ancienne et médiévale* 36 (1969): 78–99.

———. "Ralph of Flaix on Leviticus." *Recherches de théologie ancienne et médiévale* 35 (1968): 35–82.

———. *The Study of the Bible in the Middle Ages.* 2nd ed. Notre Dame, IN: University of Notre Dame Press, 1964.

———. "William of Auvergne, John of La Rochelle and St. Thomas Aquinas on the Old Law." In *St. Thomas Aquinas: Commemorative Studies.* Ed. Armand A. Maurer, C.S.B. Vol. 2. Toronto: Pontifical Institute of Medieval Studies, 1974: 11–71.

Smith, J.C. "Christ as 'Pastor,' 'Ostium' et 'Agnus' in St. Thomas Aquinas." *Angelicum* 56 (1979): 93–118.

Somme, Luc-Thomas. *Fils adoptifs de Dieu par Jésus Christ: La filiation divine par adoption dans la théologie de saint Thomas d'Aquin.* Paris: Vrin, 1997.

Sonnet, J.-P., S. J. "Le Christ et l'accomplissement de la Loi: La *halakhah* du Juif, l'éthique du Gentil." *Nouvelle revue théologique* 122 (2000): 353–368.

Soulen, R. Kendall. *The God of Israel and Christian Theology.* Minneapolis, MN: Fortress Press, 1996.

———. "YHWH the Triune God." *Modern Theology* 15 (1999): 25–54.

Southern, R. W. *Saint Anselm.* Cambridge: Cambridge University Press, 1990.

Spence, Brian J. "The Hegelian Element in Von Balthasar's and Moltmann's Understanding of the Suffering of God." *Toronto Journal of Theology* 14 (1998): 45–60.

Spicq, Ceslaus. "Saint Thomas d'Aquin exégète." In *Dictionnaire de théologie catholique.* 15a: 694–738.

Stohr, Johannes. "Bewahrt das Sittengesetz des Alten Bundes seine Geltung im Neuen Bund?" In *Lex et Libertas.* Studi Tomistici 30. Ed. Leo Elders and K. Hedwig. Vatican City: Libreria Editrice Vaticana, 1987: 219–240.

———. "Die Thomistische Theozentrik der Theologie und neuzeitliche Auffassungen vom Wesem und Ziel der Theologie." In *Prospettive teologiche moderne.* Studi Tomistici 13:4. Vatican City: Libreria Editrice Vaticana, 1981: 87–107.

Stump, Eleonore. "Atonement according to Aquinas." In *Philosophy and the Christian Faith.* Ed. Thomas V. Morris. Notre Dame, IN: University of Notre Dame Press, 1988: 61–91.

———. "Atonement and Justification." In *Trinity, Incarnation, and Atonement.* Ed. Ronald J. Feenstra and Cornelius Plantinga, Jr. Notre Dame, IN: University of Notre Dame Press, 1989: 178–209.

———. "Revelation and Biblical Exegesis: Augustine, Aquinas, and Swinburne." In *Reason and the Christian Religion: Essays in Honor of Richard Swinburne.* Ed. Alan G. Padgett. Oxford: Clarendon Press, 1994: 161–197.

Sweeney, Eileen. "Rewriting the Narrative of Scripture: Twelfth-Century Debates over Reason and Theological Form." *Medieval Philosophy and Theology* 3 (1994): 1–34.

Swierzawski, W. "L'exégèse biblique et la théologie spéculative de saint Thomas d'Aquin." *Divinitas* 18 (1974): 138–153.

———. "God and the Mystery of His Wisdom in the Pauline Commentaries of St. Thomas Aquinas." *Divus Thomas* (Piacenza, Italy) 74 (1971): 466–500.

———. "The Mystery of Christ in the Ministry of St. Thomas Aquinas." In *Prospettive teologiche moderne.* Studi Tomistici 13:4. Vatican City: Libreria Editrice Vaticana, 1981: 207–219.

————. "St. Thomas Aquinas as a Master of Theological Syntheses." In *Problemi teologici alla luce dell' Aquinate.* Studi Tomistici 44:5. Vatican City: Libreria Editrice Vaticana, 1991: 104–113.

Sykes, S. W., ed. *Sacrifice and Redemption.* Cambridge: Cambridge University Press, 1991.

Synan, Edward A. "Aquinas and the Children of Abraham." In *Philosophy and the God of Abraham.* Ed. R. James Long. Toronto: Pontifical Institute of Mediaeval Studies, 1991: 203–216.

————. *The Popes and the Jews in the Middle Ages: An Intense Exploration of Judaeo-Christian Relationships in the Medieval World.* New York: Macmillan, 1965.

————. "Some Medieval Perceptions of the Controversy on Jewish Law." In *Understanding Scripture.* Ed. Clemens Thoma and Michael Wyschogrod. New York: Paulist Press, 1987: 102–124.

Synave, Paul, O.P., and Pierre Benoit, O.P. *Prophecy and Inspiration: A Commentary on the Summa Theologica II-II, Questions 171–178.* Trans. Avery Dulles, S.J., and Thomas L. Sheridan, S.J. Tournai: Desclée, 1961.

Tanner, Norman P., S.J. *Decrees of the Ecumenical Councils.* 2 vols. Washington, DC: Georgetown University Press, 1990.

Tekippe, Terry J. "Towards a Systematic Understanding of the Vision in Christ." *Method* 11 (1993): 77–101.

Te Velde, Rudi A. *Participation and Substantiality in Thomas Aquinas.* Leiden: E. J. Brill, 1995.

Tonneau, Jean, O.P. "The Teaching of the Thomist Tract on Law." *Thomist* 34 (1970): 13–83.

————. Translation, notes, and appendices to *Somme théologique: La loi ancienne,* by Thomas Aquinas. 2 vols. Paris: Desclée, 1971.

Torrell, Jean-Pierre, O.P. "La causalité salvifique de la résurrection du Christ selon saint Thomas." *Revue Thomiste* 96 (1996): 179–208.

————. "Le Christ dans la 'spiritualité' de saint Thomas." In *Christ among the Medieval Dominicans.* Ed. Kent Emery, Jr., and Joseph P. Wawrykow. Notre Dame, IN: University of Notre Dame Press, 1999: 197–219.

————. *Le Christ en ses mystères: La vie et l'oeuvre de Jésus selon saint Thomas d'Aquin.* 2 vols. (continuous pagination). Paris: Desclée, 1999.

————. "*Ecclesia Iudaeorum*: Quelques jugements positifs de saint Thomas d'Aquin à l'égard des Juifs et du judaïsme." In *Les philosophies morales et politiques au Moyen Âge.* Ed. B. Carlos Bazán, Eduardo Andújar, and Léonard G. Sbrocchi. Ottawa: Société Internationale pour l'Étude de la Philosophie Médiévale, 1995: 1732–1741.

————. "Imiter Dieu comme des enfants bien-aimés: La conformité à Dieu et au Christ dans l'oeuvre de saint Thomas." In *Novitas et Veritas*

Vitae. Ed. C.-J. Pinto de Oliveira. Fribourg: Éditions Universitaires, 1991: 53–65.

———. "La pratique pastorale d'un théologien du XIIIe siècle: Thomas d'Aquin predicateur." *Revue Thomiste* 82 (1982): 213–245.

———. *Recherches thomasiennes*. Paris: Vrin, 2000.

———. "Le sacerdoce du Christ dans la *Somme de théologie*." *Revue Thomiste* 99 (1999): 75–100.

———. *Saint Thomas Aquinas*. Vol. 1, *The Person and His Work*. Trans. Robert Royal. Washington, DC: Catholic University of America Press, 1996.

———. *Saint Thomas d'Aquin, maître spirituel*. Paris: Cerf, 1996.

———. "Le savoir théologique chez les premiers thomistes." *Revue Thomiste* 97 (1997): 9–30.

———. "Le savoir théologique chez saint Thomas." *Revue Thomiste* 96 (1996): 355–396.

———. "Le semeur est sorti pour semer: L'image du Christ prêcheur chez frère Thomas d'Aquin." *La Vie spirituelle* 147 (1993): 657–670.

———. "Le thomisme dans le débat christologique contemporain." In *Saint Thomas au XXe siècle: Colloque du centenaire de la "Revue Thomiste*." Paris: Éditions Saint-Paul, 1994: 379–393.

———. "Le traité de la prophétie de S. Thomas d'Aquin et la théologie de la révélation." In *La doctrine de la révélation divine de saint Thomas d'Aquin*. Ed. Leo J. Elders. Vatican City: Libreria Editrice Vaticana, 1990: 171–195.

———. "La vision de Dieu 'per essentiam' selon saint Thomas d'Aquin." *Micrologus* 5 (1997): 43–68.

Torrell, Jean-Pierre, O. P., and Denise Bouthillier. "Quand saint Thomas méditait sur le prophète Isaie." *Revue Thomiste* 90 (1990): 5–47.

Tugwell, Simon, O. P. *Human Immortality and the Redemption of Death*. Springfield, IL: Templegate, 1990.

Turner, H. E. W. *The Patristic Doctrine of Redemption*. London: Mowbray, 1952.

Valkenberg, Wilhelmus G. B. M. *"Did Not Our Heart Burn?"*: *Place and Function of Holy Scripture in the Theology of St. Thomas Aquinas*. Utrecht: Thomas Instituut te Utrecht, 1990.

———. "The Functions of Holy Scripture in Aquinas' Theology on the Resurrection of Christ." In *Storia del tomismo*. Studi Tomistici 45:6. Vatican City: Libreria Editrice Vaticana, 1992: 13–22.

———. "How to Talk to Strangers: Aquinas and Interreligious Dialogue." *Jaarboek of the Thomas Instituut te Utrecht* 16 (1997): 9–47.

———. *Words of the Living God: Place and Function of Holy Scripture in the Theology of St. Thomas Aquinas.* Rev. ed. Leuven: Peeters, 2000.

van der Ploeg, J. P. M., O.P. "L'exégèse de l'ancien Testament dans l'épitre aux Hebreux." *Revue Biblique* 54 (1947): 187–228.

———. "The Place of Holy Scripture in the Theology of St. Thomas." *Thomist* 10 (1947): 398–422.

———. "Le traité de saint Thomas de la loi ancienne." In *Lex et Libertas.* Studi Tomistici 30. Ed. Leo Elders and K. Hedwig. Vatican City: Libreria Editrice Vaticana, 1987: 185–199.

Van Steenberghen, Fernand. *Aristotle in the West.* 2nd ed. Trans. Leonard Johnston. Louvain: Nauwelaerts, 1970.

Velecky, Ceslaus, O.P. Appendices to *Summa Theologiae,* vol. 6: *The Trinity.* New York: McGraw-Hill, 1965.

Viviano, Benedict T., O.P. "The Kingdom of God in Albert the Great and Aquinas." *Thomist* 44 (1980): 502–522.

Vodopivec, Janez. "La 'gratia capitis' in San Tommaso in relazione all'ecclesiologia di comunione." In *Prospettive teologiche moderne.* Studi Tomistici 13:4. Vatican City: Libreria Editrice Vaticana, 1981: 327–338.

Wainwright, Geoffrey. *For Our Salvation: Two Approaches to the Work of Christ.* Grand Rapids, MI: Eerdmans, 1997.

Waldstein, Michael M. "On Scripture in the Summa Theologiae." *Aquinas Review* 1 (1994): 73–94.

Walsh, Liam, O.P. Introduction to *Summa Theologiae,* vol. 49: *The Grace of Christ.* New York: McGraw-Hill, 1974.

———. "Liturgy in the Theology of St. Thomas." *Thomist* 38 (1974): 557–583.

Wawrykow, Joseph P. *God's Grace and Human Action: "Merit" in the Theology of Thomas Aquinas.* Notre Dame, IN: University of Notre Dame Press, 1995.

———. "Luther and the Spirituality of Thomas Aquinas." *Consensus* 19 (1993): 77–107.

———. "Wisdom in the Christology of Thomas Aquinas." In *Christ among the Medieval Dominicans.* Ed. Kent Emery, Jr., and Joseph P. Wawrykow. Notre Dame, IN: University of Notre Dame Press, 1999: 175–196.

Weber, E.-H. *Le Christ selon saint Thomas d'Aquin.* Paris: Desclée, 1988.

Weinandy, Thomas G., O.F.M. Cap. *Does God Change?* Still River, MA: St. Bede's Publications, 1985.

———. *Does God Suffer?* Notre Dame, IN: University of Notre Dame Press, 2000.

———. "The Human 'I' of Jesus." *Irish Theological Quarterly* 62 (1997): 259–268.

Weingart, Richard E. *The Logic of Divine Love: A Critical Analysis of the Soteriology of Peter Abailard.* Oxford: Clarendon Press, 1970.

Weisheipl, James A., O. P. Appendices to St. Thomas Aquinas's *Commentary on Gospel of John.* Albany, NY: Magi Books, 1980.

———. *Friar Thomas d'Aquino: His Life, Thought, and Works.* Washington, DC: Catholic University of America Press, 1983.

———. "The Meaning of *Sacra Doctrina* in *Summa Theologiae* I, q.1." *Thomist* 38 (1974): 49–80.

White, Kevin. "Aquinas on the Immediacy of the Union of the Soul and Body." In *Studies in Thomistic Theology.* Ed. Paul Lockey. Houston: Center for Thomistic Studies, 1995: 209–280.

Wilken, Robert Louis. "In Defense of Allegory." *Modern Theology* 14 (1998): 197–212.

Williams, A. N. "Deification in the *Summa Theologiae*: A Structural Interpretation of the *Prima Pars.*" *Thomist* 61 (1997): 219–255.

———. *The Ground of Union: Deification in Aquinas and Palamas.* Oxford: Oxford University Press, 1999.

———. "Mystical Theology Redux: The Pattern of Aquinas' *Summa Theologiae.*" *Modern Theology* 13 (1997): 53–74.

Wippel, John F. "Thomas Aquinas and Participation." In *Studies in Medieval Philosophy.* Ed. John F. Wippel. Washington, DC: Catholic University of America Press, 1987: 117–158.

Witherington, Ben, III. *John's Wisdom: A Commentary on the Fourth Gospel.* Louisville, KY: Westminster John Knox Press, 1995.

Wohlman, Avital. *Maïmonide et Thomas d'Aquin: Un dialogue impossible.* Fribourg: Éditions Universitaires, 1995.

———. *Thomas d'Aquin et Maïmonide: Un dialogue exemplaire.* Paris: Cerf, 1988.

Wright, N. T. *The Climax of the Covenant: Christ and the Law in Pauline Theology.* Minneapolis, MN: Fortress Press, 1992.

———. *Jesus and the Victory of God.* Minneapolis, MN: Fortress Press, 1996.

———. *The New Testament and the People of God.* Minneapolis, MN: Fortress Press, 1992.

Wyschogrod, Michael. *The Body of Faith: God and the People Israel.* 2nd ed. Northvale, NJ: Jacob Aronson, 1996.

———. "A Jewish Reading of St. Thomas Aquinas on the Old Law." In *Understanding Scripture.* Ed. Clemens Thoma and Michael Wyschogrod. New York: Paulist Press, 1987: 125–138.

———. "Letter to a Friend." *Modern Theology* 11 (1995): 165–171.

Index

Aaron, 77
Abelard, Peter
  on charity, 5, 58, 60, 148n.20
  on salvation, 5, 60, 148nn.18, 20
Abraham, 182n.127, 186n.39, 193n.19
  God's covenant with, 68, 112,
    156n.20, 193n.20
  relationship of to Christ, 68
Acts, 18, 28, 30
  2:24, 189n.93
  17:24, 92
Albert the Great, 5, 183n.20,
    198n.79, 202n.20
Alexander of Hales, 6
Ambrose, Saint, 170n.100
Anselm of Canterbury, 147n.8
  on eternal life, 4
  on salvation as satisfaction, 4–5,
    57, 58, 147n.10, 148nn.15, 21
Aquinas, Thomas
  on acquired knowledge, 74–75
  on beatific vision, 32, 33, 39,
    59–60, 61, 62–63, 73–75, 125,
    129–30, 134, 135–36, 137–40,
    143, 162n.9, 200n.97, 202n.22,
    205n.59
  on beatitude, 38–39, 65, 72–73,
    128, 131, 160n.59, 180n.99,
    200n.97, 201n.11, 202n.22
  on ceremonial precepts of Old
    Law, 7–8, 16, 17–18, 24–30,
    53–58, 88, 126–27, 128, 143,

158n.46, 159nn.49, 51, 55,
  160n.64, 173n.16, 184n.26,
  196n.61
on charity, 5, 25–26, 40, 58–61,
  65, 70, 77, 115–16, 121, 125,
  127, 139, 144, 150n.37, 171n.1,
  173n.19, 175n.28, 189n.90,
  190n.109, 196n.55, 203nn.27, 33
on Christ as king, 41–43, 47–48,
  53, 66–73, 78–79, 109,
  143–44, 170n.101, 178n.71,
  179n.88, 180nn.93, 99, 100,
  182n.136, 198n.80
on Christ as mediator, 39, 58,
  76, 79, 92–93, 96–97, 100,
  105, 118–19, 120, 125, 139,
  141, 143, 157n.33, 175n.27,
  194n.27
on Christ as priest, 41–42, 43,
  46–47, 53, 54–58, 66–71,
  76–79, 105, 109, 123, 139,
  143–44, 170n.101, 178n.71,
  181nn.124, 127, 182n.136,
  198n.80, 200n.6
on Christ as prophet, 41–42,
  43–46, 47, 48–50, 53, 54,
  66–71, 73–76, 78–79, 109,
  143–44, 170n.101, 178n.71,
  179n.88, 180nn.103, 110,
  181n.119, 182n.136, 198n.80
on Christ's baptism, 41, 43,
  101–2